Policing The Nation

Diaries of a Country Cousin

Attention Authors

'We Convert Fighters into Writers'. That's the motto of Manas Publications for more than four decades. Our message to the world is that India can win the battle not only by bullet but also by the pen. There is no dearth of intellectuals in our country, but their knowledge is confined to them only. No sincere effort has been made by any other publisher to channelise their knowledge in national interest. That is why the talent of a large number of intellectuals remains latent. An author transforms his knowledge into a manuscript, and it is our job to spread his/her knowledge by converting it into a beautiful book. For over four decades, Manas has been motivating the intellectuals by publishing their manuscripts and would like to publish your manuscript too. If you or your colleagues have any manuscript ready for publication or are working on it, kindly contact us with detailed synopsis and list of contents. We will transform your work into a valuable publication. If you wish, we can also suggest you the suitable subjects for writing the books related to your area of expertise. Manas is known for its publishing quality and commitments. We take utmost care in production and give wide publicity to the book as well as its author through our national and international distribution network.

Policing The Nation

Diaries of a Country Cousin

AB Tripathy, IPS

Former DGP: Orissa

Manas Publications

(We Convert Fighters into Writers)

New Delhi-110002 (INDIA)

MANAS PUBLICATIONS
(Publishers for IAS, IPS, IFS, IRS, Defence, Press, Judges etc.)
(Publishers, Distributors, Importers & Exporters)
4402/5-A, Ansari Road (Opp. HDFC Bank)
Darya Ganj, New Delhi-110 002 (India)

Off: ✆ 011-23260783, 23265523, Res: 011-23842660
Fax: 011-23272766
E-mail: manaspublications@gmail.com
manaspublications@yahoo.com
Website: www.manaspublications.in

2015

ISBN: 978-81-7049-506-2
₹ 795/-

Designed at
Manas Publications

Printed in India at
R.K. Print Services, Delhi
and published by Mrs Suman Lata for
Manas Publications,
4402/5-A, Ansari Road, (Opp HDFC Bank),
Darya Ganj, New Delhi-110 002 (INDIA)

Preface

When I started writing this book, it was with considerable reluctance and hesitation because of two factors: firstly, whether what I, seemingly just a retired police officer, write about myself deserves the attention of readers and secondly, its susceptibility to acquire a subjective tone, as the writer may tend to exaggerate his achievements and underplay the failures. I dreaded the prospects of truth becoming a casualty. In 1999 when I was catapulted into limelight, there were requests and suggestions that I pen the landmark events in my life. But I resisted the temptations. On hindsight, I feel that it was a sensible decision. The post-retirement period for me has been immensely fruitful and rewarding and the book of 1999, had it been written then, would have missed that rich mosaic of my life.

Once, I sat down to write my life's story in Oriya but gave up after the initial 50 pages. It was from 2011 to 2012 when I very consciously reduced my public engagements and time was at my disposal that I decided to write about the important events in my life. Then the dilemma was how was I to sequentially define the importance of events in my book? Could I exclude the period of Indian Independence followed by annexation of more than 500 princely states with the Indian Union, including the one I came from, where as a child I was a witness to the upheavals? Having decided in the affirmative, the writing took on an autobiographical tenor, landing me on sensitive turf.

Apart from objective presentation of facts another factor that weighed in my mind was that I should not appear as a preacher airing views on several issues which plague our democracy today, such as deficit in trust and governance, the pervasive corruption eating into the vitals of our system, criminalisation of politics, fall in values, loss of accountability and last but not the least Police and Policing, which had brought considerable hardships and suffering for me and for my family. I hoped that many of the ills which have become systemic over a period of time would be reflected in my experiences in service life which I have incorporated in this narrative.

Reminiscences in an autobiography are bound to have a personal note. As such, references to family, colleagues and those who we meet in our lives on a social basis are unavoidable. Certain observations on some people may appear to be harsh; but even after drastic moderation in my book, they are the nearest to the truth. At this age, there is no desire to hurt someone's sentiments and feelings.

Coming back to the objective of the book, I will say that it depicts the life of an IPS officer struggling, getting mauled and crushed in the initial years, almost giving up, yet trying to bounce back with a resolution to keep his head high, with what measure of success that is for the readers to judge.

My preface will remain incomplete without acknowledging the help, cooperation and encouragement I received from various sources. Four ladies stand out who, I think, deserve specific mention.

My wife Usha Rani has provided rocklike support not only by way of encouragement, but also assuming the role of a secretary, taking charge of typing and on the way, doubling up as a content editor.

My grateful thanks to Amita Patnaik of the IIPA who has been assisting me for the last several years. During her leisure hours she has typed the bulk of the handwritten manuscript, putting up with my ire and irritation.

Vijaya Sharma, based in Delhi, and who has spent her childhood in Bhubaneswar took up the onerous task of editing the draft which she did painstakingly with commendable expediency. I convey my thanks to her.

And, of course, my younger daughter Anuradha, unburdening me of the worries of following up at the end of the editor and publisher. My thanks and blessings to her.

I am sure the writing of a fumbling country cousin, polished and finished by the elegant touches of such refined feminine sensibility and grace, has now become an assemblage of readable pages.

Gautam Kaul, an IPS officer of the UT cadre of the 1965 batch, with whom I have worked in tandem in Delhi, has vetted a portion of the book. For this I am deeply grateful to him.

Last but not the least, I convey my thanks to Manas Publications for having agreed to take up the publication readily.

Amiya Bhusan Tripathy

Contents

Part-7: The Great Human Drama

Part-8: Concluding Chapter

Author as a probationer in Mount Abu

Entering into a new phase of life with Usha Rani

Receiving trophy from Shri R.K.Padhi, Director (Vigilance) Orissa

With HE Shri B D Jatti, Governor of Orissa along with Shri Narayan Chand and Shri Narsingh Swain, outgoing and incoming Police Chief

With Shri Yogendra Makwana, Union Minister of State for Home Affairs

At National Police College, Bramshil, UK

HE Shri Biswambhar Nath Pandey, Governor of Orissa inaugurating Prison Training School at Berhampur

With Shri N K Singh after receiving President's Police Medal for Distinguished Service

On the occasion of Nabakalebara of Lord Jagannath at Puri in 1996 with Shri P C Mishra, IG HQ, Shri B B Panda DG Crime and Daitapati Shri Jagannath Das Mahapatra

Shri J B Patnaik, Chief Minister Orissa at the DG's residence at Cuttack on the occasion of the Annual Police Conference

With Chief Secretary Shri R K Bhujabala and GOC Northern Command (Lucknow) at the Civil Military Liaison Conference at Bhubaneswar

Bidding adieu to Police Service after nearly 36 years

With Justice J S Verma, Chairman NHRC

In a conference of Human Rights bodies of Asian Region in New Delhi with Justice J C Verma, Chairman NHRC

Receiving the National Award for Best Investigative Feature Film from HE Shri A P J Abdul Kalam, the President of India in 2003

Being honoured by Chief Minister Shri Naveen Patnaik on the occasion of Police Raising Day in the presence of Shri B B Mishra, DGP

At an INTACH Conference on conservation of heritage in New Delhi

With HE Shri Rameshwar Thakur, Governor of Orissa on the occasion of 2050th Buddha Jayanti Celebrations in Bhubaneswar

With family
Vishwapavan, Padmini, Anuradha, Subhasish (standing right to left)
Charu Padma, Usha Rani, the Author, Anwesha, Ankit (sitting right to left)

Part-1

The Nest and the Bird

- Growing Wings
- Stepping Out
- Taking Flight
- Ravenshaw College: Hall of Fame

Chapter-1

Growing Wings

My childhood was unremarkable. Born into a middle class family in a village called Jaloi in Sonepur, an erstwhile princely state of Orissa, now a district, where my father served as a sub-inspector of police. I was the eighth child after six successive deaths of children in infancy. The seventh child was a daughter, who survived, but remained sick throughout her short span life. For my parents, the death of six children was a divine curse and I have often wondered if my elder sister lived to suffer from lifelong illness to purge my parents from that curse.

By the time memories dawned and lived on me, it was the mid-forties. Things had changed for the better. My mother had given birth to another daughter and a son; my father was the Chief Police Officer of Sonepur state – enjoying power, privilege and prestige. But intermittent death seemed to run like a pattern in our family. My youngest brother was born in 1951, the last and the 13th issue of my parents. Going by numbers, eight children had died, leaving five to survive.

My father, who did not pursue studies beyond matriculation, was lucky to be selected as a sub-inspector of police and was sent for training to the Hazaribag Police Training College, in the undivided Bihar and Orissa province against quotas reserved for princes. During his training, he excelled in horse-riding and law, which fetched him prizes in the passing-out ceremony – prizes that I still preserve.

My preliminary education started mostly at home as I was reluctant to go to school. Tutors came to our house in morning and evening and taught us – me and my two sisters. I remember, I went to a school for a few days in standard III to pass the examination and was admitted to standard IV in the Maharaja High School, sometime in 1947–48.

The mid-forties were the time when the freedom struggle had reached its penultimate stage. In spite of the lack of communication facilities and unavailability of newspapers, its heat was felt in remote Sonepur. Leaders had emerged, giving fiery and provocative speeches against the British, which, by implication, meant their voices were against the King. There was a child brigade of the Congress party. My elder cousin brother, whose father was SDO Sonepur, enrolled me as a member. I was so excited that I shouted at the Yuvraj one day while he sped away in a motorcycle. He, of course, took it lightly as my father was a favoured officer of the royal household.

In those feverish days, one name that echoed and re-echoed everywhere was that of Mahatma Gandhi, indicating the extent of his appeal in the remote parts of the country.

August 15, 1947. I remember the day vividly. There was subdued joy on the occasion, as apprehensions about the future had started looming large. In the morning, a parade was held on the ground behind our house to unfurl the national flag. I went to see the parade. An added attraction for me was my father, who was commanding the parade. At the appointed time, the Maharaja did not turn up and sent his son, the Yuvraj, instead. For me it meant nothing. As a young boy, I was not in a position to grasp its significance. Years later, when grown up, I realized that following the departure of the British, uncertainty over the future of the princely states had already started haunting the rulers. Their premonition came true with rapid developments during the next six months.

By January 1948, their exit was a certainty. Apart from the King, the most affected section of people were his officers, for whom it was a huge psychological setback. Now, they were sure, that they had to go out of Sonepur till the end of their career. For them, barring Sambalpur, Cuttack and Puri, any other place in Orissa was alien land.

My father was more familiar with Calcutta and Bombay, as it was much frequented by the royal household, with him in tow. For them, it amounted to being rooted out of their soil, displaced and banished. There was pervasive gloom in all the families. Some considered resigning and not leaving Sonepur; my father was one of them, but good sense prevailed after the representatives of the state government came and interacted with the local officers.

Sonepur was a closed society. Social life was limited to interactions amongst family members, who were quite large, and the locally prominent people, most of whom were officers. The pace was placid, with religious rituals taking precedence over other social activities. Our home was the hub where all family members would converge. During Dussehra, mothers observed fast for the sons for a day and sisters for their brothers. In western Orissa and Chhattisgarh, these were called pojiuntia (for son) and bhaijiuatia (for brother). Mothers and sisters needed to be rewarded with sarees. I remember mountains of sarees being stacked on cots and tables for the ladies to choose.

Meat and fish figured prominently in the menu of the day following the fast. On Vijay Dasami, goats were sacrificed and from each place of sacrifice, a portion would come to the residence of the Chief Police Officer. The quantity was so large that it was distributed liberally and anybody who came took a portion.

One incident from those days, indelibly imprinted on my mind, is the visit of Major General Iskandar Mirza, the then Political Agent of the Eastern States Agency, who rose to become the Governor General of Pakistan. Such visits were dreaded by the Kings whose fortunes depended on the report of the Political Agent. There were instances of some Kings getting deposed for tyranny and maladministration. In Orissa, Dhenkanal was an example.

So the Maharaja and his son left no stone unturned to keep the General – a striking personality, with an English wife and a pet tiger cub to boot – in good humour.

Mirza visited the police station where my father presented a semblance of guard of honour. He then walked into my father's office and enquired about his pay. On paper, my father was being paid Rs 200 per month, the highest in Sonepur, next only to the Diwan, who was a contractual employee of the King, most of whom came from Calcutta. In effect, my father would get Rs150 per month.

The Political Agent took umbrage at the lie and ordered that he should be paid Rs 300/- per month. Nervous that he was, my father fumbled for words. Instead of being happy, he saw the shadow of royal wrath and retribution ready to descend on him, very soon.

After Mirza's departure, he visited the Maharaja in the evening as was the daily custom, with a heart full of trepidation. To his great surprise, he found that the King showed no anger, but only asked him to accept Rs 200 per month. My father heaved a sigh of relief. This pay cheque became the envy of others, particularly magistrates, who were graduates and doctors.

Within the geographical boundaries of Orissa, there were 26 feudatory states, out of which six were Salute A states. Sonepur was one. Contiguous to these states were many princely states such as Raigarh, Sarangarh, Sakti and Sarguja in the present day Chhattisgarh. After independence, the Kings of the Eastern States agencies, led by the Maharaja of Balangir, mooted the idea of an Eastern States Union within the Indian union in the line of Saurashtra, Pepsu and Rajasthan. The demand gathered momentum and, most importantly, Sardar Vallabhbhai Patel was not averse to the idea.

But Orissa had a very strong and ambitious Prime Minister (later Chief Minister) in Dr Harekrushna Mahatab, who had excellent rapport with both Pandit Jawaharlal Nehru and Sardar Patel. He was keen that the states be merged with Orissa. His views prevailed and barring two states, Saraikela and Kharsuan bordering Bihar where the kings instigated unrest and violence against the proposal, the remaining 23 were merged with Orissa, on January 1, 1948. Mayurbhanj followed a year later. The decision of Dr Mahatab has been questioned by many, who blame him for the loss of two princely states to Bihar.

By January 1948, we in Sonepur had become a part of Orissa. In our houses, there were frantic discussions and speculation about the shape of things to come. The state government sent two officers – an administrator and a senior police officer – to take stock of the affairs in Sonepur. The police officer, Sripati Nanda, known for his efficiency and integrity in Orissa police, assuaged my father's misgivings. The Member Board of Revenue, Nilamani Senapati of the ICS, visited Sonepur.

In the midst of all these hectic developments, the biggest tragedy of the time struck India. Mahatma Gandhi fell to an assassin's bullets. The nation was shocked and dazed. I remember all these events vividly and sometimes have felt that the attainment of freedom and the accompanying events bestowed upon me premature maturity.

I have earlier mentioned an instance – regarding my father's salary – of the whimsical manner in which the King functioned. Another disservice he did to the officers was not mentioning their equivalent ranks.

The state government had decided in principle that an officer would be posted out in a rank below the one he was holding. In all Salute A states, the chiefs of police serving as Superintendents of Police were posted as Deputy Superintendents. In Mayurbhanj, which was known to be the most well-administered state, the police chief, Ramchandra Dash, was called IG of police. He was posted as SP and in no time became DIG. He retired as IG of police of Orissa. The post of my father was treated as Deputy Superintendent. He was posted to Balasore in February/March 1948 as Circle Inspector of Police, which was a big disappointment. We made preparations to move to Balasore. A chapter in our life had come to an end.

Chapter-2

Stepping Out

My father first proceeded to Balasore, leaving us with my maternal grandparents in their village in Sambalpur. We followed later. Going to Balasore was quite a journey in those days of scarce travel facilities, still worse in Orissa, a poor and backward state. We crossed Mahanadi by boat, and then took a bus to Sambalpur. From there we took train rides to Jharusuguda on the Howarh-Bombay (now Mumbai) route, and then to Kharagpur. From there we took another train to Balasore on the Howarh-Madras (now Chennai) route. Balasore in north Orissa bordering West Bengal was one of the oldest districts in the undivided Bengal province. Situated on the coast of the Bay of Bengal, the land in Balasore was fertile and people better educated than the western part of Orissa, with a visible Bengali presence.

There is a historical reason for the dominant presence of Bengalis in Orissa. After the British occupied the state in 1805, the local Brahmins were reluctant to serve them. The kayastha community came forward and got the clerical assignments. In the districts, apart from the District

Magistrate, Superintendent of Police and the Civil Surgeon, other functionaries were Bengalis and a few Muslims. Some lumninaries of Bengali literature, who frequented Orissa, acquired lands and built houses. Famous historian Rajendra Lal Mitra wrote the first ever book on Orissan architecture, "Antiquities of Orissa".

With Bengali officers dominating the administration, there was an attempt to bury Oriya language and replace it with Bengali in all schools as the vernacular language. This led to protests from Oriyas. The debate reached the Asiatic Society of India in Calcutta (now Kolkata), where intellectual discussions shaped many events in modern India.

Luckily, in the later part of 19th century, there emerged on the Orissa literary horizon some talents who wrote prose and poetry with a vengeance to establish that Oriya was a separate language, as old as, or even older than Bengali, and succeeded in their mission. Foremost among them was Fakir Mohan Senapati, writing great and wonderful prose. He hailed from Balasore. Ironically their efforts were supplemented by an English civilian, John Beams, who was the Collector of Cuttack. A linguist and a scholar in Sanskrit, Beams wrote copiously on the separate identity of Oriya language and even risked going to the Asiatic Society to establish his point, only to be shouted down by some Bengali intellectuals.

So that was Balasore, also a port town, which saw the entry of the Dutch and Portuguese. The city is still marked by Dutch and Portugese monuments. The Oriya language, which was then being threatened, received the status of a classical language in 2013.

I was blissfully ignorant of all these developments in Balasore and knew it by the fact that had been drilled into my mind: that Balasore was infamous for its malarial climate, which in fact it was, and we were recommended preventive doses of quinine which we had to swallow periodically.

I was admitted to Class IV in the Balasore Zilla School in March with only a month left for final examinations and found that the textbooks and syllabus were totally different. It was just not possible on my part to cope up with the syllabus. I flunked the examination and withdrew into a shell of shame. After summer vacation, I was readmitted to Class IV. I studied in that school for three years and completed my Class VI. Then onwards began the journey to finish my matriculation – five schools in the next five years, covering the length and breadth of Orissa.

I cherish the memories of my three-year stay in Balasore. The opprobrium my father apprehended of being a highlander or a Gadjati was not to be experienced there. He was accepted and by dint of his hard work commanded respect of his juniors. My father's honesty was his special strength and which, from time to time, he would drill into my ears, in the form of advice and anecdotes.

After I entered service, I heard officers speaking about him with undisguised admiration for his qualities. One such officer was B K Ray, the first direct recruit of the 1948 batch to come to Orissa. He was the ASP under training in Balasore and, according to him, he learnt the basics of policing from Balaram Babu, my father. The other gentleman was K Ramamurthy of the 1949 batch who, while he was DG BSF, used to come to my office room in RK Puram in Delhi and enquire about Balaram Babu, speaking nostalgically of his days in Balasore as SP.

Of the friendships I built at Balasore, many endured for years and one continues till today. He is Dr Sanjibit Jee Jachuck, now a resident of UK. He shifted to UK, rose to become a famous cardiologist, was a consultant to British Medical Services, suffered a stroke while lecturing and has recovered from near paralysis. His younger brother,

Indrajit, joined IPS in 1968 and served under me in various capacities.

In September 1952, my father was transferred to Cuttack as Circle Inspector Sadar (rural). Before he joined, we went to Puri where my thread ceremony was performed and I became a Dvija, the twice born. The area where we stayed was a suburb of Cuttack, east of the railway station, beginning from the First Battalion Orissa Military Police to Chauliaganj, Nayabazar, Central Rice Research Institute and beyond. Surprisingly, there was no high school in the area. I was admitted to the Middle English school in standard VII. The one-year stay in Cuttack was marked by visits of relatives from Western Orissa and cousins studying in Ravenshaw College, SCB Medical College and Law College. The state capital had just been shifted to Bhubaneswar, but Cuttack continued to remain the hub of educational, cultural and business activities.

My uncle Ram Chandra Tripathy, a first class magistrate posted at Jajpur, a sub-divisional headquarters, used to come to Cuttack once in a while. He was fond of theatre and I used to accompany him to see plays staged by Annapurna theatre, one of the oldest professional theatres in Eastern India, which faded into oblivion by the 60s. While I was DG Vigilance at Cuttack in the early nineties, we tried to revive it. The government gave a grant and a hall, Kala Vikash Mandap, was earmarked for staging plays on fixed dates. I, along with my wife, saw all the plays. But since they were ticketed shows, not more than 20 spectators were to be seen in the large hall. Currently, Orissa, in particular the cities of Bhubaneswar and Cuttack, are flooded with cultural shows, all staged free of cost, thanks to the largesse by the government. The halls are overflowing, leading one to think that in Orissa people do not like to pay to see shows.

The visit of Pandit Jawaharlal Nehru, the first Prime Minister of India, to Cuttack left a deep impression on me.

He drove from Bhubaneswar to Cuttack in an open Jeep. As the motorcade passed by the OMP crossing, my father's responsibility for his security covered the area from the Kathjodi river to the railway level crossing, I was excited at the prospect of seeing Pandit Nehru and was thrilled when the jeep came into view. My first impression was that of an angel emerging from the horizon. I was thrilled to see him accepting flowers, patting children and smiling, waving to the crowds gathered right up to the Cantonment Road, after which he addressed a meeting.

Later, when as DG police I made police arrangements for the visit of Prime Minister Narasimha Rao, I remembered Nehru's visit, when not a fraction of that massive security apparatus was put in place. Crowds surged back then; they came to see Nehru of their own accord and applauded him with spontaneity, for he symbolised their hopes, aspirations and dreams. Over the years there have been some people who have become my ideal, my source of inspiration. Nehru was the first. His humanity, statesmanship, learning, compassion, vision, patriotism and concern for the Indian people had influenced me profoundly, so much so that that I overlooked his many failings, blindly.

In 1953 my father was transferred to distant Koraput, a district in the south, and was posted as Circle Inspector of police, Nabarangapur, which was a subdivision. We covered the 600 km distance by boarding a train up to Vizianagaram from where we took a bus to Jeypore, the main town of Koraput district, from where we took yet another bus to Nabarangapur.

Koraput was then the biggest district of Orissa, next only to the adjoining Bastar district in Madhya Pradesh, which was the largest in India. The district lies in the Eastern Ghats, its terrain full of hills, rivers and streams. Koraput town, the district headquarters, at an altitude of 3000 feet, had a pleasant climate. In the old Madras presidency in which the district lay, Koraput used to be the summer workplace of the Collector and Superintendent of Police, for both of whom beautiful bungalows had been constructed.

If Balasore had Bengali influence, Koraput, bordering Andhra Pradesh, had a sizeable Telugu community. The southern influence was evident in the life of the local people. Though lying in the plains, Nabarangapur, surrounded by dense forests and hills -- which stand denuded today -- had pleasant weather even in the summers.

I was admitted to the Sir C D High School in standard VIII. Our Headmaster R C Patro was a strict disciplinarian and used to be very watchful. I remember vividly his daily visits to the classes. Dressed in dhoti and full-sleeve shirt tucked in, with tie and coat, he would interact with the students. His clarity in teaching English grammar was excellent and that further sharpened my continuing efforts to improve my English. In those days, our English teachers had excellent command over the language, although without the anglicised accent common in the Convent schools. To my mind, they were better than their counterparts in the English medium schools.

A landmark in my young life was the journey I undertook alone, when I was just 13, to places that almost encircled Orissa, with the exception of the northern districts. Communication was sparse, transport undependable and transit accommodation uncertain. But I was determined to go out to indeterminate places without any plan.

My parents agreed reluctantly and, one morning, I took a rickety bus to Vizianagaram where I should have reached by afternoon to take the night train to Cuttack, but after several breakdowns, reached Vizianagaram early next morning, sleepless and famished. After bath and breakfast, I took a train to Cuttack, reaching the city in the evening. I stayed with a cousin for a few days, ran out of money, borrowed some from my old friends and proceeded to the western part from the eastern coast. There was a local train leaving Cuttack in the evening for Talcher. I got down at a station called Meramundli at midnight, ran to the bus stand and boarded a bus, which reached Sambalpur in the morning. There I stayed with my mausi (maternal aunt). My destination was our ancestral village Meghla in Balangir district, where my paternal grandparents were staying.

I took the Balangir bus, got down at a place called Dungiripali, where I was received by my piusa (uncle). We walked about five km to reach his village. The next day, he arranged his bullock cart to go to Meghla. After dinner we left; sleep was by fits and starts. The only saving grace was the moonlit night and the night-long journey in a bullock cart, under the open sky, which was an exhilarating experience.

My grandparents and a widow piusi (aunt), who was staying with them, were overjoyed to see me and my grandfather spared no effort to make my weeklong stay with them comfortable.

The next stop was the village where my parents had purchased about fifty acres of land, on the other side of Mahanadi, the main river of Orissa. We travelled again by bullock cart to a place called Binka, took a bus to Sonepur, crossed the Mahanadi by boat and walked about five km to reach our village Paikpali.

There was a big mud and thatch house where we stayed and my grandfather had to arrange everything for cooking such as utensils, firewood and food items. He cooked food during our stay, drew water from the well behind our house for our bath and cooking and would not allow me to do anything. The lands had been given to share croppers, who were making hay in our absence in distant places. Collecting our annual share was tough. It used to be less than our due and the loss was routinely attributed to damage of crops either due to scanty rain or heavy rain.

We collected our share and exchanged the same with money, and I embarked upon my return journey home. We came to Sonepur where my grandfather parted company with me, giving me plentiful of advice. I took a bus to Balangir, from where I proceeded to Titilagarh, a railway station on the Howarh-Raipur route. It was the west of Orissa, and my train took me to Rayagada, down south, a sub-division in Koraput district. My uncle Parsuram Tripathy was serving there and I stayed with them. My parents heard about my arrival at Rayagada and felt relieved. After reaching Nabarangapur, a day-long bus journey from Rayagada, I was filled with a supreme sense of achievement. I felt that I had arrived.

Towards October or November 1953, my father was promoted to the rank of Deputy Superintendent of Police and posted to Sambalpur. We packed and proceeded to Sambalpur, where I was admitted to the Chandra Sekhar Zilla High School, in Standard IX. The school was one of the oldest in Orissa and my fourth on way to passing matriculation. The high school had some highly reputed teachers who commanded respect throughout the state. Our History teacher Sib Prasad Das was a reputed historian. But the school jewel was our English teacher, Manmohan Patnaik. Impeccably dressed, he would teach us with a grace and style that kept us mesmerised. Sadly, such stellar personalities are not to be seen in the present day high school education.

Our stay in Sambalpur lasted about seven or eight months and was largely uneventful. Temperamentally, by that time, I had become somewhat pensive, thinking about too many things. Two things, which intrigued me, were human suffering and social taboos in my religion, which I abhorred. I had started reading the Oriya translation of the book Uncle Tom's Cabin, which dealt with slavery in the USA and Nehru's letters to his daughter Indira. .

At this time, a particular family incident dealt a psychological blow and turned me into a rebel. We received news that my sister's husband had taken another wife. The shock waves that followed engulfed the entirely family. It was not only the jeopardy that had set in the marriage, but its future implications that were disturbing: what would happen to my sister in a tightly tradition-bound society?

I argued with my parents that she should be given in marriage to another suitable person as she had not seen her husband after her marriage at the age of eleven, which, I said, was nothing but a sham. But bound by religious traditions and social norms, my parents would not venture to embark on such a course. I felt that their lack of courage was also due to the illness of my sister and their concern for her health.

Cruel fate had condemned her to a life of suffering. I was so disgusted.

Everything of Hinduism was bad and perverse, I decided, and resolved to become a Buddhist. I told my parents in so many words. While my mother did not realise the significance of my decision, my father showed serious concern and gave a lot of indulgence to my criticisms of the traditional Hindu way of life. He believed that my resolution would melt in the course of time, and in fact it did. In retrospect, I think that a single incident, occurring during an impressionable and formative period of a person's life, has the power to deeply unsettle him or her.

In the summer of 1954, my father was transferred to Keonjhar, a feudatory state till 1948 and rich in mineral deposits. Surrounded by forests and hills, the climate was salubrious and pleasant. It was my last destination before matriculation and the penultimate one for my father, before he retired. I was admitted to standard X in D N High School and had a memorable stay till 1956, when I passed my matriculation and moved to Sambalpur for collegiate classes.

In the high school, we had some highly talented teachers who used to take personal interest in students. Our headmaster, Harihar Nanda, was our teacher in English, a subject he taught with great care. Our class teacher, Nrusingh Charan Das, was a versatile scholar, teaching us many subjects. His son Gouri was our classmate and a friend of mine. This friendship continues till date. While Gouri was far ahead of me in academics, I used to take the lead in debating and English essay writing. After studying at IIT, he went to the USA and settled down there. Every year, when he comes to Bhubaneswar, we make it a point to meet and catch up on each others' lives.

On the political scene, there was turbulence ahead and I was drawn to it irrevocably. In 1956, the report of the States Reorganisation Commission was released. There were high hopes that the two princely states, Saraikela and Kharsuan, which went to Bihar in 1948 because of the machinations of the local Kings, would be restored to Orissa. The demography of the area favoured Orissa. But it was not to be. The area remained in Bihar and it was ascribed to the influence of Dr Rajendra Prasad, the first President of India.

The people of Orissa felt let down and agitations broke out and spread across the state like wildfire. The agitations got a boost as the then Congress government led by Nabakrushna Choudhary, a simple and honest politician, and a favourite of Nehru, had the courage to direct the police to treat the agitators with leniency. I came to know this as I used to scan the wireless messages received from police headquarters. The messages issued by ORPOL (IG Police) to all district Superintendents of Police were issued on similar lines.

Keonjhar was no exception; with the support of the Congress leaders who remained in the background we hit the streets. For the leaders, their visible front was the students and willy-nilly, I had to take the lead. Gradually the situation went out of control with eruption of violence, leading to use of force by the police. The home ministry intervened, asking the state government to bring the situation under control and offered Army help. Now the approach of the government swung from show of leniency to the opposite – tough measures were put in place. For my father, it was a delicate situation. He had to balance the two ends – his professional duty with his fatherly responsibility towards his son, who was leading the protests.

A few days later, the provincial Congress Committee President, Biswanath Dash, who was the Prime Minister of Orissa after the state was formed in 1936, came and addressed a meeting near the Town Hall. I was there, and at the prompting of a journalist, he called me to his side and asked the crowd to listen to a young leader. My moment of glory had come. I delivered a fiery and passionate speech, commanding all demagogy at my disposal and received wide applause.

The foundation of my political consciousness had been laid.

My participation in the movement seriously hampered my preparations for the matriculation examination, knocking at the door. I threw myself into studying for the examination with a passion, trying to make up for the lost time, appeared in the examination and managed to secure a first division.

It was at Keonjhar that I developed my lasting hobby of reading books, other than text books, both English and Oriya. I remember that after the examination, I finished two novels of Marie Corelli, Vendetta and Sorrows of Satan, and switched over to Somerset Maugham. Soon, I undertook another trip to my village, again traversing a circuitous route, and returned with the proceeds of our crop with which the thread ceremony of my second brother Akshya was performed.

A lasting relationship which I built was with Sashi Bhusan Mishra, the government pleader. A scholar and a man of erudition, he was informal, warm and friendly. As a youngster, I would listen to him talking about ancient Indian culture, epics and puranas. Fifteen years later, when I joined Keonjhar as Superintendent of Police, he was still the government pleader, discussing with me the Specially Reported (SR) cases, which he prosecuted in the courts.

For me our stay in Keonjhar was a memorable one. I had grown physically, mentally and intellectually. The idea of conscience, which later helped me to evolve certain basic principles of life, was getting rooted in my psyche. I had become tall and lanky; my chest and face were becoming hairy. I thought I was presenting an odd picture of myself.

I had decided to shave after passing matriculation. After shaving, when I looked at my face in the mirror, certain narcissism filled my mind. My standard apparel till then consisted of half pants and a bush shirt. I changed to trousers now. I started becoming conscious of the opposite sex.

Dressed in trousers and a shirt, with my face neatly shaven and strange ideas disturbing the mind, I looked at myself and said: "You are now grown up." I began my preparations for college.

Chapter-3

Taking Flight

The route to higher education in those days for students with good marks particularly from Western Orissa used to be to study Intermediate Science after which go for either medicine or engineering or continue in the stream till post graduation. One could after I.Sc switch over to humanities or commerce and continue in that stream. Another avenue was law after graduation. Job opportunities were mostly in government sector, doctors, engineers, lecturers or a placement in the Civil Service in the state.

With only a hand full belonging to the All India Services from Western Orissa, these services were yet to catch the imagination of the students. Management and IT were far away.

Following the footsteps of all cousins in our larger families, I had to study I.Sc although I was more inclined towards humanities. As for college, Ravenshaw College in Cuttack, which considering all parameters was one of the leading colleges in India, was the first choice. I applied to the college but could not get a seat in the first list.

Avoiding the uncertainty of a second list I proceeded to the next best in Orissa, the government college in Sambalpur, which was named after a famous poet of Western Orissa, Gangadhar Meher. Incidentally, in those days Orissa did not have more than 15 colleges of general studies. By the end of 1970, colleges mushroomed, mostly private ones, and by the end of the century, the number was more than 1,000, doling out abysmally poor standard of education.

The rain had cut-off the fair weather road from Keonjhar to Sambalpur and I had to take two buses and two train journeys over 24 hours to reach Sambalpur, which now can be reached in five hours by car on the National Highway 6. After reaching Sambalpur, I saw the hostels and dreaded at the prospect of staying there.

There were two hostels, the new hostel, an asbestos roof affair, where students of BA, BSc and B.Com were staying. For a bed in the main hostel meant for the intermediate students, enrolment in the National Cadet Corps was compulsory. The main building, a concrete one had three barracks and a temporary shed, built of mud and thatch with several rooms. Initially, I was assigned to the temporary shed, which so aggravated my despair that I wrote tearful letters to my father to take me away.

Luckily in the final list, I got a seat in one the brick and cement barracks, which gave me some consolation. There was no electricity, no modern toilet, no place for bath. There was a single well, half of which remained in the Superintendent's residence. One had to stand in queue for toilet, for bath and for breakfast in the overcrowded canteen.

Our Principal was Dr Mayadhar Mansingh, father of diplomat Lalit Mansingh, famous in Orissa as a romantic poet. A poet, visionary and idealist, and embodiment of fearlessness, he was a source of inspiration to the students. His famous tiff with the district administration during the 1956 SRC agitations on the issue of entry of police to the college premises had made him a darling of the students. In no time I forgot the hardships and inconveniences of hostel life and settled for a normal life with an ever increasing circle of friends.

My lack of interest in Science saw me spending more time in idle gossip with friends and watching films. Financially I was fairly well off. While most of my friends were getting Rs. 50 to 60 for their monthly expenditure, I was getting Rs 70, which helped me to have good tiffin in the morning and afternoon to get relief from the substandard hostel food and watch films.

Enrolment in NCC sharpened my sense of discipline and punctuality. In the annual camp, which we attended in Charbatia near Cuttack in 1957, we came to blows with our traditional rivals, Ravenshaw College in the last night in an entertainment show which I was compering. Next whole day the cadets from Ravenshaw and GM College were on punishment drill.

The most memorable event during my stay in Sambalpur was the visit of Pandit Jawaharlal Nehru in 1959 to commission the Hirakud Dam, the 'Modern Temple' of his dreams. To us, it appeared to be a fabulous affair. People were flocking to Hirakud, a distance of 10 km by bus, truck, cycle and on foot. So did we and saw Nehru commending the Hirakud Dam to the people of Orissa. It certainly cast an impression on my young mind as it would have on others about a glorious future.

Without exception our teachers were good, friendly and affectionate. Unforgettable was our English teacher Prof K P A Pillai, whose simple and effortless English flowed from his sonorous voice holding us in rapt attention. Then came the final examination and I paid heavily for my negligence. In 1958, I scraped through I.Sc with a third division which deeply hurt my sensitivity. But in retrospect I find that I deserved it. The brighter side was had I got a better class, I would have been persuaded to go for medicine or engineering, but destiny had willed otherwise. My switchover to humanities became a certainty.

At the home front, my father had been transferred to Dhenkanal. He had just a year to go before retirement. With scarce saving he was yet to build a house to live after retirement. My sister had passed matriculation and was waiting to go to college. My parents were getting worried as the financial outlook appeared gloomy. When my father retired in later part of 1959, he with my mother and children had nowhere to go. My uncle was at that time Executive Officer Puri Municipality. He asked my father to come and stay at Puri temporarily in a rented accommodation. Once there, his meagre savings got depleted. All that he could do was purchase a plot in Sambalpur in 1960, where he could not construct a house for the next six-seven years.

Chapter-4

Ravenshaw College: Hall of Fame

In June 1958, I joined Ravenshaw College in Cuttack which was going to be my alma mater for next four years and from where I would proceed to Mussoorie for my foundation course in the Indian Police Service (IPS) at the National Academy of Administration. I joined BA with honors in Political Science, a subject that had just been introduced and we were the first batch. My four-year stay in Ravenshaw was the defining period of my life. It sharpened the contours of my attitude, values, and intellectual curiosity and was also the most enjoyable to say the least.

Founded in 1869 by Thomas Edward Ravenshaw, the then Commissioner of the Orissa division in the then greater Bengal, the Ravenshaw College was the first institution of higher studies in Orissa. Started in the aftermath of a famine which ravaged Orissa taking thousands of lives, out of the remains of the famine relief fund, the college became one of India's premier institutions, churning out alumni who shaped the destiny of Orissa in course of the next century, be it separate statehood for Orissa in 1936, a separate university in 1944 and nurturing students who joined the cauldron of freedom struggle.

It had one of the finest faculties in the country and the embrace of Ravenshaw was so enveloping that anybody who mattered in the state came out of the portals of the college irrespective of his profession, be it chief ministers, educationists, judges, bureaucrats, doctors, engineers and businessmen. When Cuttack was the state capital, it housed the state museum, the university and the state Assembly. When I joined Ravenshaw, its glory was shining and I became a part of that tradition. Our head of the department, Professer Sriram Chandra Dash, was a formidable person, controversial for shooting off his mouth. He was a brilliant teacher as well. He used to evaluate the individual performance of all 32 Honours students and announce his assessment openly in the class, chiding me for my answers off the textbook while saying a few good words about my English. My friend Rajendra Narayan Dash, who joined the Indian Administrative Service (IAS) in 1962, and was allotted Bihar cadre was superb in writing off textbooks, but scoring above all of us for his analytical skill.

When I joined Ravenshaw, our Principal was Dr Sadasiv Mishra, a well-known economist and teacher par excellence. An amiable person with a charming personality and effortless sophistication, he represented all that one could aspire for—achievement through struggle, smartness, wit, suavity, keen intellect and, most important, values of life. As a young boy, he sold newspapers and later rose to be one of the prominent public faces of Orissa. Dr H. K. Mahatab, the Chief Minister whom he used to treat on an equal basis, asked him to join IAS, which he did not accept. Mahatab also offered him the Finance Secretary's post, which he declined and preferred the life of a teacher.

After Pandit Nehru, who had cast a deep impression on me, it was this iconic teacher who influenced me profoundly.

I recollect an incident when he took me to task for no fault of mine. Pandit Govind Ballabh Pant, the then Home Minister, visited Orissa and we wanted to submit a memorandum to him on the injustice meted out to Orissa by the States Reorganisation Commission. We requested Dr Mishra to facilitate our submission of the memorandum and he agreed after extracting a promise that we would behave and there would be no slogan shouting. The Home Minister, on his way from Raj Bhavan at Cuttack to Bhubaneswar, would pass via the college crossing where his car would stop to enable us to submit the memorandum. Unknown to us, another section of students belonging to the students federation affiliated to the Communist Party stopped the convoy near Mangalabag Police Station, which came before the college. There was stone-pelting, followed by use of force by the police. The convoy was cleared and it zoomed without stopping at college square. We were disappointed and felt let down. It was only at night that we learnt about the incident that led to it.

Next morning Dr Mishra sent for us. Like us, he was also feeling let down and thinking that we were part of the previous night group, he lashed out at me with the words, "It is better to die a thousand deaths than to live a life like yours". I was stunned and shocked and my explanation to prove our innocence and ignorance of the incident fell on deaf ears.

There were two hostels attached to the college building, east and west. I got a seat in the west Hostel. With the number of students increasing every year, the rooms were getting congested and in my third year I shared a room with four others. In my final year, because of good scores in the annual examinations, I got a single room which became the den of all my friends, inmates and day scholars to gather and gossip.

Yet another unforgettable incident took place in my final year BA. The annual play of Ravenshaw was a famous affair, lasting for three days. We did not know that a fourth year student of Science, had a crush on a girl who was the female lead in the play. She later became a well-known actress in Oriya films. Spurned by her, he planned to abduct her from the drama pandal, by creating confusion through a novel way—exploding a bomb.

As our final examinations were approaching, I was in no mood to see the play and was studying in my room when suddenly I heard an explosion followed by the sound of a motorcycle racing past our hostel. Dr Mishra was very upset with what had happened and tried to locate the accomplices. His needle of suspicion naturally fell on people who were prominent in college activities. One evening, dressed in a cotton towel and vest, much sloven by Dr Mishra's standard, while I was studying in my room, there was a knock. Opening the door, I was surprised to see the Principal. He looked disapprovingly at my attire, came inside and made detailed enquiries about me, my family and background and left. He was perhaps satisfied that I was innocent.

I was a keen debator right from my school days and kept my interest alive in Ravenshaw, taking part in all debating activities. A substantive part of my time was spent reading books, a hobby I had developed after matriculation. The Jaico Publishers used to print books of famous writers, which were available at two rupees a copy. My monthly allowance of Rs 80 a month was sufficient for me to purchase a book every month and see films. Of the several books which I read, the notable ones were Siddhartha by Herman Hesse, Old man and the Sea by Ernest Hemingway, Myth of Sisyphus by Albert Camus, Yogi and the Commissar by Arthur Koestler, Story of Philosophy by Will Durant, Brothers Karamazov by Fyodor Dostoyevsky, and Lolita by Vladimir Nabokov.

While the Beatles culture was taking root in the West, Existentialism was becoming a very popular tenet in literature and I read the books of Sartre and tried to understand the underlying philosophy. This stood me in good stead later in my viva voce for IPS where I got an opportunity to speak on the subject at length. Visiting the Kanika Library, which had a collection of more than one lakh books, was a daily ritual, not always for studying textbooks but other books including journals. My favourite magazine was Encounter, edited by the famous literary critic Stephen Spender. In fact, the magazine gave me a perspective of the thought and philosophy of contemporary literary figures and thinkers.

The Kawas Nanavati case was the talk of the day. The Naval Commander had shot dead Prem Ahuja, paramour of Nanavati's wife Sylvia. Blitz magazine had started a campaign in favour of the Commander during the trial and we readily responded to it. If I remember it right, he got away with a sentence less serious than murder as the offence was treated as outcome of grave and sudden provocation.

In 1960, after graduation, I joined MA in Political Science, resisting all temptations to go to Allahabad, the Mecca of Oriya students for postgraduate studies. Several friends who had gone to Allahabad persuaded me to join them, but I had made up my mind in favour of Ravenshaw.

As the permanent campus of the Utkal University was coming up in Bhubaneswar, some university post graduate subjects were taught from Ravenshaw. Political Science was one with Professor K. V. Rao as the head. He later proceeded to Benaras Hindu University as professor in political science. Dr Sriram Dash, our head in BA (Hons), and Dr Rao were bitter rivals reason being Dr Dash's perceived deprivation of the University post that went to Dr Rao. So we landed from Dr Dash to Dr Rao's arms and had to do some tightrope walking.

The other members of the faculty became eminent, rising in course of time. Sitakanta Mahapatra, who joined IAS in 1961, became a famous poet and is a Padma Vibhusan awardee and Jnanpith award winner. P C Hota joined IAS in 1962 and rose to become the Chairman of the Union Public Service Commission. Lalit Mansingh, after completing his Masters from Utkal University, joined as a lecturer in 1961 and joined IFS in 1963. Later, he became the Ambassador to UK and USA and then the Foreign Secretary. Of them, Hota was the most friendly, joining us over tea and Pakora in a nearby Gujarati restaurant.

One event that the students looked forward to in the beginning of the session was the annual election to the college Union. There were two groups: the Union, seemingly independent, but enjoying the support of the Congress, and the Federation backed by the CPI. For the 1962 elections, the Union group approached me to be their candidate for the post of President. I declined as I had decided to appear in the Civil Services Examinations. They also approached my friend D K Roy, who was in final year English. When he showed reluctance, we decided to put up Binod Chandra Kar, from Psychology, who was a popular figure and a poet to boot. Binod agreed and we started organising his campaign when we learnt that D K had decided to contest as the Union candidate. We were upset as we knew that Binod would be no match for the versatile D K.

This made us determined to put up an independent candidate and while drawing up the strategy we concluded that the candidate would have to be from the Science stream to draw the Science votes. I approached S B Mishra, a final year Physics student. He flatly declined as it was beyond his comprehension that a Science student could contest and win an election. We explained to him that he would not only get an overwhelming majority of votes from the Science block, but also majority from humanities with the exception of fourth year Arts, which had committed voters for DK. He agreed and the epic battle started, epic because there was no violence, no mischief and no mud-slinging.

It was all the strength of voice and the articulation flowing from it. I had the herculean task of taking S B Mishra to all classes, introducing him and appealing for votes. On the penultimate day debate, I listed as many novel ideas as possible for him to speak. He won with a comfortable majority prompting Dr A P O'Brien, professor of English and advisor of the Union, to say that he had witnessed a unique election. The clouds of misunderstanding among friends vanished in no time and we all became one. S B Mishra later joined IAS in 1965.

My participation in the campaign seriously affected my preparation for the Civil Services examinations, which were only a little more than a month away. I found that it would not be possible to study in my room, which was always crowded, nor in the college library, where I would be distracted by the sight of girls and signals from friends. I decided to go to the university library, not very far away and study there.

Everyday, after early lunch I would proceed there, occupy a booth and study till 4.30-5.00 pm, then go to the nearest South Indian hotel and kill my hunger. After that, life used to be normal for the remaining hours of the day—friends and fun.

In the winter of 1962, I was selected to participate in an inter-university debate in the Delhi University . I went there and stayed in Gwyer Hall with my friend Suresh Patnaik. I decided to put on a suit for the occasion. I borrowed one from a senior, as also his shirt and tie and tried several times to make sure I did not make a fool of myself.

I also thought, somewhat foolishly, that this dressing-up would be a prelude to my wearing a suit for my UPSC interview.

I participated in the debate initially with diffidence at the sight of the smart Delhi boys in suits and pullovers and girls in sarees, salwar kameez and cardigans (no jeans and tops in those days). I did not win but was gratified by the compliments I received from the chief judge.

On my way back, I stopped in Allahabad to see my friends. I stayed in the PC Banerjee Hostel, dominated by Oriya students and had a whale of a time. I purchased a suit piece in Allahabad and gave it to a tailor. My friend Achutanand Mishra took the responsibility of delivering it to me in Cuttack.

There were moments when coming out of the euphoria of college life I was struck by the million arrows of stark realities at home. My parents had shifted to Sambalpur and were staying in a rented accommodation. My elder sister had become a permanent fixture in our house, my parents always concerned about her health. My younger sister had joined college and my second brother was on his way there. My father's paltry pension was only a fraction of their basic needs to subsist. I would ask myself, if I did not qualify in the Civil Services examinations then what? I did not apply for the State Civil Service examinations as the next profession I preferred was that of a teacher's.

Those were the days of uncertainty.

Two all-India Congresses were held in Ravenshaw in 1962 —the All-India Political Science Congress and the Indian Science Congress.The former, conducted under the supervision of two rivals Dr Sriram Dash and Professor K V Rao, saw us sandwiched between two sets of functionaries each at loggerheads with the other. In the Science Congress, the attraction was Jawaharlal Nehru talking on scientific temper.

Apart from P C Hota, our teacher, several final year MA students like me, R N Das, Preet Mallick, Surendra Mishra were taking the Civil Services examinations. Many who did not qualify had turned out successful in the State Civil Service examinations and, by the end of the session , were waiting for their appointments. Our batch of 1962 had contributed a record number of candidates to the Orissa Civil Services and most of them retired from IAS in course of time. Hota, Das and Preet received interview calls for the IAS. For the IPS and Central Services, the Union Public Service Commission (UPSC) used to hold the interview on a regional basis. I got a call letter along with Surendra Mishra to appear before the Board in Calcutta.

The IAS results came first. P C Hota, R N Das and Preet Mallick along with four others from Orissa got through. The IPS and Central Service results came a few days later. Three from Orissa had qualified: Pyari Mohan Mohapatra, Manbesh Mukherjee and me.

The Oriya newspapers did not print my name assuming that Tripathy was from Uttar Pradesh. Instead, they published the name of my namesake from West Bengal cadre, Amiya Kumar Samanta, as Samanta is a common Oriya surname. I had to send an express telegram to my father, informing him about my selection to IPS. Apart from jubilation, it was for me a great relief which I find difficult to describe. I was filled with a great sense of gratitude to the divine power as I felt that the penury in which my parents, brothers and sisters lived would be alleviated to a considerable extent.

When I think in retrospect, the year 1962 was a significant year for many of us in different contexts. Several of my batch mates were selected for the State Civil Services, three of us— Rajendra, Preet and myself—qualified in the All India Services before passing MA; the year had till then sent the largest number of candidates to the All India and Central Services, seven to IAS, three to IPS and three to Income Tax. Last but not the least, we of the 1962 IPS batch over the years, have been meeting every two years after retirement. In 2010, we met in Orissa, in 2012, it was at NPA Hyderabad for a 50 year reunion, and Kanya Kumari in 2014.

It was time now to leave Ravenshaw and make preparations for my journey to Mussoorie for the foundational course. Ravenshaw, which had shaped my personality, was igniting many thoughts which then appeared wondrous and joyful and now, with wizened wisdom, unfulfilled and unredeemed.

Did we join the service only to earn money? The honest answer would be both a "yes" and a "no". We took up the service because we had to provide wherewithal for us, our family and the family we were planning to raise. No because we were the pre-midnight children who had tasted the thrill of freedom, had grown up reading the saga of freedom struggle, the sacrifices of the leaders, the ideals with which they started administering the country. We became dreamers led by the Olympian dreamer, Jawaharlal Nehru, of a golden future for our country.

This idealism which had imbued our mind and spirit may look unpractical and foolish in the present days. Examples will be cited how Nehru's many dreams crashed and how that vision of a glorious future has turned sour today. But, for me, that should be no reason to become a prophet of doom, become a cynic treating everything with cold calculation without a touch of humanism. We joined the All India Services, which were specifically incorporated in the Constitution on the insistence of Sardar Patel who could visualize the shape of things to come. The All India Services were to act as unifying agents to guard the unity and integrity of the nation, and not be a part of the divisive political forces which grew and have been growing in strength with the passing years. Regional parties formed on the basis of caste, community and religion, all contrary to the spirit of the Constitution, are virtually derailing the very spirit of India on the pretext of federalism. Our Constitution is federal, but there is an underlying spirit of unitariness that will be evident from several provisions. The shrill voice of regionalism under the garb of federalism is doing untold damage to our national fabric.

I went to Sambalpur to spend a few days with my family before proceeding to Mussoorie. After receiving telegraphic instructions, I proceeded to Mussoorie via Calcutta in July 1962. I reached Dehradun by the Doon Express on a rainy morning and was received by Rajendra who took me to the National Academy of Administration for a four-month stay. I became a public servant for the next 35 years of my life. Another chapter in my life had begun.

Part- 2

Training and the Refinement

- IPS Training, Mussoorie: Chugging Along
- Police Training, Mt Abu: Polishing
- Training in The State

Chapter-5

IPS Training, Mussoorie: Chugging Along

Mussoorie was a vast impersonal cauldron. Trainees from all parts of India were pouring in. The academy had been shifted to Mussoorie from Delhi, to provide better ambience for training. The main campus was an erstwhile hotel called Charleville. New buildings were yet to come up. So, by the time we reached, most of the rooms on the main campus had been occupied by IAS probationers. The academy had hired a number of houses near and around it to accommodate other probationers. I was assigned accommodation in a building called Chapleton, about a kilometre from the campus. As food was available at the mess on the the main campus, my daily routine was to go to the campus every morning around nine, take breakfast, attend classes, have lunch, attend afternoon classes and then go to the mall or market. I would return by 7 pm, head for the dining hall, then walk back to my place of stay, before 9 pm. I used to spend my leisure hours mostly in Rajendra's room. The road from campus to Chapleton was dimly lit, almost dark; during the rains, the journey back was pretty frightening. We used to return in groups, but there were nights when I used to walk back alone, imagining the worst—ghosts and landslide, and what not.

Soon after arrival, I had to buy warm clothes, a suit, and the prescribed combination of gray flannel trousers and blazer. I also had to learn to familiarize myself with the standard English greetings. In fact, that remained the sole conversation with many probationers throughout my stay because of the impersonal nature of interpersonal relationship. People tended to group themselves generally on the basis of regional and institutional identity. Prominent were the Presidency group from Kolkata, the Allahabad University group, the St Stephenian group from Delhi, the Bombay University group and the Loyala group from Madras. The Oriyas, who had done their MA in Allahabad, such as P C Hota, Nila Madhab Mohanty and Pyari Mohan, were more a part of the Allahabad crowd.

Being basically shy, I was not able to open up and interact freely with other groups. So I was often seen in the group consisting of Rajendra Das, Narasing Sahu, an income tax probationer and Manabesh Mukherjee from IPS. We were joined occasionally by P C Hota, Nila Madhab Mohanty and Pyari Mohan. It was only after joining the Central Police Training College, Mount Abu that I was able to shed my inhibitions. Thereafter there was no looking back.

Frankly speaking, there was nothing remarkable about the teaching in Mussoorie. Professors taught us Economics, History, Sociology, Public Administration and Governance. Of the teaching staff, Professor Rama Swamy was notable, not only for his lucid explanation of economic issues, but also for his ribald jokes, many verging on the erotic, leaving the faces of the women probationers red.

Lectures by some guests were instructive and interesting; but the teacher who stood tall was A N Jha of the ICS, the Director. His scholarship, erudition, versatility and articulation held the class spellbound. What was unique about him was the choice of subjects. He rarely spoke on a prescribed subject. He would come to the class, take the views of the students, pick a topic and deliver a memorable speech while rolling his pipe for a smoke. As a man, he radiated warmth and friendship, and although always suited and booted, being as he was from the ICS, he was never stiff-necked. He later went to Delhi as Lt. Governor and died in harness.

At the end of the course, I found that the sum total of our learning was neither significant nor substantial. The only useful purpose it served was the congregation of probationers of All India and Central Services for exchange of thoughts and ideas, in spite of the limitations I have explained earlier. Conceptually, however, the course was laudable, as probationers from all parts of the country, from all communities, all faiths and strata, converged. Bharat and India became one.

As far as the IPS probationers were concerned, there was only one occasion when the probationers gathered to meet E L Stracy, an IP officer from Tamil Nadu, who was the Deputy Commandant in Central Police Training College, Mount Abu (Now Police Academy, shifted to Hyderabad) to listen to his pre-training briefing. In the relaxed atmosphere of Mussoorie, the presence of Stracy, an Anglo-Indian, tall and handsome, radiating discipline and speaking to us with precision and clarity in his sonorous voice, had a magical effect on our young minds. The prospects of going to Abu appeared both tantalising and challenging.

A tragedy hit the nation in October 1962: the Chinese aggression. We were shocked, sad and confused, trying to follow the progress of war, the lack of preparedness of the Indian Army, the deficiencies in the war apparatus and the frustrations of a Prime Minister. American intervention came, and the Chinese declared unilateral ceasefire. The war ended, but the wounds remained, and are hurting even now. Later in 1966–67, when I was posted at Tezpur in Assam in an ITBP Battalion, I heard from the local people that the Chinese were only 20 miles away from the town.

A tragedy that struck the academy was the death of a probationer of the Central Services, while on a trekking adventure. He fell into the Yamuna, and was swept away by the turbulent currents. The probationer, Krishna Murthy, happened to be my roommate. The news hit me like a bolt of lightning. He was an unassuming, gentle and friendly soul and my journey mate from Chapleton to Academy every day. As his body could not be traced, there were rumours making my nights restless and fearful. The situation became worse as neither his relatives came to take his belongings, nor did the academy make arrangements to shift those from the room. The sight of his belongings would only aggravate my sense of fear and insecurity.

Getting introduced to Bacchus was something that many probationers considered important and necessary to maintain the lifestyle befitting an All India Service officer. There were some who were already proficient in the art of drinking and the demonstration effect was telling. Many probationers, who started drinking in Mussoorie, later, became alcoholics that affected their family life as well as health.

I was never a prude, and had no reservations about drinking. I just took a decision not to drink during my training period and stuck to it. Temptations would stare at me; my drinking friends would try to take me into their fold by telling that if I considered whisky risky, beer certainly was no fear. One night, a friend staying at Chapleton, Kishen Dis of Postal Service, in an inebriated state, poured a bucket of cold water on me while I was asleep.

What helped me to stick to my decision was perhaps the company I kept. The others were non-drinkers. It was while at Mussoorie that we got our cadre allotment. Four probationers were allotted to the Orissa cadre: Pyari Mohan Mohapatra, who joined IAS in 1963, followed by me, Manabesh Mukherjee and Samir Prasanna Mallik from West Bengal. At that time, the principle of allotment was fifty per cent insiders and equal number of outsiders. While Pyari and I came from the insider quota, Manabesh, though from Orissa, got Orissa as he had shown Bihar his home state, where his family had some assets.

The end of the foundation course was followed by a break when we all left Mussoorie and went to our native places. I came to Sambalpur and from there proceeded to Mount Abu for my one year police training.

Chapter-6

Police Training, Mt Abu: Polishing

Going to Mount Abu from Sambalpur was quite a journey. I went to Jharsuguda from where I took the Howrah-Bombay Mail, reaching Bombay one late evening. I was a little nervous having heard many stories about life in that megapolis. I was accosted by a hotel agent who promised me good accommodation. There was no other option and I went with him to spend the night in the hotel on a daily tariff of Rs 10. At night there were noises from all the rooms. I kept my fingers crossed. Next evening I took another overnight train to Ahmedabad. After reaching, I went to the first class waiting room, had my bath and breakfast and took a train to Sirohi, the rail head for Mount Abu on a middle gauge line. I booked a first class ticket and spent most of the time in the dining car which had fine white linen and gleaming cutleries, which are now things of the past.

I reached Sirohi in the afternoon along with some other probationers. We were dumped into a one tonner, and started climbing to Mount Abu, which is located at about

3,500 ft. above sea level. Central Police Training College, as it was then called, was the training centre for IPS officers from 1948 to 1970 when it was shifted to Hyderabad and the name changed to Sardar Vallabhbhai Patel National Police Academy.

At Mount Abu, every thing was well-organized and streamlined to avoid the slightest confusion. I was allotted a room in the main block, the Rajputana House, and shared the room—room No 21—with BJK Tampi from Kerala. Accommodation was spacious with an anteroom but toilet was primitive without flush latrines. Water was scarce and regulated.

Next day we all got our kit for physical training, drill and sports, working uniform, dinner jacket, etc, and underwent elaborate briefing, mostly by the redoubtable Stracy, whose commanding presence was truly awesome. The briefing covered each activity, right from getting up early in the morning till you retire for the night. Each room had a bearer, who was our Man Friday and on whom we depended for everything.

Apart from the IPS probationers, CPTC had trainees from other states and forces. The CRPF had sent four deputy superintendents; there were two deputy superintendents from Nepal, three from Goa, a few from Delhi Police and about eight or nine from Madhya Pradesh. The deputy superintendents included, we numbered more than 75. Some deputy superintendents from Madhya Pradesh were excellent sportsmen and later proved to be successful officers. They remain friends till today.

On reaching there we learnt that the training of one year had been cut short by two months as a part of economy measure arising out of the Chinese aggression. This affected us in many ways. Our daily routine was overloaded as all the training inputs had to be compressed; our Bharat darshan was cancelled, later to be revived to cover only two places of eastern India—Patna and Calcutta. Also, the army attachment was confined to 10 days at the Jhansi Armoured Brigade instead of going to Kashmir and visiting the India-Pakistan border.

Training started with a bang and its tempo was an ascending graph, culminating in a crescendo in our passing out ceremony. The interregnum witnessed the transformation of a young man—from a fumbling, reluctant, hesitant wannabe to a man exuding confidence, courage and conviction. The regimen that appeared to be formidable in the beginning became moments to be cherished at the end. The mettle of an IPS officer was unparalleled in the world police brotherhood, a compliment I received 15 years later from the Director of the National Police Training College Bramshil in the UK, where I had gone for a training course. Sadly, many an IPS officer lost this sense somewhere in the midst of their career, in terms of physical fitness, intellectual pursuits and professionalism.

The daily routine, to say the least, was tough. Getting up by 5 am, and afterbed tea and morning ablutions, getting into the physical training (PT) dress, running to the gate at the sound of a whistle and then to the college ground, doing PT, then changing to uniform for drill practice—there was no breathing space. Putting parade dress was quite a problem, particularly while tying the putties over the ankle boots with the prescribed folds, ensuring symmetry of the layers, for which we always fell back on our bearer . From the college ground, we moved to Trevor Oval, a parade ground bigger in size in the heart of the town. Even while going back to mess after parade, we had to march in our respective squads. The only liberty we had was to utter inane profanities in hushed tones at the rigor of the routine.

Spadigam, our Chief Drill Instructor remains unforgettable. Drawn from the Malabar Special Police, he was one of the toughest officers I have seen in my life. An epitome of discipline, he was a hard taskmaster, taking us to task with whatever language came to his mouth. His abuses were legendary. He would call us bandicoots, jokers, lousy pregnant women, bringing shame to IPS and cursing the UPSC members for selecting us for IPS. If a probationer committed a mistake and became the object of his wrath, all hell would break loose. He would tear him to pieces in the open field with his sharp tongue, unleashing the choicest abuses. We were mentally prepared for a hard life in Mount Abu but what jolted many of us was the lashing we got from Spadigam.

We decided to meet Stracy and complain against him. Some of us went to his office and ventilated our feelings. He heard us with patience, did not take us to task, but said very firmly, "No complaints, no complaints; Hats off to Spadigam." That was enough for us to come to reality and adjust our life for the rest of our stay at Mount Abu and also to see the other side of the coin.

Spadigam, the man, while on the parade ground, was the unquestioned monarch; outside he was a gentle soul, polite, reticent, restrained and respectful. During the dinner nights, whenever he came, we could see the soft side of his personality and regretted that we had complained against him. The most poignant moment came in the passing out dinner when, what he said I am trying to reproduce: "During the past 10 months you have received so many abuses from me. My utmost concern was your training. If I have hurt your sentiments, please forget and forgive. Hence forward many of you will be my bosses." Indeed in Stracy's language, 'Hats off to Spadigam".

While Spadigam was a daily fixture, other senior officers used to come to the parade ground by turn —S C Mishra, the Commandant , Stracy, and Burge, the Assistant Commandant. The mornings marked by the presence of Spadigam and Stracy were dreaded by all of us.

Two other components of our outdoor police training were horse riding and range practice both in rifle and pistol. Horse riding was an activity many probationers hardly looked forward to. The Chief Instructor, Dharam Singh, was equally biting in his comments, chiding us all the way. There were falls from the horseback resulting in minor injuries which were simply ignored. Usually, to gain confidence, a probationer stuck to a horse which would get familiar with its master. My favourite horse was Chetak. With him I learnt to trot and graduated to canter and then gallop a few times. As some horses were getting old, new ones came and amongst them was a mare christened 'White Lady', which fascinated me. In one class, I chose White Lady which was yet to be tamed to the stable.

That morning Stracy was present. I trotted, started cantering and then there was an order to gallop and my miseries began. White Lady just ran wild, did two or three rounds in the field, would not stop and started moving out of the field when Stracy, who used to call me Trips, said "Bye bye Trips". I thought it was going to be permanent adieu to the world as I was sure that I would fall off and die or get seriously injured and clutched its neck in mortal fear. It ran through the town, encircled, it and started slowing down near the quarter guard, which was close to the ground where I got down alive and unharmed.

Range practice was interesting. I was good at pistol shooting and used to score very high points in all the range practices consistently.

Now, coming back to the daily routine, after reaching our room, we took bath, changed to working uniform, slacks and bush shirt and rushed to the mess to fill our famished stomach and then proceeded to the college for our classroom sessions.

In the absence of a campus, various buildings of the CPTC lay scattered all over the town although not faraway from each other. The mess had three buildings, all separate:

Rajputana House, where I stayed, Jodhpur House and Palanpur House, which accommodated the advanced course officers and visiting dignitaries. The administrative and teaching block, gymnasium and parade ground constituted the main college campus. Trevor Oval was in the midst of the town, so also the quarter guard. The horse riding course was yet in another place. The senior administrative functionaries were Commandant S C Mishra, Dy. Comdt. E L Stracy and Asst. Commandant Burge, who were also part of the faculty apart from teaching staff in Law, Police Theory, Police Procedures, Administration and Hindi.

The emphasis in teaching was on Law and Police Procedures/ Administration, which then highlighted the main functions of a District Superintendent of Police like (a) man management (b) investigation including scientific aid and prosecution of cases (c) law and order and (d) collection of intelligence. Meticulous care was taken to drive these cardinal principles into the mind of the probationers. Talk on police community relationship had started gathering momentum. Our top two trainers, being members of the Indian Police, put professionalism as the core value of police, leadership in man management, pursuit and doggedness in investigation, mastery over law for successful prosecution and devising strategy for tackling law and order. Later, looking back particularly in the seventies, when the general regimen of training was somewhat relaxed, I used to wonder, was our training inadequate? But the post-mortem to me revealed no deficiency with the exception that lessons in History and Sociology could also be beneficial to enlarge and widen the vision of the probationers. With change of times and in tune with the change, the syllabus now is much more broad-based as it should be, but the fundamentals remain the same.

At that time, the police, particularly the Superintendent of Police, had two major responsibilities which are no longer there and which have become two major departments in the government, independent of the police. One was the implementation of the Motor Vehicle Act, which is now administered by a Transport Commissioner at the state level. The SP used to be the licensing and registering authority of vehicles and for this there was a separate division in each District Police Office, headed by a Deputy Superintendent of Police. It was only after the implementation of the Marani Committee report in 1964–65 that a separate department was created in all the states. The enforcement provisions, however, remained with the police in many states for quite some time. In view of this,the provisions of the MV Act were very carefully explained in the law classes. Other major Acts, which received attention, were the Indian Railway Act and the Forest Act.

The other major responsibility with the police till 1974 was the prosecution of criminal cases in the courts. In 1974, through an amendment to Section 25 of the CrPC it was taken away from the police and separate prosecutors from the Bar were appointed to prosecute cases. The result was disastrous as it became a convenient tool to dole out patronage to lawyers loyal to the party in power. With change of the political setup, the prosecutors changed. The yardstick was loyalty to party in power and not legal knowledge. The system collapsed in no time and rate of conviction, which was between 65% and 70% suddenly dropped to 10 to 15%. This distortion which has done lasting damage to prosecution is yet to be corrected even after creation of a separate cadre of prosecutors. In our training, emphasis was laid on knowledge of law to enable the SP to monitor prosecution and take corrective steps before prosecution of a case started.

An overflow of social legislation was predictable in a democracy dedicated to the welfare of the people. Three major social legislations were the Suppression of Immoral

Traffic in Women and Girls Act in 1956 following the UN convention in Paris in 1946 on exploitation against women, Prevention of Untouchability Act, as ordained in the Indian Constitution, in 1955 and the Children Act in 1960 setting the tune for a separate Juvenile Justice system. Several were in the offing. We had two Law Instructors, Mr Tiwari and Mr Deb. Tiwari was a perfect gentleman and punctilious in his teaching of Law, the major Acts of IPC, CrPC and Evidence Act—the Bible of a police officer. He would emphasize and re-emphasise a point to make sure we understood. He recently passed away. Deb had the look of a serious intellectual teaching us the nuances of Law like an academician.

The important aspect of teaching Law and Order was tackling agitations, which were various in many fields, prominent being labour, students, farmers, employees union, backward communities and linguistic issues, including the anti-Hindi movement. Separatist movement was taking its root in the Northeastern states, apart from Kashmir. Linked to Law and Order was the teaching of Intelligence in which communism figured significantly. It might appear strange that in spite of very good ties with the USSR, its credo Communism was a subject which was taught at great length. America and CIA hardly figured, because I think America had no imperialistic design. Politically maintaining a policy of isolation, America came to the world stage after World War I. On the other hand, Communism, still not divided, believed in the policy of expansionism and that was the cause of worry for India. So friendship with Russia meant killing two birds with one stone, i.e. to prevent Communist expansionism and to get support in India's conflict with Pakistan, which had already become a stooge of the USA whose policy was to build allies to counter Communism through alliances like NATO.

Communism had become fashionable all over the world.

Marx's Das Capital has enough material to ignite the young intellectual rebels with romantic notions of a stateless society. It had followers in capitalist Europe, Germany, France, Italy and England and in the poorer countries of Latin America and in South and South East Asia. Che Guevera was the romantic hero who inspired many including Fidel Castro who dared to have a Communist state close to the USA. All these implications were taught to us including what was predictable and a certainty which the world would witness in a short time, that was the challenge within.

Two biggest countries which were ruled by kings had embraced Communism—Russia and China. But these two countries, which were fighting capitalism, became rivals and by midfifties Russia found that it would be difficult to contain Chinese ambition. Occupation of Tibet was a milestone that not only brought turmoil in the Communist world, but also sounded a warning signal to India.

By mid-60s, China declared that its party would be known as Communist Party (Marxist) in contrast to Communist Party of Russia and would advocate power as the main instrument of State, power flowing from the barrel of a gun. In India, the Communist Party in India was split, CPI led by Shripad Amrit Dange and CPM lead by B T Ranadive. Establishing its stronghold in West Bengal, the CPM unleashed a reign of terror and its more radical wing CPML emerged in the shape of the Naxalbari farmers movement where the credo was only violence. Naxalism jumped over Orissa, took its roots in Andhra Pradesh and rapidly spread to Orissa, Bihar and Madhya Pradesh while it was rooted out of West Bengal by the famous Calcutta Police Commissioner Ranjit Gupta, an IP officer, with the support of Chief Minister Siddhartha Shankar Ray, his classmate.

Our Hindi Teacher, the gentle Mr Gupta, took immense pains to teach us Hindi, but my proficiency in Hindi was only marginal, in spite of having a surname that had its origin in Uttar Pradesh. Remaining alert in the classes was indeed a herculean effort after the gruelling training we got in the morning. I remember the visit of B B Mishra, IP, an officer of the Orissa cadre who was DIG CRPF at Ajmer. He came to Mount Abu to deliver talks on CRPF. I was attached to him to look after his comforts. Stracy, who introduced him in the class, remained throughout the lecture and saw me dozing off and on. After the class, he summoned me to his room to tell me that I should be ashamed of sleeping in the class of a senior police officer, that too from Orissa, and I should proceed to Palanpur House where he was staying and beg apology. Although I was quite reluctant to express my regret which amounted to double punishment, having already been taken to task by Stracy, I had no alternative but to proceed to meet B B Mishra and tender an apology.

Mess life in Mount Abu was strictly formal, except for Sundays, when we would take our breakfast leisurely, then go on a long walk, return to have a hearty biryani meal and then, indulge in the luxury of sleeping the afternoon away. Initially, Stracy was a regular visitor, teaching us table manners at which he excelled. His observant eyes would follow the motions of the probationers, right up to the opposite table in the long hall and suddenly, someone would be called to be faulted with. Once, when I was having a toast, I heard my name called from the head table: "Trips, don't anticipate, don't anticipate; let the toast reach your mouth, then open it." Obviously I had opened my mouth a bit earlier than the prescribed moment. The quality of food was better than Mussoorie; one item that figured regularly was Stracy's favourite rasam, which also found favour with my palette.

I was in the mess committee for two consecutive months, mess secretary in the ninth month and a member of the executive committee in the final month. During my mess secretaryship, the menu tilted towards south Indian cuisine, which invited complaints from our northern friends, particularly the Punjabis. So, in the final month, the balance was in favour of north Indian menu. The last mess night dinner was meticulously planned; I took active part in the selection of the menu. What was interesting, however, was the allotment of seats in the main dining hall. As the main hall would not seat all the probationers, the spillover went to the annexe, a sought after destination as, there, all mess manners were given a go by. While the Commandant and Deputy Commandant were bound to their tables with other invitees in the main hall, there was nobody to supervise the annexe.

I allotted myself to the annexe and we had a roaring time, eating liberally.

After the afternoon games, which were compulsory, and by which time our fatigue was stretched to its limits, we would quickly change for dinner and proceed to the dining hall to fill our hungry stomachs. Pre-dinner gossip in the lounge was not very frequent, exceptions being Saturday nights and Sundays. As for entertainment, it was limited to an occasional film show in the gymnasium through a 16 mm projector; that too depended on the vagaries of transportation. There was a cinema hall in the town and the Saturday and Sunday shows audience consisted mostly of probationers.

Socially, life was homogeneous. The IPS probationers were the dominant constituents with the deputy superintendents of police coming next. Friendship was easy. There was no dearth of camaraderie; what was in dearth was time. Of the four Orissa cadre officers, Pyari, as was his wont, played the big brother. Manbesh was friendly, a perfect gentleman, Mallik grave and withdrawn.

My great buddy, however, was Dibakar Dasgupta, a Bengali from Allahabad University, fluent in Oriya having spent his time mostly with the dominant Oriya group in Allahabad. He was a Deputy Superintendent of Police and, later, joined IPS in 1964. He was allotted the Madhya Pradesh cadre. We used to go out frequently.

This is no place to speak about individual officers, but apart from our professional training, there were probationers who were talented otherwise. Devendra Singh was the foremost, with his versatility. Serious in studies and good in sport, he would enthrall us with Hindi ghazals and English songs. He was awarded the best cadet award, a recognition which he richly deserved. My roommate, B J K Tampi, would narrate jokes, not manufactured or culled from books, but from his life's experiences. During our training, we came across a scam, this term not in vogue then, minor in nature.

One of our instructors, Gopal Krishnan, who was in charge of the co-operative store supplying everything to us— our uniform, civil clothings, stationery and other day-to-day needs—was charged with misappropriation of funds, which constituted our uniform grant of Rs 1,000 each. I think, he was placed under suspension, and later committed suicide.

Each day, a probationer, by turn, had to act as duty officer whose duty was to visit all premises of the college, scattered all over the town. He then had to make an entry that would testify to his visit. At night the streets were dark and empty, and the lone probationer would move, armed with his baton and a torch light, and with a beating heart heavy with stories about eerie sounds, unseen movements, ghosts walking and weird animals.

Training in Abu was marked by three outings — training in civil defence in Nagpur, army attachment, and Bharat Darshan. Due to the national emergency arising out of the Chinese aggression, the last component was dropped. We visited Nagpur at the peak of summer for our training in the Central Emergency Relief Training Institute, met our income tax friends who were undergoing their basic course, went to Kamptee to witness an army passing out parade, where, the then Army Chief General J N Choudhary was taking salute, and attended a reception given by the Senior Superintendent of Police, Nagpur.

Our army attachment was with the Armoured Division at Jhansi, where, in the mess, our batchmate Bhaskar Rao would match the army officers over a peg too many. We were invited by the Indo-Tibetan Border Police (ITBP) to a passing out parade at Babina, where, pleasantly, I met N R Patnaik, a directly recruited Deputy Superintendent of Police from Orissa, working as Assistant Commandant, and we became friends. Professionally sound and thorough, ITBP became his favourite organization, from where he retired as Inspector General.

Bharat Darshan, in a truncated form, was revived in mid-1964, dividing the batch into groups for visiting a limited number of places. My group was assigned Calcutta and Patna. In Barrackpur, DIG Training, the famous Ranjit Gupta of the IP, while talking to us, gave us advice, short and sharp "Deserve and Desire."

The cycle of life moves ineluctably. While at the beginning, feeling tortured by the dispensation designed for us for the next ten months, we were looking forward to the end; we saw time slipping by and, lo and behold, the end was in sight. There was, no doubt, a feeling of elation at the prospect of going home, but also there was, in our subconscious, a feeling of being overwhelmed by the enormity of the impending departure.

Preparations started in full swing for the passing out ceremony: examinations, ceremonial parade practice and mess dinner. We took exams in theory, physical training, parade, horse riding, first aid and rifle and revolver shooting. Rehearsals for the ceremonial parade were gruelling and unsparing, to ensure perfection in every movement and faultless symmetry.

The last days were hectic. We all received intimations of our next port of call, mostly the state police training colleges. In our case, it was the Police Training College at Angul for three-month training. Pyari had left Mount Abu to join IAS, and so, we were three now.

The passing out parade was commanded by Devendra Singh, the best cadet, and, to say the least, the parade was perfect. It was not a surprise, given the rigorous training we had received during the preceding ten months. But the poignant moments were yet to come. After the parade and accompanying formalities came the last item, peeling off, to the soulful tune of "Auld Lang Syne".

As we were peeling off, our mind was surcharged with emotion, an intense feeling of togetherness and impending separation, a contrast of life, contrasts that are the laws of nature, life and death, brightness and darkness, happiness and sorrow, laughter and tears. The feeling was accentuated by the realization of what is going to happen next, embarking on a course of life that held tantalizing challenges and promises.

Evening mess dinner was fabulous. While perfection ruled the roost in the main dining hall, with the trainees and invitees following each prescribed motion, culminating in a toast to the head of the state, there were noisy scenes in the annexe, where, the chosen left over that included me, savoured their dishes liberally, sans table manners, with reckless ease. It was in the mess night that Spadigam was at his humble best and Stracy, the star of the show.

Thus, came to an end a chapter of our life, the most decisive one in the Central Police Training College, Mount Abu. We made preparations for our departure and journey to our respective states for the third phase of our training in the state police training colleges, bidding adieu to Mount Abu and friends.

Chapter-7

Training in The State

We reported in the Police Training College (PTC), Angul which was a sub-divisional town in the undivided Dhenkanal district. The institution started as a school in 1936, after separation of Orissa from Bihar, and became a college in 1948. It was one of the most backward and ill-equipped training institutions, highlighted by the annual visit of the modernisation team set up by the Ministry of Home affairs to monitor the modernization scheme in 1973–74, when I was the AIG of Police from 1973 to 1976.

We were given accommodation in the Mission Bungalow, which was earmarked for assistant superintendents and deputy superintendents of police. Our Principal was Biswakesh Tripathy, an officer of the 1954 batch, a hard task master, who would never smile on the parade ground. He proved to be tougher than Spadigam, who rarely punished us. But BK, as we called him, was the opposite.

Once, while we were in the midst of drill, for some reason we could not suppress our laughter at a certain incident, inviting the wrath of BK, who ordered four of us—three IPS trainees and one deputy superintendent, Prem

Ranjan Mohanty—to run around the field for one hour, with kits on the shoulder and rifle in hands. Manabesh and Prem Ranjan were stocky in their built. After some time, they started gasping, a sight which made me laugh, to be again taken to task by the Principal. Off the field, he was a friend, inviting us to his residence for dinner and joining us in the mess quite often. He had returned from deputation to CRPF; he was to go to it again and return in 1977, to go again as Inspector General, BSF and then to Nagaland as Police Chief, where he took premature retirement.

The most memorable event during our stay in the PTC was our deployment during Nehru's visit. I think we were the last batch to have performed duty during Nehru's visit to different parts of the country. The annual session of the Indian National Congress was held in January 1964 in Bhubaneswar, and elaborate police arrangements had to be made.

At that time, police resources were limited. There were just two armed battalions—one located at Cuttack, the second, a Gurkha Battalion, at Jharsuguda in Western Orissa. Crowds would swell to see Nehru, who would drive, at times, in an open jeep from the aerodrome. The only saving grace was that the crowd, which came spontaneously, would generally pose no law and order problem. While on the road Nehru would virtually be piloted on foot by senior officers clearing the way, step-by-step.

JC Ghosh, a member of IP, was the IG Police. He ordered that the ASPs and DySPs, under training, would proceed to Bhubaneswar for duty, which we did under the supervision of our Principal. In Bhubaneswar, we stayed in our tents in the Stewart School compound, which was functioning as the main control room and mess for visiting officers, under the overall supervision of B K Panigrahi, an officer of the 1952 batch.

Each major aspect of the law and order arrangement

was under a Superintendent of Police. I was attached to traffic, which was the responsibility of P C Ratho (1956), SP Sambalpur. I was assigned the independent duty of supervising route lining during Nehru's drive from airport to Raj Bhavan and from there to the venue and back. It was certainly a tall order, and I was feeling very diffident till I received a reassuring pat from P C Ratho. On the day prior to the arrival of Nehru, extensive rehearsals were carried out.

On the morning of his arrival, I was taking a few rounds from Raj Bhavan to the airport and back, when I saw a PHD tanker swerving strangely from the opposite direction. It lost its grip, swung to the left of the road, dashed against a tree and stood, half-turned. I was at a loss as to what to do. The vehicle could be removed either by a crane or by towing, which I was not in a position to organise. I was pacing restlessly when the SP Puri G C Senapati (Bhubaneswar was then a subdivision in Puri district) came, looked at the ugly sight and told me to remove it by using my discretion and left.

My confusion was further confounded: how could a young ASP from the PTC, who had no idea about the system and no contact whatsoever, remove the tanker. After some time, Damodar Chotray, DIG Central range, an emergency recruit after independence, a seasoned and experienced officer, came by. He got down from his vehicle, inspected the sight and asked me what I was planning to do. I expressed my utter helplessness and what he told me still rings in my mind: "Do not bother. Let it lie; it may be hidden by the crowd." His words were like elixir to my sagging spirit. My confidence restored, I started performing my duty.

Nehru's drive to Raj Bhavan passed off smoothly. What Chotray displayed that day was not only leadership quality, but also empathy, which I found, in subsequent years, was an integral part of man management.

But the real faux pas was yet to come. The general session in the evening passed off smoothly. Next afternoon, Nehru went to attend a working committee meeting in a building close to the venue. On the eastern coast, evening falls earlier, and, in winter, darkness sets in still earlier. The front half of the venue was not properly lighted. There were parked two identical cars – one for Nehru and the other, for Morarji Desai. D N Singh, an officer of the 1958 batch, then SP Kalahandi, was Nehru's protection officer.

I had parked my vehicle about 100 metres away from Nehru's car. Ahead of me was Alam, a Reserve Inspector, in the advanced pilot vehicle. It was arranged that I would receive a signal from the protection vehicle the moment Nehru came out of the building, relay it to Alam, who would go ahead, clearing the crowd. Morarji Desai first came out of the building and got into Nehru's car by mistake.

The darkness hindered recognition. The security staff thought it was Nehru, and gave me the signal. I, in turn, asked Alam to proceed. It was only at the Raj Bhavan crossing that I heard in the VHF that Nehru's car was held up by the surging crowd. When I got down, I saw Morarji Desai sitting in the car which I piloted. I got into my vehicle and rushed frantically to the place where Nehru was held up, jumped out and started clearing the crowd. A gigantic task it was.

Luckily, Prafulla Kumar Mishra, an officer of the 1960 batch, who later became a hardcore Intelligence Bureau (IB) man, arrived and both of us steered Nehru's vehicle all the way to Raj Bhavan. P K Mishra died in a tragic car accident in 1986.

At night, at the pre-dinner gathering, I was waiting for a heavy dressing down. Surprisingly, there was none. It was D N Singh who was at the receiving end of light-hearted remarks, thanks to the predinner ambience. It was, no doubt, a security lapse.

Perhaps, beyond the police, and, if anybody was to be faulted, the finger would point at Morarji Desai. But, in the context of present times, with media pouncing on every single event, either the SP Kalahandi or I would have been made the scapegoat.

Next day, early in the morning, Nehru was to go to Tikarpara to lay the foundation stone of the multi-purpose dam on Mahanadi. I was there in the Raj Bhavan square controlling traffic. Time kept ticking, but Nehru would not come. People whose vehicles had been stopped were getting restless, and so was I. Around 9 am, news came that the programme had been cancelled. Nehru had a stroke, which later was famously described as "Bhubaneswar was the beginning of the end". That was to happen a few months later.

Our Bhubaneswar duty was towards the last leg of our stay at Angul. When we met the IGP, he informed me that I was being posted to Sambalpur.

We returned to Angul and after getting relieved, proceeded to our respective districts in the latter half of January 1964. Soon after joining, practice for the Republic Day parade started. SP P C Ratho ordered me to command the parade.

My father suggested that for my convenience I should take a house in the Reserve Police lines, if available. I approached the SP and he readily allotted an old type sergeant's quarters with three big rooms, a courtyard and some open space. This became the den of the 1963 IAS probationers coming for training in the Administrative Officers Training School in Hirakud. P C Hota, my batch mate in IAS, who later became the UPSC Chairman, shifted to my place from the Circuit House, where, every now and then, depending on the visit of VIPs, he was asked to vacate his room.

Here, it will be relevant to discuss the political scenario then prevailing in India in general, and Orissa in particular, as I would be dealing with the system for the next three decades. At the national level, the Congress party held undisputed sway, with its iconic leader Pandit Nehru, who was in his fourth term as the Prime Minister. He had touched Olympian heights as a world statesman and commanded great respect all over the world, drawing admiration even from critics. A dreamer, a visionary and an idealist, he very often failed to see the realities and was battling his biggest humiliation after the Chinese betrayal. His failings notwithstanding, he continued to be the darling of the masses.

In Orissa, politics was like quicksand. The Congress, no doubt, was the dominant group, but formidable challenge was emerging in the shape of a political outfit called Ganatantra Parishad. It was founded mostly by the former rulers of the feudatory states with R N Singhdeo, former ruler of the Balangir, as its president.

The Parishad enjoyed wide support of the people in Western Orissa. The first Chief Minister of Orissa after independence, Hare Krushna Mahatab, went to Centre in 1950 to join the Union Cabinet and Nabakrushna Chowdhury, a bhoodan leader, unassuming, principled and honest, succeeded him. Mahatab lost his cabinet berth after the 1952 elections, and then began an era of intrigues that plagued the Congress. Nehru sent him to Bombay as Governor, but his three famous disciples, Biju Patnaik, Biren Mitra and Nilamani Routaray, the troika who would be ruling Orissa in the succeeding years kept the flame of intrigues alive.

Choudhury resigned in disgust in October 1956. Mahatab staged a comeback, but had to lead a coalition ministry with his bete-noire R N Singhdeo. His admirers termed it a masterstroke, but the critics would not spare him, highlighting the fundamental differences in the ideologies of both parties one talking about society based on socialism, the other advocating free enterprise.

The three disciples of Mahatab were disillusioned by the strategy adopted by their Guru to remain in power. Biju Patnaik, who had ingratiated himself with Nehru, led the Congress in the 1961 Assembly elections to a convincing victory, bagging 89 seats in the 140-member House. The troika came to power, with Patnaik as the Chief Minister. An industrialist-turned-politician, Patnaik was ambitious, amoral and impatient, verging on recklessness. What he did have, though, was a vision for Orissa, which endeared him to Nehru.

The troika, however, had a patchy rule. Patnaik had left his Chief Ministership in the Kamraj plan. His friend, Biren Mitra, was the Chief Minister when I started my life in IPS in Orissa. The Gantantra Parishad, the main opposition party, had lost its identity by merging itself with the Swatantra Party, founded by C Rajagopalachari. The Communists and the Praja Socialist Party (PSP) were marginal players. The PSP later joined Congress.

The district training of an IPS probationer, lasting 10 months, was divided into different phases: attachment to district police office including motor vehicle section, reserve office, circle inspector office, collectorate and the court. The last two months comprised attachment to a police station as officer-in-charge.

My entire training schedule, however, turned topsy-turvy on account of two major law and order situations, which hit Orissa in 1964. They were communal disturbances in March and a student agitation in the latter half of the year, which virtually led to the fall of the Biren Mitra ministry after a visit by Gulzarilal Nanda, then Union Home Minister, and L P Singh, the Home Secretary.

SP PC Ratho, whose residence was just across the road, mostly functioned from his residential office. He was an outstanding field officer. He would reach a problem area without delay and immediately take command of the situation. He would not blink an eye before proceeding to a troubled area and could remain without food till he was satisfied that he had done a good job. He seemed to have taken a liking for me and we maintained a friendly and informal relationship. As mentioned earlier, I had been a teetotaller till I finished my training. It was only at Sambalpur that the SP and the Collector, Kukreja, initiated me into alcoholic beverages, starting with beer.

Hardly a month had gone by when communal disturbances erupted in Rourkela, the steel town, and rapidly spread to Sundargarh, Rajgangpur, Jharsuguda and Brajraj Nagar, the last two in Sambalpur district. The provocation was the sight of a refugee train, which was on its way to Dandakaranya, an area covering parts of Madhya Pradesh and Orissa. It had its headquarters at Koraput in Orissa, developed for settling the refugees from East Pakistan on a permanent basis. There was large scale looting, arson and killing of people leading to use of force by police. The law and order machinery in Rourkela had completely collapsed due to inadequate strength of the forces and other logistic deficiencies.

It was either a holiday or a Sunday. I was at home, when a message arrived from the Reserve Office that I should be in uniform to accompany the SP to Jharsuguda. Ratho came in no time, accompanied by Prasanta Mohanty, a correspondent of Samaj, the largest circulated Oriya daily, in a jeep. I hopped in and he drove at breakneck speed.

After leaving the town, he pulled the throttle to allow the jeep to attain its maximum speed. We kept our fingers crossed. We reached Jharsuguda in record time and as we entered the main road that led to Rourkela, we saw devastation spread before us – all the shops of the minority community were gutted, looted and damaged. The road was deserted; some casualties had taken place. We saw the culprits running towards the residential area of the minority community to attack.

We ran after them, chasing, hammering them with the cane and the butt of the revolver. Eventually we rounded them up and herded them to the police station. Later, I thought it was only because of that action, third degree at its worst, that further loss to life and property had been averted.

The second battalion of the armed police was located at Jharsuguda. Additional force was readily available. The force, Gurkha in composition, was disciplined, tough and listened blindly to the orders of superiors. Kukreja, the Collector, with great aptitude for field work, arrived. The situation had been brought under control by evening. Stray incidents, however, continued.

Brajrajnagar, an industrial town with a paper mill of the Birlas and a refractory of the Tatas only 20 km from Jharsuguda, was equally affected, although the damage was comparatively less. Armed pickets were immediately mounted for round-the-clock vigil.

We were patrolling till midnight, when the SP decided to return to Sambalpur, asking me to stay back. I requested him to allow me to go to Sambalpur and come back within three hours with the bare necessities, but he would not listen. I went to the IB, got some night clothes from a friend, and slept for a few hours.

The next day and for the third day, I remained in one set of uniform without shaving, and left for Sambalpur only on the fourth day. I wonder if it would be taken in good spirit now-a-days, but, back then, we accepted it as routine of a police man's life.

The entire stretch on the Howrah–Bombay line, starting from Rourkela to Rajgangpur, another industrial town, to Sundargarh, Jharsuguda and Brajarajnagar became vulnerable to sporadic incidents for quite some time. The state government decided to call the Army, which was deployed under a Lt Col in all these places. I continued to stay at Jharsuguda, overseeing the situation till May, i.e., for more than two months.

In the wake of the riots, the police force underwent massive overhauling. J C Ghosh, IP, was replaced by S K Ghose, an IPS officer, who had started his career as a directly-appointed DySP. Ghose emerged as one of the toughest and most seasoned officers in the police force, with the added advantage of being very close to the then Home Minister, Nilamani Routaray. He flew to Rourkela, ordering B K Panigrahi, an IPS officer of 1952 batch, another efficient, and honest officer, to join as SP Rourkela replacing S Sinha, a 1956 batch officer.

Soon thereafter, a new range was created, the Western Range, carved out of the Northern large. Iqbal Singh, an officer of the 1950 batch, who later went to R&AW was posted as DIG at Rourkela. Two battalions of the armed police were sanctioned —one at Rourkela and the other at Koraput, the southernmost district of Orissa, bordering Andhra Pradesh.

By that time, a 1961 IAS probationer, P K Patnaik, academically senior to me in college was sent to Jharsuguda by Kukreja to join me. We shared a room in the IB. Ratho's visits to Jharsuguda were unpredictable, coming at unearthly hours to check if things were in order.

One such midnight, when we were asleep, there was a knock on the door. I opened the door to find the SP, who light-heartedly said, "I came to check if you are sleeping with a woman!" Jharsuguda had a history of corrupting IAS and IPS officers.

The Army demanded the entire IB for their accommodation and office. So, we had to vacate the IB and were shifted to an industry guest house. We marked our time, waiting to be recalled, which happened only in May.

Within a few days, I proceeded to Cuttack, to appear in the departmental examinations conducted by the Board of Revenue. For the accounts paper, all that we had to do was to send a question paper to the District Police Office (DPO), where an accountant would write the answers and send the same to us for reproduction in our answer paper. For the non-Oriya probationers of IPS and IAS, I literally wrote the answers, all within the knowledge of the Secretary, an IAS officer, wondering why he showed this indulgence to me, till I received an invitation for tea, at his residence.

It was in Cuttack that I received the news of Nehru's death. I had been staying with S P Mallik, my batchmate. We were glued to the radio to the very last, listening to the funeral proceedings, to the famous commentator, Melvin De Mello, whose choked voice uttered the poignant words: "My leader is gone." Tears brimmed over. Nehru's departure had created a gaping void.

Lal Bahadur Shastri took over as Prime Minister. He did the very best in his tenure, cut short by his untimely death in Moscow. But the gentle colossus that Nehru was could never be replaced.

I returned to Sambalpur and resumed my training, but within a few days proceeded to Bargarh, one of the busiest trading centres in Sambalpur on NH 6 (now a separate district) for my two months of Police training as officer in charge of the police station. I stayed in the canal IB and had a fruitful stay at Bargarh. In fact, this was the only period of my training when I was my own self, registering first information reports, investigating into a few simple cases, checking motor vehicles and submitting prosecution reports, doing night patrol, all under the guidance and supervision of the Circle Inspector Judhistir Babu. He had a lot of patience and would explain the nuances of various records of the police station like crime directory part I, II and III, history sheets, case diaries, charge sheet and final report, confidential weekly reports so on and so forth.

My leisure time was spent in the house of my cousin sister whose husband was a well-known advocate or with S K Lal, an IAS officer of 1960 batch who was Sub Collector of Bargarh. While there was one visit by the Range DIG Narayan Chand, a former princely state officer who rose to become the Chief of Orissa Police, there was surprisingly no visit from the SP who I learnt was preparing to go on two months leave.

An important charge like Sambalpur could not be kept without a full-time SP and by the time I returned to Sambalpur T Ananthachari, an officer of 1958 batch, was posted as SP Sambalpur. The next major law and order situation in Orissa was in the offing, this time the students' agitation of September 1964. It engulfed the entire state for the next three months, disrupting the last leg of my training and surcharging the political climate in Orissa.

The provocation for the students was a minor incident of scuffle between a student and a shopkeeper in Cuttack, followed by marching of hundreds of students from Ravenshaw College to the Assembly in Bhubaneswar and ransacking the House without any opposition.

In a major incident in Cuttack, the students who were planning to hold a meeting near Saheed Bhavan were dispersed by tear gas, and lathi charge resulting in injury to many. Public cried foul, condemned the police for excesses, even questioned the role of the IG Police S K Ghosh who came under severe scrutiny. The agitation spread like wildfire across the entire state. The main reason for the prolonged agitation was the unpopularity, which the ruling troika of Biju Patnaik, who was now not in office of CM but in control of the state, Biren Mitra, the functioning CM, and Nilamani Routaray, the Home Minister, had gained over several alleged acts of irregularities, nepotism and malpractices. Vernacular dailies and sometimes the English papers published from Calcutta, particularly The Statesman, carried scathing criticisms of the regime on their pages. What also sustained the agitation was the support, both direct and tacit, it was receiving from all political parties including Congress, the ruling party. There was violence in all major towns, causing loss of life and property.

My duty everyday was to come and report at the control room located in the Town PS and rush to a spot with force and Magistrate to control the situation. Ananthachari, the new SP, proved his mettle at Sambalpur. Never shy of facing a crowd, he would take command of a situation with minimum response time. Collector Kukreja was an ideal counterfoil.

Chari, as the SP was popularly called, was yet to get married and lived a spartan life in one room in his official residence, but he would entertain people over dinner where drinks were served. His was an eventful career shuttling between state and Centre and pioneering new technology in police like IT. Later he would become the first Director of the Directorate of Coordination Police Computers (DCPC) where I would be joining him as his deputy in 1977 to succeed him as Director in 1979. He retired as the Director General of Border Security Force. He was a leading figure in fighting for police reforms and the lot of IPS by remaining a frontrunner activist of the IPS Association in the state and the Centre, foot prints which I followed.

In a major incident in the sub-divisional town of Rairakhol, the mob attacked the police station and caused considerable damage to properties and records. The ineptitude of police, coupled with the inaction of the Sub-Divisional Officer, only escalated the situation. I was at the control room in the company of the Collector and two Additional Superintendents of Police —Md. Fida Rassol and Janardan Pattanaik, a promoted officer. Chari was out.

On receiving the news, Kukreja contacted Chari over phone and then asked me to proceed to Rairakhol with a platoon of force. I was surprised as the seriousness of the situation demanded that an Additional SP should go. But I had no option and reached Rairakhol late in the evening. I saw the ghastly look the police station presented with the SDO and Circle Inspector sitting with gloomy faces. Immediately we posted pickets, rounded up the mischief-mongers and after patrolling the small town I went to the IB for dinner. The SDO, crestfallen, short of crying implored me not to give any adverse report as he had already received a dressing down from Kukreja in his typical Punjabi style. I suddenly felt important, an ASP under training being supplicated by the SDO to save his skin.

Yet another incident comes to my mind vividly. It was, to say the least, an enactment of courage, displayed by the range DIG Narayan Chand. When it was known that Union Home Minister Gulzarilal Nanda and Home Secretary L P Singh would be visiting Cuttack to listen to the grievances of the students, the students of the GM College, Sambalpur, marched *en bloc* to submit a memorandum to the Collector, violating 144 CrPC.

The Collectorate, the DPO and District Judge court were adjacent to each other but without a boundary wall. So a human cordon was formed, barricading the area that included the nearby DIG's residence and RDC's office. I was guarding the point near our office. We saw the slogan-shouting students breaking the barricade near the DIG's residence and coming towards the Collectorate. As they came, they started pelting stones which could only be prevented by use of force and at that point in time —the fag end of agitation—any casualty would have had serious repercussions on the visit of the Union Home Minister.

I was in no position to take a decision. Chari had gone out of Sambalpur to control the situation elsewhere. Kukreja, who was in his residential office, talked to the DIG and suddenly I saw a jeep emerging from the gate of the DIG's residence with Narayan Chand inside. He got down from the jeep in the midst of the students and started walking towards the entry point where I was positioned. When I saw him, I thought the man was mad, handing himself over to the vagaries of angry students. To my surprise, the pelting of stones stopped and students started shouting, booing and jeering at Chand with a repeated refrain "Narayan Chand Kukur (dog) Chand'. Regardless, the DIG walked confidently with a baton in his hand followed by the students who on nearing the gate directed their abuses with the choicest epithets at me: "Down, down Amiya Tripathy, betrayer of the students of his college", alluding to the fact I was a student of GM College in my Intermediate classes.

Chand came inside the cordon and with a patronising look asked the students to select a group to be allowed inside the cordon to proceed to the Collector's residential office to submit their memorandum; that done, he went to the SP's residence and waited in the residential office while the students went to submit the memorandum. Thus, the DIG's act of valour averted a major crisis.

My district training, seriously fractured, was coming to an end. I received my transfer order, to Berhampur as Sub Divisional Police Officer, but was faced with impediments to get relieved as Chand wanted me to continue as ASP at Sambalpur, a prospect I did not like as I was keen to go to a field posting. Chand relented and, after more than two years of training in four phases at four places—Mussoorie, Mt Abu, Angul and Sambalpur—I prepared myself for more than 33 years of active police life.

What impact did the four officers, BK Tripathy, Principal PTC, P C Ratho, SP Sambalpur succeeded by T Ananthachari and DIG Narayan Chand, had on me? I should say substantial, two important features being leadership quality and treating an IPS officer as a friend, for they knew that an IPS officer was a potential police chief. B K Tripathy, a hard task master in the field, was a friend off duty. Ratho and Ananthachari, both high voltage and high octane, treated me as a friend and brother both on and off duty, and Narayan Chand's tough exterior was a deceptive facade necessary in police. His softer side was revealed when he asked me to continue in Sambalpur after training. I tried my very best to maintain these qualities in my professional career.

Part-3

Life Of A Nomad

- Berhampur
- Bhubaneswar
- Puri—Failed operations
- Cuttack—Incurring Chief's Wrath
- Balasore
- Tezpur and Shivpuri
- Koraput
- Bhubaneswar—Barred entry to Raj Bhavan
- Mayurbhanj—Hot Seat
- Koraput, Keonjhar, Cuttack: Wiser by the Day
- Berhampur: Beginning of Stability

Chapter-8

Berhampur

I joined Berhampur in December 1964. The students' agitations were just over with Home Minister Gulzarilal Nanda's personal intervention at Cuttack Circuit House. A Commission of Inquiry, headed by Justice S K Burman of the Orissa High Court, was set up to look into the students' grievances. Berhampur, which was very badly affected, was limping back to normalcy. The students had caused damage and destruction to property, attacked a police station and burnt the local church, the last act being the consequence of their anger against my predecessor Samuel Mahapatra, a Deputy Superintendent of Police, who was a Christian.

There was no residence for the SDPO. Mahapatra continued to stay in the rented house as he was posted as Deputy SP, Special Branch, at Berhampur. I occupied the resting room in the fire station and stayed there for nearly three months out of my seven months' stay till I was allotted an Inspector's quarters by the DIG, Southern Range, which covered the vast area of south Orissa comprising four undivided districts of Ganjam, Phulbani, Koraput, then the second biggest district in India, and Kalahandi.

Berhampur, which was Orissa's second biggest town then, next only to Cuttack, was a throbbing trading centre in the district of Ganjam, whose district headquarters was located at Chhatrapur, a small seaside town 20 km away. The Revenue Divisional Commissioner, DIG and many other divisional level officers, including SP Vigilance of the State Anti Corruption Bureau, were located at Berhampur. BK Roy, the first direct recruit allotted to Orissa in 1948, was the DIG. A Majid, an IPS officer promoted from the rank of DySP and a renowned football player who represented India in Asian Games, popularly known in Orissa as Bachan, was the SP. While BK Roy was a hard task master going to unnecessary details during his prolonged inspections of district police office and reserve office, Majid was a gentle soul -- polite, suave and friendly. I called on both, received instructions from them and settled down to my duties. I also called on the RDC, the DM and, as directed by the DIG, some divisional level officers of other departments.

When I started police life in Berhampur, with fond dreams of contributing to nation building and with robust idealism and a tremendous sense of dedication, little did I foresee that all these feelings would be put to severe test by a whirlwind of events in the next seven years during which I would be clocking 14 postings, an average of six months each -- moving from one end of Orissa to the other like a nomad, antagonising the all powerful IGP SK Ghosh, the state Governor SA Ansari and two Collectors in two districts.

Finally, when I found some stability in 1971, also in Berhampur, I found myself emerging unscathed and my cherished values intact.

Berhampur was a small subdivision with a few police stations in and around the town. So workload was not heavy. Most problems centred on Berhampur, which reported a high crime rate. As it was situated on the Howrah—Madras railway line, criminals from outside would commit crime with local contacts and slip out in the morning. Another problem was smuggling of fertilisers, which underutilized in Orissa found way to Andhra. Enforcement of the Essential Commodities Act was a prime responsibility of the police. The strength of police was woefully inadequate to match the criminals and over a time the situation, instead of improving, deteriorated.

Berhampur also became notorious by the end of the 60s for killings by rival political groups—in the open and in broad daylight. The Khallikote College, then one out of the two private colleges in Orissa, and the second biggest in the state, was a breeding ground of indiscipline.

In the first few days, I got a taste of political interference in a case in which a group of students, supporters of the Congress party, were charged with assaulting and obstructing the Civil Surgeon (now called CDMO). One of the students later became a Union minister. I supervized the case and gave orders for charge sheet. The students ran to the Chief Minister and sought his intervention. Biren Mitra, the then Chief Minister, rang me and told me clearly that no charge sheet should be submitted. Puzzled, I spoke to the DIG who asked for my supervision note that I had written without adequate command over the nuances of supervision. After going through it, the DIG agreed with my findings and sent it to the IGP with his views. The case, however, remained pending till I left Berhampur.

Talk about police, public relationship was yet to get momentum. SK Ghosh did, however, take some measures in that direction, notable being introduction of a postcard system in investigation. The OIC, while registering a case, would give a self-addressed postcard to the complainant for getting his feedback on the investigation. This was considered a novel idea and response from public was encouraging, but it withered way in no time. Ghosh had taken several steps to streamline the police administration. A very useful measure was to compile the police orders and police circular orders issued after independence and publish them in book form. These books became very useful to officers at all levels as they covered many areas not spelt out in the Police Manual. The contents were professional and not pedantic. Later, however, some police chiefs, perhaps swayed away by their importance, issued circulars recklessly more out of the urge to see their names in print than to bring in any improvement.

After the Chinese aggression, the small Himalayan kingdoms of Nepal, Sikkim and Bhutan were becoming strategically crucial for India's security. Prime Minister Lal Bahadur Shastri and the Bhutanese King were scheduled to hold parleys at Gopalpur-on-sea, in the Oberoi Palm Beach Hotel under my jurisdiction.

Elaborate security arrangements were made with several rehearsals supervised by the DIG and IGP. On the day of arrival, we were all in the air field. IGP, RDC, DIG, DM, SP and I to receive the VVIPS, but at the last moment the visit for some reason was cancelled.

It was at Gopalpur that I met the famous owner of Oberoi Group of hotels, Rai Bahadur PS Oberoi. Over a glass of beer, he narrated the fascinating story of his acquisition of the hotels. Palm Beach was the third, for which he had paid Rs 20,000. The previous owner had one condition, that the name Palm Beach be retained and so the hotel was named Oberoi Palm Beach. A Swiss lady, Madam Lutse, who was the caretaker, was very much there taking meticulous care of the hotel. Matronly, gregarious and affectionate, oozing warmth and charm, she developed a great liking for me and used to treat me and my friends with delightful dinners at a heavily discounted price.

Yet another VVIP visit was that of His Holiness the Dalai Lama, who used to be accorded full state honours at that time obviously under instructions from Nehru. The Dalai Lama was to visit a Tibetan refugee camp in Chandragiri in Ganjam. He came to Berhampur from Calcutta in a special coach attached to a train. The coach, which reached Berhampur early morning, was parked in a yard and it was arranged that he would come out of the coach at 8 am to receive the greetings of people and give blessings. I along with the Sub Collector reached the yard much in advance and when the Dalai Lama learnt about our arrival, he called us inside and talked to us. A little later when I came out, I saw RDC KC Ray, the DIG, DM and SP waiting to receive His Holiness. Ray, a highly religious person, fell at the feet of His Holiness, seeking his blessings, leaving all of us surprised. The Dalai Lama, who was very young then, looking radiant and benign, waved at the eager crowd and proceeded to Chandragiri.

While I was at Berhampur, the other subdivisions, Paralakhemundi (now a district) and Bhanjanagar, had two IPS officers as SDPOs, NK Singh of 1961 batch, and my batchmate Manbesh Mukherjee respectively. There were two IAS probations under training. Nilmadhab Mohanty, my batchmate in the last leg of his training, and R K Bhujabal, my classmate and of 1963 batch. MY Rao of the 1963 batch came after Nilmadhab left. When all would gather at Berhampur-- and that was quite frequent -- my small room in the fire station would be witness to heated and loud discussions, gossips followed by eating food brought from Girija restaurant, an old eating place. Occasionally, we would visit Gopalpur for dinner in Palm Beach and be treated royally by Madam Lutse or watch films at the local cinema halls.

When I shifted to my residence, there was privacy and

space and freedom of speech was more in display. NK Singh went on earned leave and I was asked to remain in charge and had an unforgettable experience of supervising a murder case.

I had to go to a remote corner of Paralakhemundi, not accessible by road, to supervise the case. I went to RU daygiri, where the Circle Inspector was located, and was planning to return to Berhampur next day. At RU daygiri I was told that the spot was more than 30 km, which had to be traversed by foot. Spot visit was a must and was unavoidable although the Circle Inspector gave me indications that witnesses could be brought to the circle office. I decided to start early next morning, hoping to reach the spot by evening in spite of imponderables like rain as monsoon had set in, and the terrain full of forests and hills. We started as scheduled and made good progress. After about 20 km when we stopped in a village for lunch, I found the Inspector, an elderly person, totally exhausted. Since I was determined to reach the spot, I asked the Inspector to stay in the village and proceeded onwards with an ASI and some gramrakshis.

We reached the spot late evening, completely fagged out, took some food and blacked out. Next morning I supervised the case and left the village by early noon. Halting for the night midway was inevitable. On the third day, we resumed our journey; the Inspector had joined me by then, hoping to reach RU daygiri by afternoon. Clouds were becoming thick and heavy rainfall started. We moved regardless through the slush and mud. Then came a mountain stream and, as we were crossing it, water came rushing with a speed that threatened to swallow us. I could feel water rising and covering different parts of my body—my feet, then knees, waist and then chest. The gramrakshis encircled me in a tight grip and we stood still. They said the water level would recede and it happened that way. The water level receded and we crossed the stream. This, I was told, was a common natural phenomenon in the mountainous region. We reached R Udaygiri late evening. My feet had swollen and I was disoriented.

By April 1965, my marriage had been finalized. It was slated for July 7. I applied for one month's leave beginning July 1. I left the place with a sense of anticipation that I found exciting. There was no way of knowing that I would not be coming back to Berhampur.

Chapter-9

Bhubaneswar

I went to Sambalpur and from there we came to Bhubaneswar for the wedding. My wife, Usha Rani, was a student of Political Science in Utkal University, where Dr Sriram Dash, my teacher in Ravenshaw, was her Professor. Her sister Bani followed her and then my youngest brother Anugraha too.

We returned to Sambalpur the next day. My father, even after six years of retirement, had not been able to build a house; so a bigger house had been temporarily taken on rent.

I had about Rs 1,000, which I thought I would spend on a visit to Ranchi, with my wife. My friend Rajendra Das (1962), IAS, who had been allotted Bihar cadre, was SDO Gumla and had extended an invitation. My second brother, Akshya, who had passed ISc wanted to do MBBS, but my father had no money for it.

This presented me with a moral crisis. I decided to call off our Ranchi trip and handed over the money to my brother for his admission in the medical college. I certainly was not happy, but that was the way it had to be when one was the eldest son in a traditional family. Duties must be discharged.

Ananthachari, who was SP, arranged a party in our honour. We took a rickshaw to his residence as no taxi service was available in Sambalpur. I find it important to mention these little details to highlight that the style of and approach to our life then would be considered obscure, funny and perhaps, outlandish in the present days.

I received a telegram with the intimation that I had been posted at Bhubaneswar as SDPO on expiry of leave. Bhubaneswar, till then, had an IPS officer as SDPO. In view of its growing importance, a post of Additional SP was created, and Ranjan Roy (1961), who was SDPO, had taken over as Addl. SP. I was not at all keen on going to Bhubaneswar. SK Ghosh, who was a friend of my father-in-law, perhaps thought that he was doing a great favour to me.

I went to Bhubaneswar with my wife and joined my new assignment in the first week of August 1965. Luckily, I was allotted a good house from the general pool, and settled down comfortably there. My office was less than one kilometre and I would walk to the office.

As the 1961-batch IPS officers were promoted to the senior scale only after completing four years and inspection of their work by the DIG as per the declaration of SK Ghosh, I planned to settle down at Bhubaneswar for a year. When I joined duty in Bhubaneswar, the monsoon clouds on the northern border were getting thicker with skirmishes by the Pakistan army in the Rann of Kutch. These were successfully repelled by the Indian Army, but the blame game continued.

Our diminutive Prime Minister, Lal Bahadur Shastri, initially dwarfed by giant personalities like Kamraj and

Morarji, was asserting himself, giving directions to the Army to deal with Pakistan in a decisive manner. This led to the famous second India-Pakistan war. The Indian Army in their winning spree knocked at the doors of Lahore.

Alexei Kosygin, the Russian Prime Minister, took the initiative for an Indo-Pak dialogue, and invited Lal Bahadur and Ayub Khan, the Pakistani President. A treaty not to interfere in each other's internal affairs was signed on January 9, 1966. Lal Bahadur died on the 10th, following a massive heart attack. His wife, Lalita Shastri, returned to India with his body. The Bhubaneswar telephone exchange gave the news to me while I was asleep at home.

As mentioned earlier, SK Ghosh, with his dynamism and equation with the Home Minister, had taken up the expansion of the police force as a top priority task. He was also a gregarious person, fond of spending evenings in good company. There was no mess for the officers. The ingenuous SK Ghosh obtained a grant from the government for construction of IPS probationers barracks and thus, the mess in Cuttack was born.

It was inaugurated sometime in August or September 1965. Being the freshest wedded couple, we were invited to the function to be felicitated. I dressed up formally in a '"galaband" went with my wife and was cordially received and cheered by the officers, all of whom were my seniors. The tempo of the mess activities, from then onwards, varied, depending on the attitude of the police chief.

SK Ghosh kept up the mess life; so did some of his successors like RK Padhi, whose very presence used to enliven the mood of the officers, BB Mishra, Narsingh Swain, SS Padhi and BK Panigrahi. When I look over as police chief 30 years later, I was determined to restore the ambience of the 60s and 70s.

Bhubaneswar was a small town then, mainly an official

colony. Industrial houses were yet to come, educational institutions were yet to take roots and a very small segment of the population, the retired officers, had just started settling down. So, work wise, the load was much less than Berhampur. Supervisions and inspections were divided by half with the presence of an Addl SP. Important components were VIP and VVIP duties, and checking the growing traffic particularly on the NH 5 on which bridges had been built on most rivers to ensure all-weather movements.

Crime was steadily going up. With a floating population which included criminals and anti-socials, this was no surprise. The trend continues till today without much improvement, in spite of increase in human and material resources.

By the late eighties, Bhubaneswar crime clock was ticking the fastest in the country weighed against per lakh of population, an unpleasant truth which I pointed out to the government as IG CID crime. I wrote an article, inviting the verbal displeasure of authorities. But the truth had to be faced. The SP, Bhubaneswar, issued a press statement stating that crime in the city was well under control. But the press called the bluff.

Golak Baliarsingh a smart, and agile. Inspector in-charge of Capital Police Station, one of the two police stations then functioning in Bhubaneswar, was popularly known as just Baliarsingh and that was how he would respond to a telephone call, in a resonant voice. VIPs, including the Home Minister, would speak to him directly to get things done. He was an ace investigator and a dread to the criminals of Bhubaneswar.

He proved to be a good guide to me and also, a sincere well-wisher. One day, he rang me up to ask if I was at the Khandagiri crossing on NH-5 at midnight checking trucks. No, I said. He gave me the name of an errant sergeant, who was collecting money from the highway truck drivers, posing as ASP Bhubaneswar. I reported this to Ranjan and put it in writing, as the affair was going to be a messy one, knowing that the sergeant was well-connected.

Bhubaneswar was a subdivision in Puri district. NB Mohanty, a directly recruited Dy SP with 1956 seniority, was the SP. He was a tough and thoroughly honest man. I had an excellent equation with him. It was at Bhubaneswar, however, that I first experienced the displeasure of a senior.

It was the DIG Central Range, Ghanshyam Dash. Right from my first meeting with him, I noted in him a preponderance to find fault with me, an attitude which piqued me. A reason I zeroed upon was his feeling that I had come to Bhubaneswar through a sort of "connection", and not merit. This, to say the least, was far from true as I was not at all keen to come to Bhubaneswar.

He would give me a task and after its completion, pick holes. Luckily for me, the SP and Addl SP were supportive. Once during a VVIP visit, during the rehearsal, he came to supervise and found fault with the arrangements which Ranjan and I had jointly made. His accusing finger was at me. This prompted Ranjan, son of a long-time IG, Bimalendu Roy, co brother-in-law of the legendary BN Mallik, to announce that he was completely satisfied with the arrangements made by Tripathy. Since the 1961 batch had got senior scale only after inspection by the Range DIG, he held that sword on me. His misplaced anger cost me dearly for the next two years.

In this backdrop, S K Ghosh promoted me to senior scale in January 1966 and posted me to Puri as Addl SP, months before the completion of four years in junior scale, and, without inspection by the Range DIG. Dash must have felt cornered and waited for opportunities to prejudice the IG, which readily presented itself when I was in Puri.

For us, however, everything appeared hunky-dory. My

wife was carrying our first child. I had been promoted to senior scale in record time and posted to Puri, where there was a house earmarked for Addl SP.

It was in Bhubaneswar that I acquired my first car, a second hand Fiat. In fact, it was thrust upon me by NK Singh (1961), who, on being promoted to senior scale and after a two-month stint in the third battalion OMP as Commandant, was sent to ITBP by SK Ghosh. NK Singh sent the car to me, telling me that I could pay any amount I desired, at my convenience.

I applied for a car loan of Rs 8,000, sent him Rs 6,000, and kept the remaining amount with me for small luxuries. In those times, there were three brands of car—Ambassador, Fiat and Standard. A car was the valued possession of an officer, not necessarily from the point of view of luxury, but also as a necessity. No staff cars were available back then.

Except the IG Police, who was provided with a big Impala car, no officer, not even the Chief Secretary, was given a staff car. Moreover, with liberal travelling allowance rules of the state, a touring officer could earn a handsome amount legitimately; per km allowance was 50 paisa which also the price of petrol per litre.

Chapter-10

Puri–Failed Operations

With my wife by my side, I drove my second-hand Fiat to Puri to join as Addl SP. I relieved an officer in Puri, who was from the royal family of one of the princely states. In normal course, he would have been a DIG by then.

In the earlier days, Puri, one of the oldest districts of Orissa, although it had no regular port, used to be visited by ships beyond the tides to offload passengers, mainly officers, traders and goods. When the tide was at ebb, they would come to the shore. The road, starting from Podakothi (Burnt House) towards the sea had official establishments on both sides: on the right starting with the Forest IB, the Collector's residence, SP's residence, Judge Court, DPO and Collectorate and on the left the sprawling Raj Bhavan (summer resort of Governor) complex and the Circuit House.

Puri, famous for the Lord Jagannath temple built in the 12th century, saw every year the most elaborate police arrangements during the Rath Yatra (Car Festival), when the three deities of Lord Jagannath, Balabhadra and Subhadra were carried out in three huge chariots to Mausima Temple, the abode of Gundicha Devi (their aunt) to return after a week's stay to their original abode.

The biggest problem plaguing Puri when I joined was the operation of a notorious gang of dacoits, led by two brothers, Gopi Naik and Laxman Naik, in the two subdivisions of Khurda and Nayagarh, the latter contiguous to the mountainous territory of the Kandhamal (Phulbani) district. The gang was wreaking havoc in the region, killing people, looting property and burning homes.

An ASI was killed in cold blood when he was relaxing in the evening. It was a challenge of unprecedented dimensions for the Puri police. SK Ghosh had diligently brought NB Mohanty, a tough and no-nonsense officer, to tackle the menace. Mohanty, I must say, was finely attuned to this task.

Bringing a young officer as Addl. SP, logically, meant that he would be of invaluable assistance to the SP in the police operations. I had full intention of fulfilling the task. Little did I visualise that two botched up operations would provide enough ammunition to the DIG to poison the IGP against me.

The local police had built a system of informers to get information about the gang. The more reliable of those used to come to Puri and talk to the SP directly. On one occasion, when the SP was on casual leave, an informer came and tipped me off about the likely location of the gang. Immediate action was called for. Bhubaneswar was nearer to Ranpur, where the gang was operating, than Puri, although outside the jurisdiction of the Addl SP Bhubaneswar.

I talked to Ranjan to direct ASP Balsubramanium—popularly called Bala—a 1963 officer, to proceed to Ranpur with additional force which he did. I also informed the DIG over phone and left Puri for Ranpur. Bala, reaching earlier, verified the information and found it to be bogus.

In anti-dacoity operations, this was not unusual; but when I informed the DIG of the outcome of the verification, he flared up and put the blame squarely on Bala and me for bungling the operation which it was not. Soon, thereafter, on another date, late afternoon, and again in the absence of the SP, an informer brought details about the whereabouts of the gang. In view of the distance from Puri, there was no way other than what I had done on the previous occasion.

I rang up Bala and asked him to proceed to Ranpur immediately and surround the hill where the gang was reported to be hiding. I followed with additional force. This time the information was accurate. On reaching the spot, Bala directed the force to surround the hill.

It was already night. The gang, positioned at a vantage point, opened fire on the force. A havaldar was guarding the entry on the road leading to Ranpur on the base of another hill, just opposite. I reached with reinforcement, in the midst of the fire exchange. The gang had just crossed the road and ran to the opposite hill, which had a long contiguous stretch.

I realized we had lost a golden opportunity, but lost no time in surrounding and combing the hill. Our efforts proved futile. The gang had escaped to a safe hideout. We combed the area till early morning and then returned to the IB, posting fresh pickets in the suspected areas.

In the evening, the DIG came, accompanied by the SP and the Addl SP, Bhubaneswar. While he mercilessly admonished Bala for bungling the operation, he put the blame squarely on me for the failure. All this happened at the police station, in front of the subordinate staff.

The SP, trying to save the situation, asked me to explain in detail the happenings of the previous evening. I put a map on the table, and explained everything that was done and the steps that had been taken. After listening to me, he categorically said that in the given circumstances nothing better could have been done than whatever had been done by Bala and me. Our pale and gloomy faces lit up at his words.

The DIG directed me to camp at Ranpur for seven days and left. I sent Bala back to Bhubaneswar and stayed in the IB. On the third day, the SP asked me to return to Puri as he knew that we had to wait for another chance.

I recall this amusing episode on an afternoon, while sitting in the SP's office and discussing the police operations, he said, "Let us have some fun." He rang up the DIG and told him that reliable information relating to the location of the gang had been received. Since Tripathy had bungled the last operation, he added most seriously, he would be proceeding to Ranpur. So, would the DIG please come to supervise the operation? The DIG instantly feigned illness.

SK Ghosh's displeasure became evident when, one day, while talking to me over the phone, he shouted at me over the failure of the recent operations, signalling that my stay at Puri was almost over.

My wife left for her parents' place for the delivery of our first child. Separated from my wife, and bogged down by the reprimands of the IGP, I was feeling quite lonely, when, in the last week of May, I received my posting order to the fifth Battalion Orissa Armed Police as Deputy Commandant, a posting considered infra-dig in the IPS for a senior scale officer already functioning as Addl SP.

The IGP had sent a clear signal of his perception of my performance, and that, no doubt, was damning. I packed my luggage and proceeded to Cuttack to join my new assignment under DN Singh, the Commandant and a known dissident. My troubles were multiplying.

Chapter-11

Cuttack–Incurring Chief's Wrath

I joined my new assignment on June 6, 1966. I stayed in a thatched and dilapidated house, marked for demolition. On June 9, at home for lunch, I got news of the birth of my daughter in Bhubaneswar. Overjoyed, I drove to Bhubaneswar and headed for the hospital. By the time I reached, the baby had been washed and cleaned and brought to the nursing room. It was there that I saw them—my wife and my baby. The elation that fatherhood brought, the many-splendoured feelings that suffused my being, but subdued by myriad questions are difficult to describe. "Padmini", my daughter's name, was a name of my choice, without discussing any other name.

My wife came and joined me in Cuttack after a few days. My parents came from Sambalpur and we were all together in that cramped accommodation. I would spend many evenings with DN Singh over drinks and dinner, listening to his flowery English and slowly getting initiated to the domain of dissidence. A big drama was in the offing with me in the role of a hapless victim crushed mercilessly.

It was the time of the famous judgment of the Supreme Court on the Wadhwa case. Wadhwa was an IPS officer of the Haryana cadre. The Supreme Court ruled that an officer recruited directly to IPS/IAS was entitled to draw pay in the senior scale, right from the day a vacancy occurred.. This judgment created ripples, and was threatening to create a divide between the direct recruits and promoted officers.

For us, it was a bonanza. We made a representation to the government to pay us the arrears on the basis of the judgment, much to the dislike of SK Ghosh, who was a promoted officer. At this juncture, in July, after less than two months of stay at Cuttack, I received my transfer order to Balasore as Addl SP.

I was faced with a huge crisis, both moral and professional. Rasik Mohan Patnaik, a promoted officer from the rank of SI who would be like a father to me and whose son, RM Patnaik in IPS, a year senior to me, was a very good friend of mine, was the SP Balasore. Going by the Wadhwa judgment, I would be senior to him in service.

I was duly motivated by DN Singh and some other friends in the IPS to represent against the posting, which I did. The situation that was created by my posting to Balasore was perhaps the first after the Wadhwa judgment. Such a representation was most unexpected for S K Ghosh, whose ego was hurt.

He hit the ceiling, and in his fury declared before two of his AIsG—SS Padhi, a well-wisher of mine, and PC Ratho, who had by now become a relative—that he would place me under suspension. SS Padhi rang me up to convey the outburst of the IG and advised that I should quietly proceed to Balasore.

By then, though, the dye was cast. I took medical leave and did not go to Balasore. My parents and in-laws and my wife were pressing me to go to Balasore. I was getting restive.

One day, PC Ratho came to DN Singh's house and sent for me. He chided DN for leading me astray. He asked me not to extend my leave and proceed to Balasore, saying, "You have registered your protest against the most powerful IG Orissa has had so far, and made your point. Now go and join." Family pressure, the advice of my seniors and an uncertain life persuaded me to proceed to Balasore.

While in Cuttack, my daughter whom we called Baby, suffered from high fever for a long time, keeping us worried. When she grew up, we noticed that she had developed knock knees. There remained a lurking doubt in my mind that this was perhaps due to the prolonged fever she had in her infancy. This created an enormous sense of guilt in me which continues to haunt me, till today.

Chapter-12

Balasore

I took a morning train to Balasore in September 1966, reaching there around midday. I was prepared for a lukewarm and indifferent reception at Balasore, considering the events of the past two months. To my pleasant surprise, it was to the contrary.

The SP had sent a DySP and some other officers to receive me at the railway station, from where I was taken to the Circuit House. I then went to the SP's residence, where Rasik Babu received me with a lot of warmth and cordiality. I had lunch with him and then he took me to the DPO, where I took over as Addl SP against a new post created.

In the evening, he took me to the Collector's residence. Collector KC Singhdeo, a member of a royal family in Orissa, was ADM Keonjhar in 1956 when I was leading the States Reorganisation Commission agitations. I reminded him of those days, which he remembered vividly. He recounted, "Then, you were challenging us; now you will be the challenged." As days passed, I was indeed moved by the treatment of the SP who was, no doubt, guided by a fatherly love for me.

Home Minister Nilamani Routray hailed from Balasore. Hence, the Collector and SP were his chosen candidates. That was also the reason why the Circuit House remained overcrowded most of the time, necessitating my shifting to the nearly IB and back again to the Circuit House.

Piqued by the state of flux, I dashed off a wireless message to IGP requesting for accommodation at Balasore. The message ended with the words, "This may be treated as my SOS message." This sentence was certainly avoidable but I wrote it as I had started becoming a little disillusioned with the service.

Ghosh, again, hit the ceiling and sent the range DIG GS Dash, who was already unhappy with me, to administer a verbal warning to me. Dash came to Balasore and asked me in an angry tone why I was sending insulting messages to the IGP. It seemed he did not know the full form of SOS and asked me what I meant by those three letters. "It means Save Our Soul," I said. There was nothing offensive about it, only desperation, I added.

He then gave me a long lecture on discipline which I heard with one ear and instantly let it flow out of the other. He, of course, discussed the matter with the SP. It was decided that the RI quarters (old Sergeant Major) would be allotted to me.

Balasore, historically rich, has many stories to tell. The Dutch and Portuguese came to Balasore before the British as traders. The oldest testing range of the country is located at Chandipur, 10 km away in the Bay of Bengal and thereby hangs a fascinating tale of heroism, perseverance and pursuit.

An English Captain, given the task of locating an ideal testing range, started walking from Bombay in the early nineties of the 19th century, along the west coast, rounded the southern tip, could not find a suitable site and decided to traverse the east coast. He stopped at Balasore, which was found to be ideal for testing of ammunitions. In 1895, the test range became functional. The advantage of the location was that the sea during ebb recedes miles inside making available vast space for testing without causing any harm to the public. Chandipur, now, has become a missile testing centre.

Rasik Patnaik's transfer from Balasore came as a surprise to many, mainly because of his proximity to the Home Minister. SK Ghosh, who himself was close to the Home Minister, was not very fond of him and perhaps shifted him on the ground that he had stayed longer than necessary in Balasore. Patnaik was transferred to Dhenkanal and in his place came NB Mohanty, my boss in Puri. I was very happy to have him as my SP. He passed orders allotting the RI's quarters to me and I was eagerly looking forward to be united with my wife and daughter when the last blow came.

The Indo-Tibetan Border Police, formed after the Chinese aggression, was expanding and its IG, SK Chatterjee, was in dire need of officers. SK Ghosh perhaps had assured him of a steady supply of officers from Orissa, IPS officers falling out of his favour. NK Singh had gone in the previous year. One day in November, I received a wireless message, communicating my posting as Assistant. Commandant of an ITBP Battalion at Salonibari in Tezpur, and was directed to get relieved within 24 hours and proceed.

I was shocked and thoroughly demoralized. I was not even allowed to wait till receipt of government notification, placing my services at the disposal of the Centre. On the basis of a wireless message from the IGP I was relieved the next day and in utter frustration left Balasore for Bhubaneswar driving my ramshackle Fiat.

Such was the power of an IG Police that on the basis of a mere wireless message, an IPS officer in senior scale was packed off to central deputation. Balasubramanian of 1963 followed me to ITBP after a few months. Later, when I returned to Orissa, I was told that SK Ghosh, after a few drinks in the faraway Koraput Circuit House, was gloating that he had packed off Tripathy to ITBP. Home Secretary Natarajan told me that the IB had asked for me, the senior most of a batch in the state in their permanent secondment scheme, but Ghosh recommended the name of SP Mallik, third in seniority.

Chapter-13

Tezpur and Shivpuri

The pervasive gloom and despondence notwithstanding, I made up my mind to proceed to Tezpur. In fact for me there was no alternative. My wife stayed with her parents with our daughter and I left for Calcutta, on way to Tezpur, not knowing when we would be united and settle down again.

I took a flight from Dum Dum to Tezpur in December 1966 where a Deputy Superintendent from ITBP was waiting to receive me. He took me to Salonibari and after keeping my luggage in the accommodation earmarked for me took me to his house for lunch. There he explained the setup to me.

There were two establishments—one a Training Centre headed by IB Negi, an IPS officer from Himachal Pradesh, and the Battalion commanded by a former army Gurkha officer. The Deputy Superintendent was staying in a makeshift house with his wife. Two houses in fairly good shape were occupied by Negi, a bachelor and the Commandant who was staying with his family.

After lunch I went to the Battalion office and joined as Assistant Commandant and received necessary briefing from the Commandant. I found that I had joined the same post vacated by NK Singh who had left Tezpur on medical leave, leaving his faithful "batman" Sitaram there. Sitaram who had come from Orissa with NK was happy to see me and took care of me.

My accommodation was a temporary structure, mud wall with thatched roof on a cemented platform. It was quite spacious though. My bedroom was big enough to serve as my bed-cum-dinning-cum-drawing room. Ration was free and good food was assured.

My job was adjutant and quarter master combined. Even as I started to settle down with work I could not shake off the feeling of being wronged that made me feel very lonely and sad.

Negi was a great party man. Every third or fourth day there was a party that would last till early next morning. At that time there were between 12 to 14 IPS officers at Tezpur, two from my establishment, some from India Reserve Battalions and others from the IB and R&AW. My batchmate OP Sharma, who later became Governor of Nagaland, was Assistant Director of the SIB. Those who were staying single like me were regular fixtures in Negi's parties. My batch mate in IPS, KV Chusa, a Naga who had joined IAS in 1964, used to come with his wife. Both had tremendous capacity to absorb drinks and would stay on after dinner for one too many for the journey home. A couple, Mr and Mrs Goswami from Tezpur, enlivened the evenings with their charm and wit. It was Mrs Goswami, a lady with considerable grace, dignity and knowledge, who narrated to me the state of alarm in 1962 with the Chinese only 30 km away.

At that time, Tezpur was a boiling cauldron with the presence of considerable central police forces and intelligence organizations apart from the Army. In 1962, with the Chinese knocking at the door, there was a state of alarm and the local population were in mortal fear of the impending occupation. Papers in the Collectorate and currency in the bank and treasury were destroyed. The Chinese declared unilateral ceasefire after the Western powers and the USA promised to intervene.

Assam, yet to be divided; Tripura, Manipur and Nagaland along with West Bengal had common border with East Pakistan, present day Bangladesh and huge tracts of Assam bordered China. Besides the sensitive border issues, several ethnic communities had taken to violence threatening to secede from India. In many areas with overlapping population, there was internal strife among the ethnic groups. Thus, the entire Northeast was sitting on a volcano that could erupt any moment.

This explained the presence of huge forces in the area. The BSF was still in its infancy. A new organization had been created after the Chinese aggression called Directorate General of Security, a brainchild of BN Mallik, with considerable input from Biju Patnaik who, axed in the Kamraj plan from Chief Minister's post of Orissa, yet a favourite of Nehru, was given a room in South Block to plan the future security setup for India. This is a little known fact, but Biju Patnaik's contribution to the creation of a separate foreign Intelligence apparatus, and a shadow organisation to fight jungle warfare, is undeniable.

The Directorate General of Security headed by MML Hooza, a former Director of IB, had three wings, the SSB consisting mainly of armed battalions, the Aviation Reasearch Centre and yet another set up.

The ARC has a major establishment in Charbatia, Cuttack in Orissa. Some ITBP battalions were seconded to SSB for operational purposes. My battalion was one. So, though on paper, I was on deputation to ITBP, I really belonged to SSB, with the DG Security as the administrative head.

In the initial stage, R&AW was also under the general supervision of DG Security. Apart from these organizations, several reserve battalions were placed at the disposal of the DG Security, mostly in the Northeast. An Orissa battalion was posted at Haflong. Later, R&AW was separated and grew to become a huge Intelligence agency.

Living in such a high voltage security environment was an experience by itself. A new battalion was to be raised and I was slated to go to places such as Guwahati and Dibrugarh for a recruitment drive. The general ambience in the battalion encouraged me to bring my family. The Commandant was not averse to the idea.

Accommodation was adequate, the only disadvantage being the biting cold. At this juncture, there came an order in January 1967, from New Delhi, deputing three companies to Shivpuri in Madhya Pradesh for a four-month training course in jungle warfare.

I was expecting the Deputy Superintendent to be sent as in-charge of the companies, but the Commandant ordered that I should proceed to Shivpuri with the contingent. His ground was that the Dy SP was the only experienced hand, there was no other commissioned officer, and, as such, could not be spared.

I was crestfallen, but it was difficult to question the ground given by the Commandant. My sagging spirit, which I had been trying my utmost to revive, fell to its lowest. In disgust and desperation, I sent an application in response to an advertisement of the ITC in English daily The Statesman for the post of a corporate executive and received an acknowledgement.

While I had come to Tezpur willingly, with utmost reluctance I made preparations to go to Shivpuri which literally amounted to yet another posting as Shivpuri was declared my headquarters. I went to Delhi, visited the DG's office, met Assistant Director Raj Gopal Narayan and Deputy Director Raturi and DG MML Hooza. From Delhi, I went to Jhansi and then to Shivpuri, by bus.

I reached Shivpuri, one afternoon, to be received by my faithful Sita Ram, whom I had sent with the unit. He showed me to a one-room concrete accommodation, which he had kept ready for my occupation. I was briefed by the company commander, and after a delicious dinner, retired to sleep.

Next morning, after breakfast, I went to the office of the Commandant of the Training Centre, the flamboyant Jaspal Singh, an IPS officer of the Gujarat cadre of the 1958 batch. Singh later came to the limelight as Police Commissioner, Baroda, became a darling of the press and still later, a politician of the BJP, bagging a ministerial berth in the Gujarat Cabinet.

During my interaction, he hardly touched upon my duties at Shivpuri, reinforcing my belief that I was in charge of the administrative matters of the men, including logistics and welfare. He invited me for tea at his residence in the evening. The evening passed off extremely well in the company of the Commandant and his wife, a lively Coorgi lady related to General Cariappa, the first Commander-in-Chief of the Indian Army. My spirits lifted. Surely, with a friendly Commandant, my stay at Shivpuri would not be a drag after all.

On alternate mornings, I used to be at the parade ground, spending the rest of the day attending some classes which I considered useful. A week later, however, came a one-line order, saying that I had to attend the entire daily activities beginning at 6 am, till late evening. I was surprised.

The other officers next to the Commandant had not given me the slightest inkling about this regimen. I was seething with impotent rage. The order was not fair, at all. I met Jaspal Singh, but found his behaviour highly officious and peremptory.

That was the last straw. I made up my mind to call it a day in ITBP. I planned my exit carefully, without antagonising

Jaspal. The first step was to go to Delhi, and meet my bosses there. I knew he would not allow me to go to Delhi on an official visit or on leave.

I lay low for a few days. I accepted his decision and started attending all the training activities with my men, every day. There was an outing which I enjoyed immensely. We went to a densely forested area, away from Shivpuri, where tents had been pitched for three-day training in jungle warfare, nocturnal encounters, etc.

A river flowed very close to our habitat, by the side of a mountain. It was a picturesque place, and when we were told that there was an abundance of fish in the river, our ingenious instructor devised a way of catching fish.

He prepared small balls of dynamite, and with perfect timing, threw the balls into the river, causing a huge explosion that propelled the fish about 20 feet high. Fish was collected in bags, taken to the camp and cooked for the dinner. All the men and staff had a roaring time, downing rum and nibbling the fish fry, followed by a sumptuous dinner.

Towards the end of January, I decided to leave Shivpuri. I dropped a casual leave application at the Commandant's office. I left my big tin trunk in Sitaram's care, instructing him to take it to Tezpur, in case I did not return.

I boarded an early morning bus to Gwalior, and from there, took a train, reaching Delhi in the evening. I went to Orissa Bhavan, where I had arranged for my accommodation. I was sharing a room and to my pleasant surprise my roommate turned out to be Ranjan Roy, who had come on deputation to R&WA.

The next day, I went to RK Puram, met Assistant Director Rajgopal and Deputy Director Raturi and expressed my desire to represent for repatriation to my state. Both were highly sympathetic and treated me well. I filed a representation for repatriation and a leave application for three weeks leave.

Raturi advised me to meet DG Security Hooza, which I did in the afternoon. To my surprise, he did not dispose me of in a peremptory manner, and agreed to send my representation to Orissa government with favourable views. I returned to Orissa Bhavan, my heart lighter.

In the evening, I went to South Extension for dinner at the residence of T Ananthachari who had come to the BSF on deputation. I returned to the Bhavan late at night, slightly tipsy, and knocked at the door, expecting Ranjan to open the door.

The door opened, and I saw the frowning face of Dr Sadasib Mishra, my revered Principal of Ravenshaw College, then DPI Orissa. He looked me up and down, and said, "You are drunk, go change and sleep." I quietly did so, without uttering a single word.

Next morning, he was his effusive self over tea, enquiring about the new security organizations that were coming up and talking about many things. It was early 1967.

The fate of my representation was linked to the outcome of the parliamentary and assembly elections, due to be held in March. The ruling troika of Biju Patnaik, Biren Mitra and Nilamani Routaray had become highly unpopular in the state. The bungling of the students' agitation in 1964 necessitating the visit of the Union Home Minister Gulzarilal Nanda to Cuttack, coupled with allegations of corruption and malpractices against Biju and Biren Mitra, the Chief Minister, had surcharged the politics of the state, leading to massive protests by people.

On the Home Minister's suggestion, Prime Minister Lal Bahadur Shastri constituted a ministerial committee to look into the allegations of corruption. The committee found substance in the allegations and Biren Mitra was asked to resign in February 1965. He was replaced by Sadasib Tripathy, an unassuming and simple man from the hill district of Koraput.

Tripathy found it very difficult to deal with the Congress veterans, who outmanouerved him at every step. The Congress party was falling apart, and the year 1966 saw blame game, recriminations and unedifying intrigues ruling the roost.

HK Mahatab, the astute politician, seeing no future for himself in the Congress, started a separate political formation called the Jana Congress, taking with him his virulent critics Radhanath Rath and Pabitra Mohan Pradhan, both senior Congress leaders.

At the national level Indira Gandhi, who became Prime Minister after Shastri's death, was sandwiched between several powerful forces.

In this backdrop, in early 1967, I returned to Orissa on three weeks leave to be extended further leaving my deputation behind and keeping my fingers crossed till the elections were over. The results of the state elections were written large on the wall, a defeat for Congress, reinforced by an unpleasant incident in a public meeting addressed by Mrs Gandhi at Bhubaneswar. There was heavy stone pelting which police did not anticipate. Biju and Biren stood bewildered. One stone hit Mrs Gandhi's nose. But she would not leave the dais and unperturbed, said, "This is an assault not on me, but on democracy." The incident sent shivers down the spine of the politicians in general and S K Ghosh in particular. His fate was now irretrievably linked with that of the troika.

The elections were held in March 1967 and Congress got a drubbing with only 30 seats in the 147-member Assembly. The Swatantra Party led by Bolangir maharaja Rajendra Narayan Singhdeo emerged as the largest single party with the newly formed Jan Congress led by HK Mahatab finishing second. A coalition ministry was formed with RN Singhdeo as Chief Minister and the first act of the ministry was to change the IG Police SK Ghosh and bring RK Padhi, an IP officer, in his place.

RN Singhdeo being a stickler for propriety, in fact, wanted to appoint JC Ghosh who had been replaced by SK Ghosh during the communal disturbances three years earlier as IG. But the Goverment of India had sent an observation that he should not be entrusted with law and order duty because of the failure of police in 1964. Singhdeo wrote to the Centre for expunction of this remark and pending that RK Padhi took over, creating a wave of joy in Orissa Police. I had to ensure that my representation reached the Chief Minister.

During the leave I met many senior police officers, including JC Ghosh and RK Padhi. Expressing their sympathy, they said, "Wait". I met Home Secretary Natarajan who with a smiling face said, "Better days are coming for you Tripathy, wait". When my file came back from the Chief Minister, it was not only a huge surprise for me, but also for the Police, Home and GA departments.

The Chief Minister not only ordered my repatriation, he in his own handwriting wrote one and half page of order, covering the events in sequence and concluding that the IGP had harassed a young IPS officer for no fault of his and desired that displeasure of the government be communicated to him. My telephone number was traced and I received telephone calls from Natarajan and AN Tiwari, Addl Secretary GA department congratulating me. RK Padhi sent a proposal for my posting as Commandant of the third battalion OMP at Koraput, it was around June 1967.

What is my assessment of SK Ghosh as IG Police Orissa? Having suffered in his hands the natural proclivity will be a damningly negative one. But no, on the contrary, it is on a strikingly positive note. SK Ghosh was the first police chief who ushered in an era of dynamism and progress in Orissa Police. Professionally, he was brilliant, his integrity was beyond question.

What is important was that he was a doer, a performer and with his equations with the political executive he was in a position to achieve, which he did in abundant measure. Orissa saw expansion of the force, particularly in the armed forces with the addition of two battalions, creation of more police districts and ranges, upgrading the SHO's post of urban police stations to the rank of Inspector. It was he who obtained government order for rent free accommodation for SP, till then a privilege enjoyed by District Magistrate only.

He streamlined the internal administration by taking several steps most important of which was compiling the police orders and police circular orders which remained valuable reference materials for all officers. And he had a presence which none in government could afford to ignore. They could be resenting him, but had to acknowledge him with deference. At another level he was the first chief to start police-public relationship programme through a specific scheme of getting feedback of people to police investigation. Earlier, as Chief of the State Vigilance organization, he had given it its present shape. For a very long time, Orissa Vigilance setup was acknowledged as the best in the country and officers from outside used to come to Orissa to study the setup. Ghosh was a prolific writer. He has authored several books on different aspects of police and policing.

On the other side, one sees this man of dynamism as a man of intrigues. Many ascribe the root of groupism and one-upmanship in the higher echelons of police to Ghosh who made his dramatic entry as police chief in 1964, replacing JC Ghosh whose morale had sunk to such depths that it could not be revived even after he was rehabilitated towards the end of 1967 by appointing him as IG Police. He ceased to function and took leave on his own volition till he retired.

There were many uncomfortable situations for RK Padhi and the accusing finger was always directed at Ghosh. After the change in 1967, he was given the equally important post of IG Vigilance in which capacity he proved to be a terror to the government officers throughout the state. A man highly volatile in temper, his likes and dislikes would swing from one end of the pendulum to the other. To sum up, this contrarian has left an indelible mark on the annals of Orissa Police.

I feel tempted to narrate two incidents of later days where I figured. RN Singhdeo had made up his mind to retire SK Ghosh compulsorily and he, on his own on a highly secret mission, had obtained the approval of the President to that effect which when implemented, created shock waves in Orissa. Ghosh left without the customary farewell and it was only in 1974 when N Swain, who was one of his favourites, was police chief that he was persuaded to accept a farewell dinner and it was my responsibility as AIG, I had become a trusted lieutenant of Swain, to organise the dinner.

SK Ghosh came and after a few drinks seeing me standing in a corner, an opportunity he was perhaps seeking for, came to me, caught hold of my hands and said: "Tripathy will you excuse me for all the wrongs I have done to you." I was speechless and overwhelmed with a feeling of nothingness at the futility of things we run after. Then in 1995, when I was DG Police we decided to introduce a scheme of honouring some outstanding retired officers for their contribution to Orissa Police and the first natural choice was SK Ghosh who had settled in Calcutta. He was sick when he received my letter but rang me up and talked to me in such an emotional voice which I cannot forget.

Chapter-14

Koraput

As for me I planned to go to Koraput, a place I liked very much, with my wife and daughter. We proceeded to Koraput with the hope of settling there for some time. I took over as Commandant of the third battalion OMP in the third week of July 1967. It was rainy season and Koraput with its salubrious climate was just wonderful. The residence of the Commandant was located on a hilltop from where one could have a commanding view of the surroundings. Two companies of the unit were manned by Gorkhas and Rajputs, thus making it a composite battalion. This was also serving as the training battalion for the state and as such several training courses were running simultaneously and the battalion premises were alive with activities. I settled down to my work which I found very stimulating.

Because of the training activities, senior IPS officers were invariably camping at Koraput as examiners in different courses that rendered life more enjoyable. Somanath Mishra of 1957 batch was SP and BP Saha of 1963 was Additional SP. My batchmate in IAS, F Moses was ADM. Social life was good.

The Dandakaranya Project, which was started in the early sixties for settling the East Pakistani refugees, covered large areas of Koraput and the adjoining Bastar district of MP (now Chhattisgarh). The Dandakaranya Development Authority had a chairman, a former central minister, a chief administrator, an IAS officer from MP cadre and a chief financial officer from IAAS and a full complement of staff. At that time the project activities were in full swing. On the law and order front the Naxalite leaders from Bengal had started establishing contact with militant groups active in Srikakulam district of Andhra bordering Koraput and a spill over to Orissa was only a matter of time.

My hope of settling down at Koraput was jolted by a signal from IG Police in the last week of August asking me to appear before the Governor for selection of his ADC. The ADC post in Orissa was a cadre post of IPS, and it was considered an attractive posting by young IPS officers. I was, however, in no mood for a change. But I had to obey the order and appeared before the Governor, Dr AN Khosla, a well-known irrigation engineer who had conceived the Hirakud Dam project on river Mahanadi.

Anticipating the results of the interview, I very politely explained to the Governor the hard days I had passed through, and my desire to continue in Koraput. Dr Khosla, a very affectionate and warm person, persuaded me to join and silenced me with his sweet smile. I returned to Koraput and waited for my posting order which came in the third week of September. Bag and baggage we came to Bhubaneswar and I joined as ADC in the first week of October.

Chapter-15

Bhubaneswar–Barred entry to Raj Bhavan

Duties of the ADC, which I need not describe here, were mostly formal and ceremonial. There were two ADCs—one from Police and one from Army, Captain Sethi. There used to be some tension in the past over their seniority. While the Police ADC was holding the rank of a major he was deemed to be senior, a fact the Army ADC would not concede. As a compromise, date of joining the Raj Bhavan was adopted as the yard stick to decide seniority. For me there was no occasion for such a controversy as Capttain. Sethi was a friendly person. One ADC used to be on duty every day from 8 am to 6 pm with lunch at Raj Bhavan and beyond 6 pm, if the Governor had an engagement. Next day he was off duty. In fact it was at Raj Bhavan, Bhubaneswar that I revived my habit of reading books which I had almost given up after getting into IPS.

I read some remarkable books like VP Menon's The

Story of the Integration of Indian States, Taya Zenkin's book on India and VS Naipaul's book which was full of uncomplimentary references to India which he subsequently revised in his book `*India: A Million Mutinies*'.

Dr Khosla was a famous expert on river valley projects and commanded high respect in Delhi. He was a Member of Planning Commission when Biju Patnaik became Chief Minister in 1961. To translate his dream of transforming Orissa to a land of plenty and prosperity, Biju Patnaik brought Dr Khosla, a visionary and a realist rolled into one, as Governor. What was remarkable about Dr Khosla was the respect he commanded from RN Singhdeo, Biju's opponent, when he became Chief Minister. He depended on Dr Khosla to pursue the projects of Orissa in Delhi with the cabinet ministers and Prime Minister Indira Gandhi. So Raj Bhavan was abuzz with activities with bureaucrats, industrialists and foreign delegations holding discussions.

The corridors are now silent as the Chief Ministers no longer look forward to the Governors as mentors. Also certain propriety used to be maintained in the administrative process. All important files used to come to Governor before issue of orders. In such an environment surcharged with activities it was a pleasure working for Dr Khosla. His wife had expired and he had become very dependent on his ADCs.

Since, he was associated with several river valley projects in advisory capacity, he used to tour quite frequently to various parts of India accompanied by an ADC and his Medical Officer. In one such trip, there was a confusion thanks to Indian Airlines when we were flying from Delhi to Calcutta to take a connecting flight to Bhubaneswar. After getting into the plane, the engine developed snag and we had to get into another plane. The crew assured that luggage transfer would be automatic. Realizing that we would be missing the connecting flight I contacted Calcutta

Raj Bhavan, requesting for transport and accommodation for the day. We reached Dum Dum Airport, the connecting Bhubaneswar filght had gone, but the Raj Bhavan staff were there. One of them took the luggage tickets from me and the protocol officer took us to Raj Bhavan whose occupant then was the famous Dharmavira of the ICS and former Cabinet Secretary.

After reaching Raj Bhavan, Dr Khosla on finding that the Governor was in town wished to see him. I passed it on to the protocol officer, requesting him to find out the convenience of Dharmavira. On learning about Dr Khosla's arrival, Dharmavira came to see him in his room instead of waiting for him in his office. That was the type of respect Dr Khosla commanded. When the luggage reached Raj Bhavan, one item was missing and that was the most important one containing Dr Khosla's medicines and changes.

Dr Khosla momentarily felt helpless, lost his temper and shouted at me. I was taken aback, but remained silent, not explaining my innocence at the fiasco. Medical Officer Dr Bhuyan intervened and assured that all medicines would be brought immediately, which was done. After lunch, I spent the whole afternoon in passing on my anger to the airlines; staff in Delhi and Calcutta and by evening received a phone call to tell me that the luggage had been located at Varanasi and was on its way to Calcutta. This news assuaged Dr Khosla.

At night to drown my gloom we were drinking in my room when Dr Khosla knocked at my door, entered and told me: "Forget what I told you in the morning it was not your fault. Draft a letter to the Aviation Minister in Bhubaneswar and put up." My wounded feelings were mollified. In Bhubaneswar, Dr Khosla blindly signed the draft, which was strongly worded, without any change and the reply came very promptly from Civil Aviation Minister Dr Karan Singh with profuse apologies. Those days the Governors during their visits to Delhi used to be the guests of the President in the Rashtrapati Bhavan, a practice which has since been discontinued. During Dr Khosla's visits to Delhi while he used to stay in his house, I was accommodated at the Rashtrapati Bhavan.

I remember one incident which put Dr Khosla in a very embarrassing situation on a day I was on duty. Chief Secretary AK Barren, a war service recruit, a no-nonsense man, scrupulously honest and very correct in official discharge of duties, had one weakness: addiction to alcohol, mainly rum. He would not depend on anybody for his drinks and knowing that the cost of vintage drinks was unafffordable for an honest IAS officer, he had stuck to his rum drinking habit from war days. When fighting a battle during the Second World War in Burma he lost his dear friend and took his widow Thelma as his wife and her three children as his own. He would not lobby for any post, it would come to him because of his sterling reputation. After retirement, he was appointed Chairman of Orissa Public Service Commission. He was by all means a remarkable man, the like of whom is rare these days.

Another war service recruit of IAS DD Suri was a contrast, fond of the choicest Scotch whiskey, crates of which would find their way to his residence at Cuttack for which he came under the scanner of state Vigilance. His house was raided, a case was started and file initiated for his suspension. The file was brought to Raj Bhavan on a day I was on duty by Rajgopalan, DIG Vigilance, for the Governor's signature after which suspension order was issued. After lunch break I got a call from Suri seeking an appointment with the Governor which Dr Khosla granted unsuspectingly.

I was blissfully ignorant of the morning developments. The Governor's engagement for the next day used to be printed and sent by special messenger to Addl. SP, SDO

Bhubaneswar, Home Secretary and Chief Secretary. Before starting his evening session, Barren saw the engagement of the Governor for the next day, saw Suri's name, flared up and rang the ADC. I picked up the receiver as I was preparing to go home and heard his booming voice: "Tripathy, how is it that the Governor has agreed to see D D Suri?" I explained the position and then he said, "Tell the Governor, he will not see Suri." It was my unpleasant task to convey this missive to the Governor who readily asked me to cancel the appointment. I rang up Suri and told him about the cancellation of the appointment only to hear him shouting obscenities at Barren. I kept the receiver down, drafted a letter and sent it by a special messenger to Cuttack to the residence of Suri and instructed Reserve Inspector Hari Singh to remain present next day at the Raj Bhavan gate and prevent Suri's entry.

Next day although I was not on duty, I came to the Raj Bhavan to ensure that there was no slip anywhere. Suri came and suffered the humiliation of being turned back.

I was also witness to two important events during the term of Dr Khosla as Chancellor of Universities. Two universities were opened, one in Sambalpur in western Orissa, the foundation stone of which was laid by President Dr Zakir Hussain, and the other in Berhampur in South Orissa, whose foundation stone was laid by Dr Khosla.

Dr Khosla during his five years stay had endeared himself to the people of Orissa whom he genuinely loved. He was to go on January 31, 1968. The entire month was full of farewell ceremonies, a phenomenon quite unusual in a state. I was with him till January 26 and after the 'At Home' left for Hyderabad in a special saloon earmarked for the Governor to escort the Governor designate Dr S S Ansari, scion of the famous Ansari family, friends of the Nehru household, to Bhubaneswar.

I stayed at the Raj Bhavan in Hyderabad, fixed up the

date and time of the wagon that would carry Dr Ansari's luggage, fixed transport to carry the same to the railway station and went to meet Dr Ansari at his residence. He and his wife received me cordially, but during the conversation I found something awkward. Dr Ansari would forget what he just uttered, which was acute amnesia. There I found a gentleman called Gupta who was to come to Orissa as his Personal Secretary and found his behaviour somewhat overbearing. I explained to him the particulars of the wagon, transport to carry the luggage that was to take place next day. He asked me to oversee this work. I politely said, it was his duty, inviting a frown from him. Seeds of my trouble at Raj Bhavan, my second tiff with authority, that too the highest in the state, were sown.

The Governor's saloon had a compartment for the VVIP and his family, a spacious drawing-cum-dining room, a coupe meant for the Secretary/ADC and another compartment for staff. I allotted a berth to Gupta in the compartment which he had to share with two members of Raj Bhavan staff. I was in occupation of the coupe. Gupta's ego was hurt, he wanted the coupe, which I declined. We reached Bhubaneswar early in the morning and at 8 am, the Governor designate was received by the Chief Minister, his cabinet colleagues and senior state officials. We drove to the Raj Bhavan for the swearing-in ceremony at the end of which I noticed a questioning look on many faces. Chief Minister RN Singhdeo giving his typical enigmatic smile asked me in Oriya, "How is he?"

Trouble started from day one. Taking advantage of the abject dependence of the Governor on him, Gupta one day sent a signed note from the Governor that he was the number two man in the Raj Bhavan hierarchy next to the Secretary. Both Captain Sethi and I strongly objected on the ground that the private staff did not figure in the official protocol arrangement. It went to cold storage. Then one day came another note from the Governor, designating Gupta as Deputy Secretary, which was vehemently protested by me and Sethi. The movement of notes from upstairs to Secretary's room on the ground floor and back again with protestations by both ADCs was quite amusing with the Secretary acting as a post box transmitting the Governor's note to ADCs and back to the sender with the views of the recipients.

But Gupta's ingenuity deserved admiration; he saw his potential threat in me, not in Captain Sethi. Yet another note came with the order that the post of Police ADC would be abolished and ADC (T) i.e. me should not be allowed to function from the next day. The Secretary showed the note to me which did not disturb me at all for I was never keen to continue in the Raj Bhavan. He advised me to go on leave which I politely declined.

The Home Secretary was BB Ratho, an IAS officer promoted from the State Civil Service. I was one of the few IAS/ IPS officers towards whom he had developed an aversion. Late in the evening, he rang me and asked me to see him which I did and requested him to give me my posting order. IG Police RK Padhi was at that time camping at Rourkela and pending his return he asked me to go on leave to which I said no and politely told him that I would continue to function as ADC till receipt of Government notification.

I came home, located IGP at Rourkela and informed him of the developments. He dashed off a wireless message to the Governor, the gist of which was that he could change me, but not abolish the post of Police ADC.

The next challenge I had to face was to enter Raj Bhavan next day. I rang up RI Hari Singh, asked him to send a car in the morning and remain personally present at the gate till I entered Raj Bhavan. Smoothly, I entered Raj Bhavan next morning, clad in mufti as I was off duty and sipped tea with Captain Sethi, a sight which infuriated Gupta who ran upstairs and told the Governor how his orders were being flouted. IGP RK Padhi followed by Chief Minister met the Governor and told him that the Police ADC post must continue. The Governor had to bite the dust.

I received my notification posting me as SP Mayurbhanj, the northern most district of Orissa bordering West Bengal and Bihar, moved there in the first week of April 1968 and assumed charge and embarked on a journey that proved to be full of thorns.

Chapter-16

Mayurbhanj–Hot Seat

Mayurbhanj was one of the best administered of the twenty four princely states in Orissa. It had a legislature, a high court, an IG Police, good road network, some medium industries. Baripada, the district headquarters, had one of the oldest colleges of Orissa. It had rich deposits of iron ore. The Tata Steel located at Jamshedpur took its first ores from Badampahad and Gurumohisani iron ore mines in Rairangpur subdivision of Mayurbhanj when the plant was started in the beginning of the 20th century. By the time I joined, the last of the deposits were mined and Tatas were planning to wind up operations. The king had opened police stations at places each not more than 20 km from the other. The town had three palaces, one for the king, another, Belgadia palace, for the queen mother and yet another on the outskirts for his sister-in-law, wife of the elder brother who was dead.

Collector Radha Kant Naik, an IAS officer of my batch, joined at the same time and we stayed together in the Circuit House till we moved to our residences. He was a good friend of mine and before leaving Bhubaneswar for

Baripada we were talking of the good days that lay ahead. He was in IPS in 1961, and after joining IAS had given me some of his uniform items.

Not very long after my joining I started feeling that our relationship was perhaps getting derailed. I smelled it when once or twice he asked me why I was not there in some meeting or discussion. I took that casually. That the situation would escalate to uncontrollable proportions in which I became the vanquished, the defeated, and the villain was beyond my comprehension. It became the talk of the town, the talk of administration, was carried to the Assembly floor where a section of the members of the ruling coalition castigated me mercilessly.

When I joined Mayurbhanj I took some hard decisions that lasted till the end of my career. I knew that as district SP I would be vulnerable to temptations of many kinds. My salary was roughly around Rs 900 and after deduction my take home salary used to be Rs 550. Out of this, I used to religiously send Rs 150 to my father or my brother who was studying his graduation and post graduation in Ravenshaw College at Cuttack. My strict instructions to my wife were to manage the household within the remaining amount and she did it. We could not afford any luxury, except a radio which my wife had brought after marriage and a transistor which I purchased to listen to radio Ceylon and Vividh Bharati and the voices of Melville de Mellow and Latika Ratnam. I had not been able to purchase a car having given the proceeds of the previous car to my father for building a house in Sambalpur. So I took the second hand Ambassador car of my father-in-law as gift as without a car it was very difficult to manage. When I had some savings I paid him Rs 5,000.

Work wise, Mayurbhanj was an ideal district for a Superintendent of Police, and I immersed myself in my work—supervision of cases, inspection of posts, welfare of the force and related matters. On the crime front, large number of dacoity cases were reported, particularly from two police stations, Muruda and Suliapada, bordering Midnapore in West Bengal, which was a dacoity prone district. The Naxalite movement was gathering momentum in West Bengal and Naxalite activities in Midnapore spilled over to both the police stations, particularly Suliapada where we had to post a special picket. Of the large tribal population, Lodhas, who were declared a criminal tribe during the British days, but got out of that tag in free India, continued their depredations by committing theft and burglary. In fact, Collector RK Naik had sent an ambitious scheme to the government for rehabilitation of the Lodhas to bring them into mainstream.

Within a few days of my joining I received an envelope which said "to be opened by addressee only". I opened it and found Rs 500 with a note written in Oriya: "This is your share from Jamsala check gate." I was horrified and scandalised and got an inkling of the reckless corruption indulged in by the composite staff of police, sales tax, forest and transport departments in the check gates situated on the West Bengal border on NH-6, from Calcutta to Bombay, through which hundreds of trucks passed every day.

My social life was limited. When I joined, one of my Ravenshaw College days friends, Bibhudendra Mishra, who had joined Income Tax service in 1964 was there as ITO. We had frequent exchange of visits. A respectable senior citizen was Paramanand Acharya, an eminent archaeologist who after merger of the princely states was the State Archaeologist, leading a retired life with whom we were on friendly terms. And as the misunderstanding with Radhakant become graver and thicker by the day, all important district level officers, the District Judge, the ADM Judicial, ADM (revenue), the Civil Surgeon, the Principal of the local college Professor K V K Rao preferred my company.

Two events we were looking forward to each year were the annual shooting meet at Dhenkanal in October and annual senior police officers' conference in January combined with annual sports. Each SP and Commmandant would make a beeline to Dhenkanal and the stay in tent for three days used to be great fun, getting up early morning and going to range by 6 am, participating in rifle competition, coming to the improvised mess for lunch, then again to the range for revolver shooting, back to the tent and after change to the mess, drinking rum till the wee hours of morning—and again get ready by 6 am for range practice. An officer tried more for not being a washout than for securing high points, for the IPS officer securing the lowest point would be presented with a big wooden spoon.

Annual conference used to be an uproarious affair with RK Padhi as the presiding deity listening to everybody with indulgence and dealing with issues with élan and eloquence. Some of us from 60 to 64 batches used to be vociferous in expressing our views. I feel tempted to cite the names of Sankar Sen (1960), NK Singh and RM Patnaik (1961), self (1962), BP Saha (1963) and BB Nandy (1964). While RK Padhi used to deal with a subject with a flourish in his brilliant English, there was another officer, BN Mishra (1952), a former IB officer, then SP Crime Branch, one of the wittiest and sharpest officers I have ever seen, who would explain a point in a way that was cut and dry, to the point and shorn of rhetoric. He used to be the hero of our group. While other senior officers asked us to exercise restraint, he would say: "Nonsense, go head." His addiction to alcohol ruined him and he died prematurely in 1972.

RK Padhi had a commanding presence exuding confidence, warmth and affection, displaying qualities of a leader. He would articulate the feelings and aspirations of the young officers in no uncertain terms before the Chief Minister. The evenings in the mess were occasions to look forward to. Camaraderie was overflowing with RK as the magnet with an abundance of pre- and post-prandial bonhomie. He became my icon in police.

I am yet to find out the reasons of my misunderstanding with Radhakant, which only goes to suggest that trivialities triggered misunderstanding. He wanted to be a very popular Collector and that was perfectly his choice, but it was not my cup of tea at that point in time. I wanted to devote myself fully to my profession and in the process had reservations about some people who were very close to him. His feeling that I was ignoring him, which was not a fact at all, may have added to the sum total of hostility which was taking shape. The saddest part was that this feeling crystallized in the form of a sinister campaign in which I, a high caste Brahmin, was looking down on him coming from the reserved quota. Never in my life have I thought of anything on the basis of caste, creed, community or religion and if Radhakant had given me the slightest hint of this I would have gone out of my way to dispel any such feeling in him. Sadly, this campaign snowballed in the print media with one section of the press out to lionize him and condemn me.

The coalition ministry of Swatantra Party headed by Chief Minister RN Singhdeo and Jan Congress headed by Dr HK Mahatab had one minister each from Mayurbhanj, a predominantly tribal district. Radhakant was close to both while my relationship with them was proper and correct. The Jana Congress party provided solid support to Radhakant and Dr Mahatab, addressing a public meeting at Baripada, showered praises on him for his work in the district. His paper The Prajatantra started a vilification campaign against me. The silver lining was, it had no material to question my integrity or professional discharge of duties. By all accounts I was naive, foolish and an ignoramus. I could have befriended the local correspondent of the largest circulated daily Samaj who was a perfect gentleman and was keeping off the controversy. I could have befriended some politicians but I kept myself off.

The manifestations of this sad story were exchange of letters on a variety of subjects. Being impulsive I would not wait and shoot off a reply in very sharp language. My DIB Inspector Mohanty, who was my genuine well-wisher, would tell me, "Sir reply to this letter later." But I would not listen till RK Padhi during his visit to Baripada advised me not to send letters to the Collector post haste. "Wait for a day. Heavens are not falling," he told me and I realized the wisdom of this advice later in life. Radhakant would—send a letter ordering deployment of force, I would not agree, he would ask me to place a SHO under suspension to which I said no, he would virtually ask for my explanation why I did not take his concurrence in availing of CL when I went to Sambalpur to see my critically ill mother, I would say copy of my CL application was sent to him, he would pass comments on the crime review and have it signed by a subordinate minion, I would question its propriety—the list would go on ad nuseam.

All these aberrations would duly filter to the press which had a field day. Then came the worst. An adjournment motion was tabled in the Assembly with the caption: "In Mayurbhanj—Brahmin SP and Pana (a Schedule Caste) Collector."

I had been discussed several times on the floor of the Assembly, but this one was the most sinister in nature. The private secretary to the Chief Minister rang me up to tell this and I did request him to prevent it if possible. He talked to the Speaker who disallowed the motion. Yet another incident which was perhaps the last straw on the camel's back was a case of rash and negligent driving where in the FIR I accused myself. JC Ghosh, who had taken long leave after serving a few months in the office of IG, was returning in his car from

Calcutta. Baripada being on the midway he had requested me to arrange lunch for him. He reached Circuit House around midday and gave me a ring. I drove to the Circuit House to see him. On the way, a cyclist suddenly crossed the road and dashed against my jeep. I got down, found that nothing had happened, he got up quickly, but to be on the safe side I took him to the hospital and admitted him.

Then the drama started which was narrated to me by the Civil Surgeon. He was persuaded to stay in the hospital for three weeks so that the injuries would become automatically grevious. I went to the police station, got a case registered showing my name in the accused column much to the reluctance of the SHO who asked me: "How can you accuse yourself." I asked him to keep his mouth shut. Then I went to the Circuit House to call on JC Ghosh.

This was a golden opportunity to drag my name again to the Assembly. A starred question was admitted, the contents of which were, how the SP driving a jeep recklessly injured a person and local people were in an agitational mood. The truth was there was not a murmur on this issue. A crash message came to the Collector, significantly not repeated to me to report forthwith. Radhakant had gone to Bhubaneswar and Murthy, the ADM had to reply. When told I asked him to report the truth, nothing but the truth which he did by reporting the registration of the case by the SP himself and absence of any tension in the town.

The RDC and DIG came to Baripada to inquire and patch up but to no avail. I had started feeling that N Swain, my Range DIG who later became police chief in 1974 and whose confidant and favoured officer I became, he knew me from my school days at Keonjhar, was somewhat lukewarm in giving his support to me, so also was PJ Joseph, a 1953 batch IPS officer who was AIG (admn). Some telephonic talks from Joseph were more on the fault finding side, than on a supportive note. In spite of trying to restrain myself,

I blurted out once or twice and there was coldness in our relationship for quite some time. I felt, I was getting support from the IGP RK Padhi, DIG Intelligence HP Singhdeo and DIG CID Crime Iqbal Singh, a 1950-batch officer who went to R&AW and stayed there till retirement.

The reports in quick succession of the Collector against me to Home Department must have made BB Rath, Home Secretary, very happy who obtained government orders for my transfer from the district. I was not very perturbed as I felt that my stay in Mayurbhanj had become untenable. But RK Padhi was not the man to give up. He wrote a stiff letter to the government that in a district it was team work and as such if the SP was to be transferred, the Collector had to go. Chief Minister RN Singhdeo readily agreed and passed order for transfer of both Collector and SP, which was not only a great precedent set by RK Padhi but also was a moral victory for me.

I was transferred to Koraput to third Battalion OMP, back to my old field having by then realised that all talks of anonymity of civil servants were bullshit and in a democracy one has to be with the politicians but not to the extent of compromising one's dignity and sacrificing the interest of the organization. This was the "Mantra" I would follow in future.

I was succeeded by SC De of 1961 batch. My one year of hard work fetched me an adverse confidential remark that did not reflect on my work performance but on my failure to maintain good relations with the Collector. Was it only I who failed? Was Radhakant communicated with similar remarks? I did not know. All that I saw was that he continued in the district.

Chapter-17

Koraput, Keonjhar, Cuttack: Wiser by the Day

I left Baripada one afternoon with an uneasy feeling. Suresh had arrived two days earlier and I wanted to hand over charge to him the following morning and leave the place. But being a highly religious person he had chosen an auspicious moment which fell the day after. Radhakant had gone out of his way to make his stay at Circuit House comfortable and Suresh spent most of the time in the company of the Collector, taking food at his residence and using his vehicle which surprised me.

He did not have food with me explaining that since I had packed my luggage, it would cause inconvenience to me, an excuse I found funny. When I handed over charge I told him about the accident case, which had turned into a specially reported case when the injuries became automatically grievous after three weeks of hospitalization of the cyclist and requested him to close the case. I did not have a driving licence, an act of omission on my part and that worried me very much. More discomfort from Suresh was in the pipeline. He became a devotee of Shri Aurobindo, later took premature retirement in the early nineties and settled in Pondicherry.

Koraput, 800 km from Baripada, was my old place. Same house, office and work environment which I found very agreeable. I settled down to work, smug in the feeling that the government would not touch me with a bargepole for a district posting and I would stay in Koraput for a full term. Koraput battalion was a training battalion and I had tried to streamline the various training courses and activities. I had an able and competent Asst. Commandant B Mohapatra, who took upon himself the task of compiling all the training manuals. RK Padhi with his flair for innovation had introduced several new ideas to consolidate the identity of police in public perception. He had started observation of the Orissa Police Formation Day on April 1, the day Orissa got statehood in 1936. In fact there was no ceremony organized by the government to commemorate the foundation day of Orissa. In line of the Police Day the government started celebrating the state formation day. RK Padhi started the concept of inter battalion competitions to be held biennially. The second competition was scheduled to be held in June 1969 at Khallikote in Ganjam district on a hilly area by the side of the beautiful Chilika Lake and we made preparations for the same.

Koraput had S Sinha, an IPS officer of 1956 batch, as SP and BB Nandy of 1964 as Additional SP. Nandy turned out to be great friend and we used to have noisy get-togethers when our friends from outside used to come to my battalion as examiners. Our main topic used to be reforming police and upgrading the service conditions of IPS. Now when I think in retrospect, I really wonder at the feelings of togetherness that was in abundance which in later years I saw diminishing.

In July 1969, I was summoned for duty in Puri for the Nabakalebar festival of Lord Jagannath. In this festival, which is followed by the car festival, the statues of the three deities (Jagannath, Balabhadra and Subhadra) are changed and the new ones made of predetermined timber and sanctified by the Daru Brahma of the old ones are in stalled.

Unlike the annual car festival, this festival attracts huge number of pilgrims from all over India calling for large scale police arrangements. While I remained in charge of crime control, B P Saha (1963) was given the charge of traffic and Bana Bihari Panda (1963) the camp arrangement. NK Singh was SP and N Swain DIG of the range. Traditionally during the pulling of chariots, the SP remains in charge of the chariot of Balabhadra, ADM in charge of Subhadra, and Collector-in-charge of Jagannath. Nabakalebara, which is held in a year which has two Asadhas was earlier held in 1951, when there was large scale violence following unruly behaviour of the Naga Sadhus. Even the ones prior to that in the 20th century had major incidents.

So we were looking forward to a smooth passage of events, but that was not to be. The chariot of Lord Jagannath had to wait till the next morning for pulling. By then the other two chariots had reached the Mausima Temple where we were all waiting with RK Padhi. Then a message came, telling us that Jagannath's chariot had collided against an electric pole and banged into a building. RK Padhi directed me to rush to the spot where I saw Collector PK Pattanaik standing crestfallen. We had to take decision. The electric pole was removed, the wheels of the chariot straightened, the ropes fitted to the right to bring the car to the middle of the road. The car was pulled out, damaging a portion of the building. This incident was a dampener which unfortunately happened again during the 1978 Nabakalebar, leading to utter confusion and chaos. The state government had to institute a Commission of Inquiry to go into the lapses of administration. I was in command of Orissa Police when the next Nabakalebar Festival took place in 1996 and I had kept my fingers crossed.

Naxalites were becoming active. Srikakulam, their hotbed, was the base from where the wings spread. Agrarian movement, which gave rise to Naxalism, was a recurrent phenomenon in Andhra Pradesh and it is said by many theoreticians that Srikakulam was as much the origin of the movement as Naxalbari, where its two fiery leaders Charu Mazumdar and Kanhu Sanyal, buoyed by their confidence in the infallibility of Mao's preachings—that power flows from the barrel of the gun —and dreaming of capturing the area from Pashupati to Tirupati found their counterparts in Srikakulam groping for direction. Contact was established and the movement hitherto known as Naxalite movement was carried forward in Srikakulam and the adjoining districts of Koraput and Ganjam in Orissa by Vempata Satyanarayan Rao, who had entrusted his daughter to constitute Dalams or squads in the area.

With the escalation of their activities, the atmosphere was getting tense. It would be naive to say that the persons caught and suspected would be accorded gentlemanly treatment by the police. Certain amount of coercion was inevitable, leading to use of third degree methods. This type of situation poses the greatest challenge to police. It would be futile to say that police should approach such incidents with restraint. We have seen West Bengal where Ranjit Gupta, given a free hand, suppressed Naxalism and KPS Gill wiped out terrorists from Punjab. At that time some rights activists, who were champions of the Naxalites, were making vocal protests against the alleged police brutalities. One group headed by Justice Tarkunde called PUCL was raising a lot of hue and cry about police excesses, so Andhra Pradesh Police were feeling considerably constrained to fight the Naxalites effectively. This was a handicap Ranjit

Gupta did not face, succeeding in virtually wiping out Naxalism from the land of its birth till the end of the century, a handicap that allowed Naxalism to flourish in Andhra Pradesh where the government was finally compelled to take tough measures by forming Gray Hounds to fight the menace effectively.

In Orissa, successive governments dithered, whether it was JB Patnaik, Biju Patnaik or Naveen Patnaik encouraging the Naxalites to indulge in mayhem, mass killings, looting of district armoury, blowing security forces, vehicles and what-not. Till the end of the nineties, Koraput and Ganjam were safe havens for the Naxalites. After the Andhra Pradesh Police successfully repelled them, they started acts of terrorism in Orissa and yet the government would adopt a wait-and-see approach. There were about 23 anti-Naxalite checkposts in both the districts and all that they did was to keep a watch on the Naxalities, who were taking shelter in Orissa. JB Patnaik's policy was 'wait-and-watch', Biju made a famous statement "Naxalities are my friends" and Naveen just did not react passing on the blame to Centre when the situation went out of control. As of now, nearly 20 districts in Orissa are affected, posing the gravest challenge to police. A unified command consisting of central paramilitary forces and state security forces is fighting a crucial battle.

In Koraput, BB Nandy and I used to go to Raygada and Gunupur and camp in the jungles for combing operations. Our target was to locate the leaders of the Dalams, who were quite active in the area.

One day, I received a copy of a wireless message addressed to SP Koraput sent by Suresh De requesting him to verify my driving licence and report its validity. I was shocked. How could Suresh do it, I thought, when I had briefed him suitably while handing over charge?

I met the SP and told him everything about the case. He assured me that he would delay the reply. But that was not the solution and I had to do something. I came to Cuttack to attend a promotion board. BB Mishra, a member of the IP who was IG CRPF and had raised the force from its infancy and subsequently IG Delhi Police, had taken over as IGP Orissa. A thoroughly competent officer he was, however, a bully in interpersonal relationship. I called on him, at his office. He looked at me and said, "You are the SP who was transferred from Mayurbhanj for quarrelling with the Collector". Determined to hit back, I said, "Yes sir, government had also passed orders for his transfer, but he did not move because of his political clout." Then he softened his tone. I left his office without calling on the AIG (admn) Joseph which was an unwritten mandate. Joseph apparently told Mishra about my lapse.

I came to the Crime Branch and met Iqbal Singh, the DIG CID Crime, for whom I had great respect and told him about the case and the signal sent by Suresh. Since the case had turned into a specially reported case, all records were available in the Crime Branch. He perused the records and said, "Why Suresh is behaving funnily?" He assured me that I need not worry.

In the evening, I went to the residence of BB Mishra with my wife for a social visit and found him very cordial. Another couple came to call on them, they were dismissed within fifteen minutes and then Mishra asked me if I would have a drink. Amazed at his gesture, I collected myself and said,"Yes". He opened a bottle of Scotch and gave me a peg. When we took leave he asked me to call on Joseph since I did not see him in the morning. I said, "Yes Sir," and we headed to the residence of Joseph. It was around 9 pm and Joseph had settled to his evening drink. He welcomed me warmly and I told him, "Sir I have come to call on you as directed by the IG." He understood and had a hearty laugh and forced me to drink Indian whiskey after the Scotch I had at the chief's residence.

While in Koraput, a signal came one day addressed to Suresh and me asking us to meet Iqbal Singh. I went to Cuttack and met Singh. When Suresh came, Singh asked him why he had sent a wireless to SP Koraput when I had briefed him at Baripada about the case. Suresh became defensive, explaining that it was a mandatory requirement of investigation. Singh told him not to teach him about investigation and close the case and send his compliance to the Crime Branch. I was eternally grateful to Iqbal Singh.

I took the shooting team to Dhenkanal in October for the annual shooting meet. There when I met the IGP he told me that he had sent a proposal for my posting as SP Keonjhar, news which totally drained out all my spirit. I was most reluctant to go as SP of a district and pleaded to him to allow me to continue at Koraput, but to no avail.

After going back to Koraput I received my posting order and we started packing for our journey to Keonjhar, my old place where I did my matriculation, was a leader as well in 1956, during the SRC agitations challenging the administration and now returning as Superintendent of Police. Many senior respectable citizens of the small town, which included some of my teachers in high school who had seen me as a young boy, now welcomed me in my new capacity as SP of the district. When I went to Keonjhar and after the beating I got in Mayurbhanj, I had became wiser and was determined to be as visible as possible in public and to remain in touch with the politicians of the district within the permissible limits. Collector Srinivas Mohapatra, promoted to the IAS from the state civil service, was a perfect gentleman, unpretentious and self-effacing. Having heard about me, he was very apprehensive of trouble from my end. His Sub-Collector DP Bagchi, an IAS Officer of 1966 batch and a friend of mine from Ravenshaw College days, had allayed his fears by assuring him that he had nothing to worry about. Braja Patnaik, a classmate of mine in college, was the DySP headquarters and three of us had a great time going out to the beautiful interior of Keonjhar, rich in hills, rivers, streams and fountains.

The importance of the district lay in mining—Keonjhar had one of the richest iron ore deposits in areas contiguous to Bihar, now Jharkhand. The areas were mainly under two police stations—Joda and Barbil and in view of the importance of the area, the SDPO was stationed at Barbil and not in the sub-divisional town of Chamupa. The other mining area adjacent to Jajpur subdivision (now a district) of Cuttack district, was Daitari from where Biju Patnaik during his chief ministership had built a 100 km state highway up to Paradip where a port had come up for export of iron ore to other countries, then mainly to Japan.

Bagchi left on transfer and Vivek Pattanayak, an IAS officer of 1966 batch, joined as ADM. He was not only a friend from Ravenshaw days but also an admirer of mine. His eldest brother KC Pattanayak of 1954 IPS was in the R&AW. To my bad luck, Collector Mohapatra was transferred and in his place came Sodrek Marwin of 1961 batch IAS. His arrival signalled turbulent days ahead from which I was again likely to emerge as a scapegoat. He was from Meghalaya and true to the nature of the people of Northeastern states, he was very simple and uncomplicated in mind, but had a mindset with ideas that would be impossible to dispel. Having heard about my days in Mayurbhanj—may be he was briefed—he was perhaps determined to exercise his authority over the SP in accordance with police manual rules.

I called on him in his office, and as we were taught at Mt. Abu, I was expecting him to call on me socially. But he would not. According to him, it was the SP's duty. He did not speak out his mind, but I smelled it and also received indications from Vivek to that effect. May be, that was the starting point. Then he would shoot off letters without any rhyme or reason. I had decided not to put my foot in my mouth, if necessary I would send a letter neither disagreeing nor agreeing with his views. Narrating my differences with him would amount to a repetition of events in my Baripada days, but I will cite three instances to highlight the whimsical orders issued by him. For me I had a great advantage of getting advance information from Vivek who would ring up and say, "Amiya Babu, a bombshell is on its way." I tried to talk things out with him, but he would cold shoulder. My dignity was more important to me than being solicitous to the Collector. Once when elephants were damaging crops, he issued an order to the DFO, DAO and the SP to remove the elephant menace. It was, to say the least, a hilarious order for such an emergency needed discussion and coordinated action. I remained silent which infuriated him asking me to send my compliances. I thought silence was golden.

Although my tour programmes used to reach him regularly, he would pass comments on my journey outside Keonjhar to Cuttack to attend a meeting in the police headquarters or to a promotion board and to Rourkela where the Range DIG's office was located. There was no way to deal with such irrational moves.

One issue inviting my reaction was deputation of armed force to Daitari, where tension was in air, with a Magistrate. One day he issued an order asking the Magistrate to return with the force. The police officer sought my orders and I ordered that the force be retained as a precautionary measure, the Magistrate could come back. He reported to the government, terming it as disobedience of order by SP and this became a cause celebre for action against me prompting Home Secretary BB Rath to teach another lesson to the errant SP.

I received displeasure of the government communicated to me directly whereas the previous adverse remarks were communicated to me by the IGP. This was the way, the government in Home department in their wisdom decided to rein in the SP.

Chief Minister RN Singhdeo visited the district to inaugurate a seminar on mining technology at Joda, which was organized by TISCO, which had a ferro manganese plant at Joda. Bipin Mishra (1967) had been posted as SDPO Barbil and had a few brushes with the TISCO management. Russi Mody, the Managing Director of TISCO, had come to Joda to receive the CM in the TISCO House. His liaison officer Manjrekar preferred to discuss the arrangements for CM's visit to Joda with the Collector who sent a note to me for making necessary police arrangements. On the basis of the tour programme of the Chief Minister received from the government I had made necessary arrangements in which the route of the CM to the meeting venue was different from the one fixed by Manjrekar.

Smug with his discussion with Collector, he had raised welcome arches in TISCO colony, which was on the route he had earmarked for the CM's journey. After tea in TISCO house, I told the driver of CM's car, who was at Raj Bhavan and knew me well, to follow my jeep which I piloted on the route fixed by me. The CM arrived at the venue from a different route to the surprise of Russy Mody and to the shock of Manjrekar. Marwin had to remain silent as copy of the police arrangements had been sent to him. Russy Mody felt things were not normal between TISCO and police. After lunch, I was sitting on the verandah when Mody came, sat beside me and asked me if there was a communication gap between TISCO and police. I told him to ask that question to Manjrekar whom he called and banged right and left for failing to maintain good relations with police, that was within hearing distance of the Collector.

Aggrieved with BB Mishra, Manjrekar wanted to shift him from Barbil and duly supported by Collector, he went to Bhubaneswar to meet the Chief Minister along with Nanda Patnaik, Tata's chief liaison officer based in Bhubaneswar and narrated the acts of alleged police highhandedness.

The CM after listening to them patiently asked, "Have you met the SP?" When they said no, he asked them to discuss their problems with the SP. I got a frantic call from Nanda Patnaik from Bhubaneswar, telling me that they were on their way to Keonjhar to meet me. They came, met me and discussed and BB Mishra continued to remain in Barbil. Nanda Patnaik, whom I met in adversarial circumstances, became a lifelong friend and admirer, showering praises I did not deserve.

In 1971, general elections were held. Biju Patnaik, ambitious that he was, disenchanted with the Congress, formed a separate outfit called Utkal Congress. Congress again failed to get majority and Biju's party along with Swatantra Party headed by RN Singhdeo bagged 69 seats, eight short of simple majority. Biju Patnaik was so confident of becoming Chief Minister that he contested from four assembly seats and one parliamentary constituency and was defeated at all places.

Utkal Congress was not willing to concede Chief Minister post to RN Singhdeo, so they chose a non-partisan Biswanath Dash, who was Prime Minister of Orissa in 1937 after the formation of the state and later Governor of UP. Biju Patnaik came to Assembly through a by-election and demanded to become CM. In short, the coalition did not work.

Utkal Congress merged with Congress taking its tally to 94. Biswanath Dash resigned in disgust in June 1972. Biju's ambition to become Chief Minister was thwarted by Indira Gandhi, who would not even allow Binayak Acharya, the elected leader of the Congress Legislature Party, to form the government. Her protege Nandini Satpathy, who was the Union Information and Broadcasting minister, was thrust on the party. In the midst of high drama, high command representative Chandrajit Yadav asked Binayak Acharya to withdraw and propose the name of Nandini for chief ministership.

Amidst all this political turmoil, I was also passing through another phase of turmoil in my life. By early 1971, I realized that my transfer from Keonjhar was a certainty. I had to see that unlike Baripada, both Collector and SP would leave the district at the same time as I was sure that the government would transfer both. This I had ensured with the help of my trusted DIB Inspector Harmohan Mohanty, who was like a member in the household of the Home Minister Nilamani Routaray in the Biswanath Das Ministry. He went to Bhubaneswar, kept track of the file and when my file reached the minister, Nilamani Babu rang up the Chief Secretary, asking him to send proposal for the Collector's transfer. I felt vindicated and also elated at the fact that people in Keonjhar town, in Joda and Barbil demanded that I should continue at Keonjhar. I was posted to the fifth battalion OMP as Commandant where five years earlier I had been posted as Deputy Commandant. I moved to Cuttack with my family in June 1971.

I knew that my stay in the battalion would be short lived as indicated by the IGP. I decided to make serious efforts to get a staff job either in the Crime Branch or Special Branch or Police headquarters or in the Vigilance organization. When I called on RK Padhi, the Vigilance Chief, I expressed my humble desire. He assured me that the next vacancy in Vigilance would go to me and asked me to brief AIG Vigilance, SK Benarjee, a jolly good man, which I did. A vacancy was in the pipeline. Sankar Sen, who was SP Vigilance southern division Berhampur, was to go to IB which materialised in October and I was posted in his place. After four months stay at Cuttack, I with my family moved to my 14th posting at Berhampur from where my nomadic life had begun in 1965. When troubled by my frequent movements and the accompanying problems, I once unfolded my sense of agonies and anguishes before a senior officer, a well-wisher, he told me, "You are a rolling stone who has gathered no moss."

Chapter-18

Berhampur: Beginning of Stability

I joined my new assignment as SP vigilance Southern Division in the first week of October 1971 and stayed in that post for two years, marking the beginning of stability in my career. The jurisdiction of SP Vigilance was coterminous with that of the Revenue Division comprising the districts of Ganjam, Koraput, Phulbani and Kalahandi. It was at Berhampur that our second daughter, Anuradha, was born on September 25, 1972.

Professionally, work was satisfying. The Vigilance organization in Orissa, apart from investigating into corruption cases, was also entrusted with detection of sales tax evasion for which there was a full complement of staff in the Directorate and in the offices of three divisional Superintendents, other two located at Cuttack and Sambalpur. There has been substantial expansion since then, but the basic structure envisaged by S K Ghosh in the early sixties remains unchanged.

Now coming to speak of the famous saying "who

guards the guardians", I always had troubled moments when I saw erring anti-corruption officials falling prey to the temptation of money and lucre; I came across some instances of delinquencies and had to face several hurdles in securing punishment for them. I have, however, come across some excellent police officers in the ranks of Sub Inspectors, Inspectors and Deputy Superintendents in State Vigilance and Crime Branch in Police, postings to which are generally avoided for obvious reasons.

One such officer was Inspector Khan posted at Bhawanipatna in Kalahandi district. A highly conscientious officer whose inquiries used to be painstaking and insightful, his output in the district was admirable going by the yardstick. While returning to Bhawanipatna after an inquiry in the extreme heat of summer, he collapsed and was declared dead in the district hospital. I felt so stricken that I went all the way to Bhawanipatna, 350 km from Berhampur, to convey my condolences to the bereaved family. These officers have brought laurels for the Orissa Police.

JM Samal (1954), the chronic dissenter, was SP Koraput and was having a running battle with BB Mishra, the police chief. He had also antagonised Home Secretary Padmanav Mishra. B B Mishra left in January 1973 to take over as Director General of the CRPF in Delhi, handing over command to RK Padhi, who in normal course would continue for next four years. Suddenly one day a news item created ripples in the entire official machinery of the state. The SHO of Jeypore Police Station in Koraput district allegedly at the behest of Samal registered a case of corruption against Home Secretary Mishra. Faraway from Cuttack, Samal stayed incommunicado and an outraged RK Padhi felt so much let down by the IPS community that he gave vent to his injured feelings as loudly and eloquently as possible. He took the Range DIG Hafiz to task for not having adequate intelligence about the incident as he had issued confidential circulars to all Range DIGs and Superintendents of Police for keeping a watch on the activities of Samal, who allegedly had caused considerable embarrassment to BB Mishra and was lying in wait for others.

RK was quite aware of my activism in the IPS Association affairs. One day, I received a telephone call from him and he reprimanded me over the incident. I was at pains to comprehend what I could have done about it. I heard him telling, "I am ashamed of leading a cadre like yours. Your head should hang in shame." This left me speechless. Then he told me, "I am bringing you as my AIG. Get ready to move." This was last week of October 1973, end of my 14th posting in seven years of service and we moved to Cuttack to take over my new assignment under a fuming and benevolent police chief who till today remains an icon to me.

Part-4

Cuttack Police Headquarters

- Cuttack Police Headquarters

Chapter-19

Cuttack Police Headquarters

I joined my new assignment as AIG at Cuttack in the first week of November. Police headquarters along with some other important institutions like High Court, Board of Revenue, Vigilance, Transport Commissioner and Sales Tax Commissioner continued to function in Cuttack even after the formation of the new capital after independence and are there till date.

Posting as a staff officer to a police chief would normally mean an uneventful stint, acting as a file pusher, conveying the orders of the chief to the field officers and overseeing implementation of various schemes. For me, however, it proved to be a highly eventful and satisfying period of my career that laid the foundation of my way of working as police chief in the event of my attaining that status. I served under three chiefs—RK Padhi, only for three months as the cruel hands of destiny would snatch him away in January 1974; Narayan Chand, who was my DIG at Sambalpur and the vigilance chief after RK Padhi took over as IGP in

January 1973, for seven months; and Narsingh Swain of 1950 batch for nearly two-and-a-half years.

In the Police headquarters, the chief was assisted by three AIGs—AIG 1, AIG 2, and AIG 3. These designations had been changed by R K Padhi to AIG (admn), AIG (finance) and AIG (qm). RNDas, an officer of 1955 batch, was AIG (adm). I joined as AIG (finance). S K Chatterjee of 1964 was AIG (qm). Das went on promotion as DIG Northern Range Sambalpur and Somnath Mishra of 1957 batch joined in his place. My responsibility was mainly police finance and all related schemes like modernisation grant, police housing schemes, police welfare projects and subsequently the Finance Commission award. My hands were more than full under three police chiefs, two of whom were dynamic, innovative, forward looking and leaders under whom it was a pleasure to work. Narayan Chand was constrained by his limited tenure. But with RK Padhi, who first became IGP at the age of 48, and Narsingh Swain at the age of 50, the future was rich in promise and both had realized that they had a commitment to their tenure.

Orissa politics then was dogged by the curse of instability arising out of emergence of new political parties, desertion by MLAs, changing loyalties not out of conviction but of convenience. The coalition of Congress and Utkal Congress headed by Nandini Satpathy collapsed in 1972 with the withdrawal of support by several members of Utkal Congress led by Nilamani Routray, the Home minister. Biju Patnaik who had been defeated in four assembly and one parliamentary constituencies in 1971 had managed to come to the Assembly through a by-election. He now joined hands with his former mentor and arch rival HK Mahatab with the hope of becoming chief minister. They formed a new party called Pragati Party and, with 82 MLAs, more than majority, walked to the Raj Bhavan to prove their strength before Governor BD Jatti, who under instructions from Prime Minister Indira Gandhi refused to accept any such claim and recommended President's rule on the ground that only fresh elections would bring stability to the government.

It is needless to say that this was a gross violation of the spirit of the Constitution, for in all fairness, he should have given them an opportunity to prove majority on the floor of the Assembly. President's rule was imposed and was in force when I joined as AIG. This act of the Governor was taken to the High Court, and its constitutionality was questioned. The High Court did give adverse remarks on the action of the Governor while not questioning the contents of his report.

RK Padhi had an excellent equation with Nandini, who held him in high esteem and also with the Governor during the President's rule. I have mentioned earlier the measures taken by him to create an identity for Orissa Police and generate a sense of pride for belonging to a unique service. He had created a niche for himself as a top intellectual and was very much in demand in public functions where he would keep his audience in pin drop silence with the brilliance of his oratory skills.

What was remarkable was that he did not have an iota of arrogance of an intellectual, but was humility personified, a quality rare in some of the self-styled intellectuals of the state with whom I would interact in later years in my life. In police he would not bother about the nitty-gritty of day-to-day administration, but would function from a higher plane, the essential component of which was leadership, a quality he had in abundance. He was accessible to all IPS officers for he wanted to groom their leadership qualities. He would say that every IPS officer is a potential police chief and needed to be encouraged to develop that potential. He would take a lot of interest in the training of probationary Deputy Superintendents of Police as they would provide second-rung leadership in police.

His fellow feeling, his sense of camaraderie was so high that he would go on leave to allow HP Singhdeo to retire as IG Police.

His self-esteem and his tenacity to maintain the dignity of a post were astounding. When his relationship with Home Secretary BB Rath became strained, he vowed not to enter into the Home Secretary's room till the incumbent was changed. He did enter the room, but only after Padmanav Mishra took over as Home Secretary. As DIG he refused to stand in line with a Deputy Secretary, which was the state protocol, claiming that a DIG should be in same article as a Secretary to Government as he was drawing more salary than most Secretaries who were either in selection grade or in senior scale. He would not bother about his posting, getting changed from IG post and placed somewhere. He would take it with effortless grace, a quality which I had seen in former Chief Secretary AK Barren. A man with such gift, courage of conviction and intellectual attainments was bound to develop a halo, an aura in which the IPS officers of Orissa joyously luxuriated. At the same time, his friendliness brooked no nonsense; he would take an errant IPS officer to task without mincing words and commend the deserving ones.

The brief period I served under him was eventful. Although there were five armed battalions in Orissa, effectively there were four; one was given to Aviation Research Centre in Charbatia with a contingent posted at Haflong in Assam. Padhi asked me to prepare a proposal for opening a new battalion at Bhubaneswar, which was demanding armed police increasingly with its growing importance.

I drafted a proposal and if I remember correctly the total financial implication was to the tune of Rs 40 to 45 lakh. He personally followed it up and obtained the approval of the Governor for creation of a new battalion in Bhubaneswar.

We selected the site later while Narayan Chand was IG Police.

The Sixth Finance Commission then was in position and grant for upgradation in the standards of administration was agreed to in principle. On instructions from RK, I prepared a case for Orissa Police which he personally presented before the Finance Commission and for the first time Orissa Police received an award from the Finance Commission for upgrading its standard. After that it was a regular feature in successive Finance Commissions.

In those days funds were difficult to obtain, the financial health of the state was poor, ways and means position was tight and the government was mostly reluctant to provide funds under the non-plan sector for police. We had to fight tooth and nail to obtain our legitimate dues. The position has changed vastly during the past 15 years, funding police is no longer a constraint. Then there was not a single staff car in police, now cars abound, the fleet has multiplied. In fact, the department is not able to spend the money it gets under various schemes. Present day officers are reaping the benefits from the toils their predecessors had put in.

Getting residential accommodation in Cuttack was extremely difficult. Many senior IAS officers who have since moved to Bhubaneswar were staying in Cuttack where all government houses were in the pool of general administration department. I persuaded Padhi to earmark funds from the Police Housing Scheme for construction of some houses for senior police officers. In the board meeting chaired by IGP, this proposal was mooted and the other three members—the Home Secretary, Finance Secretary and PWD Secretary—readily agreed to set aside Rs 5 lakh for construction of four quarters for senior police officers.

I pursued the matter with the PWD Secretary AC Padhi, who happened to be the brother of RK .Padhi and four quarters were completed in record eight months by the side of the IPS mess. Bala Subramanium (63), who had joined as AIG (qm), NC Padhi (1966), SP Special Branch, and I were the first to occupy three houses. AK Patnaik (1964) occupied the fourth one.

James Dharamraj, an IPS officer of Orissa cadre who was on deputation to CBI as IG, came to Cuttack to take an officer in place of PC Ratho, SP CBI Orissa, whose term was coming to an end. He asked me for my willingness which I readily gave, but RK Padhi said no. BB Panda (1963) joined the post in place of PC Ratho.

I went to Lucknow in January 1974 to attend a course organized by the Indian Institute of Management, Calcutta. When I met RK before leaving Cuttack little did I realize that it would be my last meeting with him. After returning from the course, I was on casual leave in Bhubaneswar when on January 23, PC Ratho rang me to tell that RK Padhi was no more.

I rushed to Cuttack, and even now I vividly remember the tearful atmosphere prevailing there. Everybody's heart was heavy, mind stricken and eyes tearful. Narayan Chand, Addl IG Vigilance, his friend, fan and admirer, speaking in choked voice, asked me and Sankar Sen to draft a condolence message. For me, the loss was so great that my mental faculties had almost ceased to function. The state government declared full state honours to be given to the departed soul.

RK Padhi died of a massive cardiac arrest while he was asleep. The previous evening, in the Rotary annual conference of the district which then covered Orissa, undivided Bihar and Madhya Pradesh, he had been elected as the Governor. Triloki Nath, a member of the IP and former IG Police Bihar and a Rotarian, was also present in the conference which was held at Gopalpur-on-sea. After dinner, he came to his uncle's place in Berhampur and fell asleep, never to wake up again. The Collector and SP were asked to escort his body to his hometown Parlakhemudi for the last rites.

In Cuttack, it was decided that a group of senior officers would proceed to attend the funeral. Agnihotri, an officer of MP cadre, who was Deputy Director ARC, readily provided a helicopter and D Chotray, the senior-most DIG of the state along with AP Mohanty, DPS Chouhan (1963) and self proceeded to Charbatia to take the helicopter to Parlakhemudi where on reaching in the evening we found all roads overflowing with people to receive their famous son.

We returned to Cuttack next morning. Thus, came to an untimely end an illustrious life of whom not only Orissa Police was proud, but also the entire state. By all accounts, he was the last patriarch in Orissa Police.

Narayan Chand, an officer of former Kalahandi princely state, took over as IG Police in an atmosphere that was surcharged with gloom, a sense of loss and dejection. A workaholic, he settled down to work in right earnest. Mid-term elections to the Assembly, which Governor BD Jatti had recommended, were scheduled to be held in early 1974. Three chief minister aspirants, HK Mahatab, Biju Patnaik and Nandini Satpathy, in their respective political formations were leading the battle. For Nandini, the elections were crucial because she was instrumental in not allowing a new ministry to come up when she lost majority in the Assembly and going for President's rule.

One of the areas which had troubled me was Police Housing. During my stay in two districts and two battalions, the acute shortage of accommodation for police personnel had hit me hard. We were not able to provide even 10 per cent satisfaction in this crucial area to people who were supposed to be on duty for 24 hours a day. The sheer meaninglessness of the weekly alochana sabhas was a stark and sad reality. The SP or the Commandant was helpless for he was not in a position to do anything other than bringing the issue to the notice of the higher authorities who were no less helpless.

This had led me to keep the welfare of the police personnel as one of the key items in my agenda in whatever capacity I would serve. I had broached the topic in the Police Housing Committee meeting, citing the example of Andhra Pradesh which was the first state to form a Police Housing Corporation, and it was agreed that this proposal should be examined in detail. I pursued the matter with Chand who deputed me to Hyderabad to study the structure, flow of funds and working of the Police Housing Corporation.

Joe Saldhana, a very senior IPS officer, was the Managing Director who personally took me to various sites of construction and explained the functioning of the corporation, including sources of funds. I prepared a self-contained report on return to Cuttack and submitted it to the IGP, who sent the same to the government, recommending strongly creation of a separate agency for police housing.

In Orissa, a Police Housing Corporation was formed five years later and SS Padhi, the then police chief sent me a letter to Delhi thanking me for my contribution towards formation of the corporation. It became functional in 1980/81 when N Swain was the chief with BP Saha (1963) as Managing Director. He was also kind enough to convey his appreciation to me. Now the corporation has grown in size, executing work not only for police but also other agencies in the state.

Mid-term elections were held in 1974. Nandini's dream of coming back to Assembly with a convincing majority did not materialize. She got only 66 seats, six short of the magical number. But with her Communist background, she got the support of the Communist MLAs and formed the ministry. After formation of the ministry, the usual game of transfer of officials, though it was on a much lesser scale then, began. The Communists who were quite influential in Ganjam district wanted the SP, RM Patnaik out. One fine morning, I received a notification, posting me as SP Ganjam, then considered a major charge, which to me was a bolt from the blue as I was not at all keen to go as SP of a district, and which much later would be held against me by my detractors as lack of experience in a major district for becoming DG Police of Orissa.

I expressed my unwillingness to Chand, met the Home Secretary and conveyed to him my reluctance to go as SP Ganjam. Mercifully the notification was cancelled.

The last days of Chand, he was due to retire in August, were full of suspense, and rumours were flying thick and fast about imminent change of police chief and speculation about the new one. General perception was in favour of D Chotray, a highly experienced officer, balanced in his approach and acceptable to many. But for Nandini there were many considerations, the most important being political proximity and, from that point of view, the decision was heavily loaded in favour of N Swain of 1950 batch.

In Orissa, he had three seniors—Chotray, Ghanshyam Dash, both said to be close to Nilamani Routray, who had defected from the previous ministry headed by Nandini causing its downfall, and Rajgopalan, who had no political equation with her. At the Centre, there were NK Ray, a member of the IP in Intelligence Bureau, Shivraj Bahadur (1949) and Iqbal Singh (1950). While the latter two were not keen to come, it was difficult to ignore NK Ray as against him nobody could level charge of being politically close to certain quarters. In fact, Nandini, basking in the reflected glory of Mrs Indira Gandhi, was in touch with him.

But following Indira Gandhi to the letter, she had made up her mind to appoint Swain as police chief and nobody could tilt that decision, least of all the bureaucracy. Only one officer could influence her: her Secretary Ramakant

Rath, an IAS officer of 1957 batch who became famous as a poet and writer, winning several awards at the state and national level. But Rath was new to the post and was in the process of finding out his roots to establish his undisputed authority and emerge as the alter ego of Nandini.

In fact, it was Nandini who started the tradition of having a Secretary whose authority was beyond question. Subsequently, this practice was followed by JB Patnaik in the eighties, Biju Patnaik in the early nineties and now Naveen Patnaik.

By mid-1974 all speculation was laid to rest and Swain was notified as the IGP Orissa with direction to take over on August 17—14 days before Chand's retirement was due. He was asked to proceed on leave.

Narayan Chand, after taking over as IGP in January, had initiated some measures to perpetuate the memory of RK Padhi. A committee was formed with N Swain as chairman and me as secretary to formulate the recommendations.

We recommended the formation of a trust with the donation of one day's salary of all police personnel, targeting Rs 1 lakh to award scholarships to deserving children of police personnel to pursue higher education and dedication of a newly constructed hall by the side of the IPS Mess to the memory of RK Padhi. Chand was following the progress personally on a day-to-day basis and his last act was to get the R K Padhi Memorial Trust launched and the hall dedicated to the memory of RK Padhi by Governor BD Jatti on August 16, 1974. The trust had IGP as the chairman and me as managing trustee.

To avoid criticism, Nandini upgraded the posts held by Chotray, Ghanshyam Dash and Rajgopalan to the rank of Addl IG and brought NK Ray from the Centre as the Chairman of the Orissa Public Service Commission.

In the above background, when N Swain took over,

bypassing several senior officers as IG Police, there was an atmosphere of distrust, intrigue and suspicion. Most of the officers did not know where they stood and I was one among them.

Swain was DIG of the central range when I was SP Mayurbhanj. As I have mentioned earlier, I did not get the type of support I expected from him in my conflicts with the Collector. When I went to Keonjhar, he was the DIG of the Western Range and his support was, I felt, lukewarm.

At Cuttack, I had just shifted to a newly constructed house, whose completion I was chasing and was in the process of settling down. I was a little apprehensive, but was preparing mentally to move out. Swain had taken over the reins of Orissa Police after completing only 24 years of service. It could be a record of sorts as he had nine years ahead of him.

A man with a razor sharp mind with excellent command over English, he was temperamental, a bit short-tempered, highly impatient, opinionated and would stick to his ground, come what may. Nobody could change his mind, except perhaps the Chief Minister. He could clearly see the herculean task ahead— the fragility of the top layer of the police apparatus with several seniors breathing down his neck.

His primary task was to bring the fractious IPS officers together, lead the team as a leader and prove his leadership qualities. Being an astute judge of men, he had gauged the attitude, competence and commitment of all middle level IPS officers, for it was they who would help him to become a successful police chief.

Most of his contemporaries had a mindset that was difficult to change; all that was necessary was to pre-empt any problem from them. Apart from me, the other two staff officers were Somnath Mishra (1957) AIG (admn) and MA

Balasubranium (1963) AIG (quartermaster), both brilliant and hard working. Being a hard core intelligence man, he was in IB and then state special branch for several years, he wanted to control the special branch on a day-to-day basis. He put SS Padhi (1951), the seniormost DIG, a perfect gentleman as DIG Intelligence, knowing that Padhi would not be proactive in the special branch The extra ordinary circumstances leading to Swain's appointment as IG Police became the cause of speculations running rife about transfer of IPS officers and I invariably figured in the various chains emanating from various sources. I thought that being a staff officer I should be clear about my position vis-a`-vis the Police chief.

I finally decided to take the bull by the horns and talk to Swain directly; but before I could do that, he called me to his residence one day and had a long chat in which he spelt out his ideas of improving the image of police, its efficiency and bringing the IPS officers together. I casually asked him if I was marked for a change.

He expressed surprise and told me that I would be one of the main instruments of his mission. He asked me to organize regular mess dinners and other activities and formulate as many schemes as possible to keep the police headquarters vibrant during office hours and life beyond the office.

We, the trio, Somnath Mishra, Bala and me, started work in right earnest and ensured that his nearly three-year tenure was brimming with new ideas and activities, full of innovations and dynamism. Unlike the present days when funds are not much of a problem for the police, our biggest constraint was funds, and, against those heavy odds, Swain marched on.

Several new measures, were introduced. The Gore Committee Report on police training was out. One of its important recommendations was matriculation as the minimum qualification for constables, which was implemented.

We all agreed that the recommendation to stop direct recruitment to the rank of DySP should not be implemented, as it would, in course of time, create a huge crisis at the senior level. This is a situation that is currently prevalent, following the populist decision of the next Janata government in Orissa (1977 - 80), headed by Nilamani Routray, to stop direct recruitment to the rank of DySP.

The uniform items of the subordinate police officers including constables underwent substantial changes. The headgear and footwear were changed for the better, and a switch was made from the cotton fabric to the terry cot. The concept of Inspectors as SHOs of police stations was introduced, this has now been extended to all police stations of Orissa.

A very significant act of modernization was to network all districts and police stations with VHF communication by erecting several towers throughout the state. Orissa was, perhaps, the second state next to Tamil Nadu to achieve such wide network coverage.

Till then, no officer in the Government had a staff car. We purchased nine Fiat station wagons on the ground that they would be used for urban patrolling, fitted them with VHF sets and gave a car to each range DIG. I had to run from pillar to post, from the departments of home to finance to get the approval of the government.

RN Das, who was Finance Secretary and later became the Chief Secretary, took an undertaking from me to the effect that the cars would not be used as staff cars. I risked that. The police department today has a surfeit of cars.

A piquant situation arose on the recommendations of the Sixth Finance Commission putting Swain in a highly embarrassing position because of a letter drafted by me.

Swain formed a committee chaired by BK Mohapatra, a promoted officer of 1951 seniority, with me as the convenor. We had elaborate discussions and brainstorming sessions and submitted a well-reasoned report for utilization of the funds under different heads like augmentation of civil police, improving the work atmosphere in police stations, mobility and communication and modernization of crime branch, special branch and forensic laboratory.

The report went to government and, after the usual delay, came the reply that the funds would not be available as the same had been merged with the larger state resources. The Sixth Finance Commission had not stipulated that the funds awarded for a particular purpose must be utilized for that only which the subsequent Finance Commissions did, and the state government, which was facing heavy financial crunch, took advantage of this omission.

There was disappointment and an infuriated Swain asked me to draft a letter to KF Rustomjee, the then Special Secretary in the Ministry of Home Affairs (MHA). I drafted the letter and being impulsive in nature worded the text strongly, which Swain glanced through and signed without toning down the language or correcting it. A copy was sent to the state home secretary, who sent it to the Chief Minister. RK Rath, secretary to CM, perusing the letter, told Nandini that the IG had bypassed the state government by writing to the MHA directly that too with complaints and suggested that the IG must withdraw the letter. Swain was called and asked to withdraw the letter which he refused. Finally, the home secretary sent a letter to MHA, informing that the letter should be treated as with drawn.

This is an example of how the real issue was relegated to the background citing reasons unrelated to the issue. When Swain narrated the events to me, I felt terribly guilty and offered myself to be shifted, which he rejected outright. This was the story of the Finance Commission award which

RK Padhi had ably advanced on the basis of a report drafted by me and the end game played by the CM's Secretariat again on the basis of yet another draft prepared by me.

I am citing the above and some other examples to highlight that an officer, even if he is a political creature, can exhibit exemplary grit, determination and courage and grow beyond the pale of his political mentor which Swain could do.

We were purchasing large number of jeeps in modernization scheme to supply a vehicle to each police station. During one financial year, we decided to procure 40 jeeps. Till then there was one agency in Cuttack for the supply of the vehicles, Patnaik & Co. Another agency had just started in Bhubaneswar owned by Panda Motors, a prominent family from Ganjam district. The oldest brother Sarat Kumar Panda was a politician of Congress Party and close to Nandini. I obtained orders from Swain to place order on 50/50 basis to the two agencies. Swain approved it by writing that undertaking should be given by both to complete supply by 31st March. I asked both agencies to give undertakings. While Patnaik & Co readily gave the undertaking to supply jeeps, Panda Motors at that time was unable to give the undertaking and stated that they would be able to provide only a particular number of jeeps and the rest would be supplied over a period of time.

I took the decision and placed order with Panda Motors for the number of jeeps indicated by them and with Patnaik & Co for the rest which happened to be the lion's share. This unfortunately created misunderstanding, and probably Nandini called Swain and suggested my transfer which Swain emphatically refused explaining the fair process adopted in the purchase with his approval.

The area where Swain excelled most, was police welfare and welfare of the deprived sections of society. The police welfare fund was augmented. He put a lot of importance on education of police children. Police high schools came up in Keonjhar, Sambalpur and other places. The quality of education in the police schools used to be far better than other schools.

A unique project that was started for the benefit of the deprived people was "Karuna", which won acclaim not only from government but also from police agencies outside the state. In this scheme, specific projects undertaken were the rehabilitation of the Lodhas, who were declared a criminal tribe during the British rule. Although that criminal tag was not there after independence, the Lodhas in Mayurbhanj district, where I was SP, used to indulge in petty thefts and robberies. While the government had started a scheme for rehabilitation of the Lodhas, the police project was more goal-oriented as it spread education amongst them and provided them with employment.

Similarly, in Keonjhar district, development of the Juang tribals whose number was on the decline was taken up with considerable measure of success. In Kalahandi district, which hit the headlines for its chronic drought conditions that attracted the visit of Indira Gandhi in 1966, relief camps were organized to supply food and clothing to the poor people.

All these activities were carried out by the district Superintendents of Police who were obviously motivated to take up the task and there in lay the leadership qualities of Swain.

PK Senapati (1967), the Kalahandi SP, son-in-law of D Chotray who had been bypassed by Swain, had serious reservations about the attitude of Swain towards him in spite of my assurance to him to the contrary. But he carried out the Kalahandi scheme with success and later realized that Swain had no prejudice against him. I was monitoring the implementation of these schemes on a day-to-day basis. For me, it was a lot of additional work as Swain had left his pet schemes in my hands for successful implementation. Ranjit Gupta, a member of the IP, then IG West Bengal visited Cuttack and was enormously impressed with what Orissa Police was doing.

In social life, Swain encouraged the districts and battalions to organize as many activities as possible–drama, shows, sports, vocational activities and the like. Life in Cuttack was abuzz with activities, regular dinners in the mess, outings, picnics, drama, welfare exhibitions and relief work, which kept the officers and their wives busy. As mess secretary, secretary of the police welfare committee, sports meet and subsequently secretary of the IPS Association, I hardly used to have time to relax.

In spite of such proximity with the police chief and enjoying his full confidence, I never asked for any favour. I made some trips to Sambalpur to see my parents and to attend my brother Akshya's wedding; I preferred to go on casual leave, driving my Fiat car for 320 km instead of making official trips. I also shared very cordial relations with the group of officers who, according to the special branch, were under watch, spending evenings with them over drinks. Once I was cautioned by an officer but I brushed it aside. Right from the day I started working under him, Swain had a feeling that I used to be very chummy with his detractors. I let that feeling remain only to see that his faith in me was reinforced.

Now it will be relevant to have a look at the political scenario prevailing at that time in Orissa. Nandini's tenure as chief minister marked a watershed in the political and administrative ethos in the state. This was in keeping with the fast moving events at the national level with Indira Gandhi at the helm of affairs. Indira introduced the concept of committed bureaucracy and judiciary with the arguments that the instruments of governance must be committed to the policies of the government for effective implementation. In effect it became the policies of the party in power whose implication would be that persons perceived to be not committed, and this is a highly subjective perception, would be weeded out or sidelined.

This violated the basic tenets of public administration of impartiality, anonymity and objectivity. Public servants are required to implement the policies of the government but by highlighting the concept of commitment, a signal was sent that mediocrity could prevail at the cost of efficiency and seniority. The bureaucracy and that included police, defence services and judiciary, all jumped into the bandwagon. The potential danger of politicization of the administrative system did not seem to have worried the higher echelons of the bureaucracy, a section of which argued that it was nothing new, it was already there. I will not say that it was not there, it was there but not announced in such a loud tone and certainly not implemented in the louder manner that followed.

Jawaharlal Nehru and his successor Lal Bahadur Shastri would not have dreamt of administering the country through mouthpieces in all sectors.

Nandini, who started her life as a member of the Communist Party in the Ravenshaw College, where she led the students agitation in 1951 and was injured in police lathi charge, was a lady with a sharp mind with flashes of creativity—writing both prose and poetry and establishing her niche in the literary circle of Orissa. With the help of Biju Patnaik, she was elected to Rajya Sabha in 1961 and worked her way to Indira Gandhi's inner circle that consisted of the Young Turks. She became the deputy minister in the Ministry of Information and Broadcasting and subsequently a state minister. Although the Young Turks disintegrated, she remained steadfastly loyal to Indira Gandhi and that is how she was thrust upon Orissa in 1971 as leader of the Congress party although the party had elected Binayak Acharya as the leader.

Nandini was intelligent, arrogant, highly opinionated, vindictive and suspicious and had strong likes and dislikes. She also formed a kitchen cabinet consisting of Banka Behari Das, Pratap Mohanty and some others which fell out in no time. Her secretary, otherwise an honest and able administrator, generally giving an impression to the people of being a highly self-effacing personality, was her advisor in matters of state.

Chief Secretary of the state was Ramkrishnaya, a war service recruit and brilliant officer, perhaps best amongst all the chief secretaries Orissa had till then. His relations with Nandini started becoming strained and he was on the look out for a berth in the Centre. He went to Centre and was succeeded by VS Mathews, another war service recruit to IAS, a highly competent field officer whose services were indispensable in all natural calamities like flood, cyclone and drought—endemic to Orissa—for relief operations.

Nandini was hardly fond of Mathews, but had to make him Chief Secretary as the latter had good equation with many politicians. But she put her trusted bureaucrat JADave, a war service recruit, as Additional Chief Secretary in charge of crucial departments like Home, Finance and GA. Mathew had to go prematurely and Dave succeeded him.

One of the most ill-advised moves by her was tinkering with higher education of the state which shocked the people of Orissa. She changed Professor Bidhu Bhusan Das, the Director of Public Instruction, without any rhyme or reason. Professor Das, who was a brilliant teacher in English, was a highly principled, honest and conscientious officer and his removal was ascribed by many to RK Rath's hostile feeling against him. Similarly, she advised Governor to dismiss Professor Sriram Chandra Das, Professor of Political Science in Utkal University and a legendary teacher in his subject on the ground that he was spreading disaffection amongst students.

Removal of Dr Dash had sent shock waves in the state, generating a fund of sympathy and goodwill for him. All these developments were not to the liking of Swain and he did all that his conscience allowed him to do without endangering his position. He was one of the first persons to warn Dr Dash about his impending dismissal, this has been recorded in the autobiography of Dr Dash.

One of her most favoured officers was NK Panda, an IAS officer of 1954 batch, Revenue Divisional Commissioner of the Central division. Possessing a very sharp and witty mind, and with a stint in the United Nations, he opened his residence to an emerging centre of political power in the person of Tushar Panigrahi, Nandini's brother. Many hangers-on used to join Tushar over drinking sessions in the RDC's residence which became the talk of the town.

And if a son was emerging in Delhi as one of the most powerful political forces in the person of Sanjay Gandhi, Orissa did not lag behind. Tathagata, the youngest son of Nandini, a budding young man, hot-blooded, tempestuous and impulsive, was making his presence felt with the District Magistrates and Superintendents of Police eager to please Nandini.

Swain did keep a safe distance from both Tushar and Tathagatha, which conveniently misinterpreted would be conveyed to Nandini by his detractors who had gained access to her. Tathagatha later fell out with his mother. Perhaps there was bitter acrimony as would be evident from the alleged diary of Tathagatha in which he vented his anger with his mother over many personal issues. He joined the Biju Janata Dal and is currently a member of the Lok Sabha, representing Dhenkanal constituency.

Yet another favourite officer was AN Tiwari, then Secretary, Department of Public Relations and Information who was entrusted with the task of projecting the image of Nandini. Here I feel tempted to cite some events which I did not know as I was not a privy to state secrets, but which I heard from my friends in the Intelligence Bureau. Nandini was amongst the favoured few of the Russian Communist political system and many officers of the Russian Embassy were said to be in touch with her. There was also speculation that Russia wanted to project her as the future leader of the country. In this backdrop there was a publicity blitzkrieg in Orissa projecting Nandini as a leader of destiny.

In a meeting presided over by Chief Secretary V S Mathews to organise a state level exhibition, where I was present as IG's representative, AN Tewari coined two catchy phrases 'dynamic decade' and 'decade of destiny' for the theme of exhibition. Mathews, a hardened realist, did not show any enthusiasm for these exuberant expressions and concluded the meeting by outlining the different roles of participating departments. Whether Nandini was in a glass house relishing all the publicity was hard for me to say, but the effect would be seen very soon.

Then came June 26, 1975, the day Indira Gandhi proclaimed national emergency. This day was preceded by several events that shook the entire nation. Indira Gandhi, who was in full glory after the 1971 liberation of Bangladesh, acclaimed as the undisputed leader of India, was passing through a turbulent period. The health of the country's economy was poor, agricultural output had declined because of drought, there was food shortage, forcing the proud lady to go to USA to beg for food.

Wages were low and labour was restive taking advantage of which George Fernandes, the militant trade union leader, brought the entire rail system to a grinding halt by engineering a country-wide strike. The Youth Congress under the leadership of her reckless younger son, who Mrs Gandhi at the Guwahati AICC session said stole the thunder and where Congress President D K Baruah declared 'Indira is India, India is Indira', was becoming a law unto himself with more of brawn than brain.

Jai Prakash Narayan, a close associate of Jawaharlal Nehru,

who later parted company with him and remained a recluse till the death of Jawaharlal and Lal Bahadur Shastri, was making his presence felt, starting the Navanirman agitation in Bihar and then in Gujarat. He had became a vocal critic of Mrs Gandhi and called upon the people for ushering in a new India through total revolution. He exhorted the defence services and the police not to obey illegal orders. The highhandedness of the Youth Congress coupled with JP's call for total revolution had created an uncertain, unstable and suspenseful atmosphere throughout the country. Sanjay Gandhi's sterilization camps were hogging media headlines. To top it all, came the Allahabad High Court judgment declaring Mrs Gandhi's election to Parliament illegal.

Things were reaching a point of no return. Instead of resigning, Mrs Gandhi stuck to her office and, prodded by her son and aided by some trusted colleagues and bureaucrats, she invoked the provisions of national emergency on the ground that the integrity and security of the country were in jeopardy with several disruptive and divisive forces at work.

Emergency meant the fundamental rights guaranteed by the Constitution were kept in abeyance. The immediate fallout was arrest of all opposition leaders throughout the country, starting with JP, all critics and worse, doling out sketchy briefs through censored media.

This is no place to write about the emergency days but I must throw some light on the happenings in Orissa and the role of the IPS during the emergency period. All important leaders, including HK Mahatab and Biju Patnaik, were put behind bars. Provisions of Maintenance of Internal Security Act were invoked for the detention of the arrested persons for whom there was no trial, but a review board headed by a High Court judge which was only a paper tiger.

Orissa had the third Intelligence Chief within one year, S S Padhi, SK Banerjee and then BK Panigrahi, an officer of 1952 batch, one of the ablest and most balanced officers in the cadre.

Though Swain had some reservations about Panigrahi, he was the right man for Intelligence, but the passing days would make him increasingly uncomfortable. Although he was 10 years my senior, he not only treated me like a friend, but one before whom he could unburden.

Speaking about the highhandedness of the Youth Congress, I feel tempted to cite an incident where I was present. Sanjay Gandhi visited Cuttack and addressed a public meeting. Ram Chandra Rath, who was a student leader in Khallikote College in Berhampur where I was SDPO in 1965, was the president of the National Youth Congress. He wanted the Barabati Stadium to be the venue of the meeting which Panigrahi did not find suitable from security point of view and I saw Rath talking to Panigrahi in a highly intemperate language. The perfect gentleman in Panigrahi must have been shocked at the behaviour of an upstart politician, but he insisted on the change of venue.

All the senior leaders of the state were lined in the meeting venue, an open field near the fort, to receive Sanjay Gandhi, but I saw him hardly acknowledging their servile salutations. A few months into the emergency, Panigrahi one day came to my house and told me that he would proceed on long leave as he was finding it difficult to carry on the work. With all persuasive ability at my command, I dissuaded him from going on leave. Nandini, who was enjoying unquestioned power and authority duly oiled by ill-considered advice from her advisors, took several decisions which lacked in grace and wisdom. She prevailed upon Indira Gandhi to change Governor Akbar Ali Khan, an aristocrat who had endeared himself to many. His sin was hosting a lunch to Jai Prakash Narayan during his visit to Orissa. As an old-timer, he did it in good faith and spirit, but saw the end of his stay in the state.

Biju Patnaik was sending feelers from jail in support of emergency which Nandini thwarted with all her might for fear of being eclipsed. Similar overtures came from Dr Mahatab, an old-time Congress veteran, with the hope of getting a CBI case instituted against him for showing favour to mining firm Messrs Sirajuddin & Co in Keonjhar closed. But he was rebuffed by Nandini. Not long after she would be taking shelter under Biju Patnaik after the end of emergency.

If there was one agency which was perceived as the instrument of oppression by the public, it was police. Hundreds of arrests were made under MISA, some at the behest of politicians in power, some on the basis of input by special branch and some on the basis of reports prepared by the district administration mostly at the instance of the local politicians. Signing of reports by the District Magistrate was a mere formality, the task of restraining the liberty of the individual was performed by the police. Apart from this, there were numerous instances of third degree methods adopted by the police in cases where they were not called for.

I will cite one example in which a friend of mine, then SP of a district, was involved. One young man was brought to the local police station on the charge of making indecent remarks at the sister of the Collector. He could have been sent to jail after registering a case under 354 IPC. Instead, the SP gave him such a sound thrashing that he fainted. His sister, from a respectable Christian family of Cuttack, was known to my wife. She came to me with her brother who opened his shirt and showed his back and arms which were full of marks of injuries, red and blue. I rang up the SP and gave him a piece of my mind and told him that the family would not lie low.

This came to the notice of Swain, who though very fond of the SP, had to direct the DIG crime to inquire into the matter. It was just a cover-up operation. Similar incidents were happening daily. This was the biggest dilemma in police and continues to defy solution even today. There will be situations in which the police will have to act on the directions of the political executive and there will be situations where they will resort to excesses. The high priests will say the police must act according to rule of law, there is no doubt about that, but that will be possible only when the police is completely insulated from the politicians and in a democracy how far and to what extent it is possible is a matter of debate.

Then insulating the police from the politicians is not the panacea unless the reforms come from within, which is the biggest challenge for IPS officers.

At the other end of the spectrum, we saw remarkable improvement in the utility services. Trains were running punctually, telephones were never dead, essential services like electricity and water supply among other facilities marked visible improvement. It was possible because of the prevalence of an atmosphere of fear. If only we could perform similarly in an environment free of coercion and fear.

As the days passed, the political climate was getting more and more surcharged. The government could censor electronic media, but could not muzzle the print press which after the initial setbacks recovered and took up a sustained campaign against the emergency. Activism in the field of human rights, although in a nascent stage, was getting pronounced. The roller-coaster ride of Sanjay Gandhi was compounding the already vitiated atmosphere.

In Orissa, things were moving faster with an element of high drama. Nandini's projection as a leader of destiny interpreted to their advantage by her detractors who carried tales to Indira Gandhi through Sanjay, was proving to be her undoing. The message of her critics was: Nandini was growing too big for her boots with the secret ambition of becoming the country's Prime Minister. The brigade of detractors was led by JBPatnaik, then a minister of state in the union cabinet, Ram Chandra Rath, president of National Youth Congress, and KC Lenka, a minister in Nandini's cabinet who was one year my junior in Ravenshaw College. Binayak Acharya, who was legitimately elected as the leader of the Congress legislature party in 1971 to become Chief Minister, but had to make way for Nandini, was also there.

JB Patnaik used to come to ARC Charbatia from Delhi by Defence service plane, hold confabulations with the dissidents and fly back to Delhi. KC Lenka used to keep me posted with the latest developments which the special branch took time to obtain. Sanjay Gandhi, who was fed with the information that Tathagatha was raising some private army to defend his mother aided by some police officers, had made up his mind that Nandini had to go. He prevailed upon his mother to fall in line and feelers were sent to Nandini to resign. But Nandini stuck to her position, declaring herself a staunch loyalist of Indira Gandhi.

Apprehending trouble, Mrs Gandhi sent Ramakrishnaya, then a Union Secretary, to oversee the transition in administration while her political emissary Chandrajit Yadav came to Bhubaneswar with Mrs Gandhi's missive to Nandini to resign. She went out of Bhubaneswar on tour; a crisis was looming large on the horizon. She was recalled to Bhubaneswar, there was talk of keeping the central paramilitary force in readiness. Finally, good sense prevailed and Nandini came to Bhubaneswar and resigned and Binayak Acharya was elected as the leader of the legislature party. Ramakrishnaya, who had been packed off to Delhi by Nandini, was now overseeing her packing off. That was the irony and the tragic finale to Nandini's Chief Ministerialover lordship.

I had good personal relationship with her and in later days, when she was in wilderness and took to alcohol to fight depression, she had called me to her house on more than one occasion to seek my advice on certain matters. Nandini never recovered from her political isolation till she died.

After resigning, she joined the Congress for Democracy party floated by Jagjivan Ram who had also fallen out with Mrs. Gandhi and who later joined hands with the Janata Party to become the Deputy Prime Minister in 1977. Nandini remained a pariah. Although Biju welcomed her to the Janata coalition, the Janata government formed in 1977 instituted criminal cases of corruption against her, and got her arrested—which drew adverse comments from the Supreme Court. She returned to the fold of Indira Gandhi in 1980 when she returned to power and continued as an MLA by winning successive elections from her Assembly constituency. Chief Minister JB Patnaik, however, kept her at arm's length in the eighties and later part of the nineties when he was in power.

Mrs Gandhi by the end of 1976 must have realized that she had committed a great blunder by invoking emergency, which did not show any silver lining in any sphere particularly the political scene. In early 1977, she revoked emergency declaring that general elections would be held as quickly as possible. By that time my tenure as a staff officer to IG police was coming to an end and in January 1977, I joined the CID crime branch as SP (1) under Durga Madhav Mishra (1952) who was DIG CID Crime. For me, it was a welcome change as during the preceding three years I had no leisure time to plan for myself and my future.

Elections were held in May 1977. The results were a foregone conclusion and the type of hostility and animosity that Mrs Gandhi had generated against herself at the national level and Nandini at the state level was enough indication of what would follow in a new political setup. As for me I was always keen for a deputation to Centre, opportunities which I missed in 1966 to go to IB due to S K Ghosh's anger and in 1974 to CBI due to RK Padhi's pleasure.

T Anantachari under whom I had worked as ASP under training at Sambalpur, a well-wisher of mine, was then Director of the newly formed Directorate of Computers Police Co-ordination (now National Crime Records Bureau). He came to Orissa and asked me if I was willing to go to DCPC as his deputy. I had to think over the pros and cons of the posting. DCPC was a newly set up small organisation where there would be no long-term career prospects. But attraction was two-fold, one would be taking over as Director in one-

and-a-half year time and two, I would be based in Delhi only. I said yes and he processed the proposal after returning to Delhi.

In the elections, the Congress lost both in the Centre and in Orissa.The Janata government, inspired by JP's movement and proclaiming commitment to his ideals, formed ministry in Delhi with Morarji Desai as Prime Minister and Charan Singh and Jagjivan Ram as Deputy Prime Ministers. Fissures appeared in no time, thanks to the obdurate nature of Morarji and the frustrated ambition of Charan Singh to become Prime Minister.

In Orissa, a ministry was formed with Nilamani Routray as Chief Minister. Routray, who had been in the Orissa cabinet as a deputy minister and as a minister since the early 50s, was not only an astute politician, but also an experienced administrator and, having remained in charge of Home Department for several years, knew almost all police officers by name and their background. He was also a remarkable human being, considerate, not vindictive or malicious.

Biju Patnaik, an architect of Janata Party who had joined the Union Cabinet as Steel Minister, sent a memo to HM Patel, the Home Minister, to send a non-controversial officer from Centre to Orissa to replace N Swain as IG Police. The choice fell on BK Roy, the first direct recruit IPS officer (1948) allotted to Orissa who was then Director, Institute of Criminology and Forensic Science. He came to Orissa and took over as police chief.

By then my deputation to DCPC had been finalized and I was waiting for government order. BK Roy after joining displayed an uncertain and unpredictable attitude towards officers whom he thought were close to Swain. Only BB Nandy was able to ingratiate himself with Roy. I was indifferent as I was marking time to go to Delhi. But an incident took place which brought me in direct confrontation with him. Those days training courses abroad for IPS officers were a rarity unlike the present times when they have become part of career development.

I was selected for an overseas command course in the National Police College, Bramshill, UK and one day I received some forms from the Department of Personnel to be filled in and countersigned by the head of the department for my placement for the training. I sent the forms to GC Senapati (1953), DIG administration who had become the relative of Routray through a marriage alliance and consequently very powerful in the new regime.

At that time, the so-called votaries of JP movement amongst the IPS officers in Orissa along with the old critics of N Swain were preparing a list of officers who were to be kicked out of the state. My name was naturally there, not because I had anything to do with emergency excesses, I was only a staff officer, but because I was close to Swain. With my name in the list of outcasts, Senapati sent the file to BK Roy with the note that my name had not been sponsored by police headquarters for the training and on that basis Roy refused to countersign. When the forms came back to me I was furious and agitated for I could not understand where my fault lay.

I rang up to Home Secretary BR Patel, an IAS officer of 1951 batch, a gentleman with a warm and affectionate disposition, and told him my predicament. He told me not to worry and bring the forms to him for countersignature. I asked him, "How can you sir, as the column says 'Head of the department'?" He just asked me to meet him with the forms. Having thus become surefooted, I went to BK Roy and requested him to sign the forms; he refused provoking, me to say, "Sir, I feel sad that instead of congratulating me, you are obstructing my training. But I will go." when he asked how, I said: "You will see."

I walked out and headed for the Secretariat to Patel's room where he made necessary entries in the relevant columns, wrote a forwarding letter, got the envelope sealed in my presence and sent it to the GA Department for sending the same to Department of Personnel in Delhi with the utmost expediency. BK Roy got a copy of the letter in due course, as I got. This was a classic example of bypassing the police chief by an IPS officer, in this case, me. I offer myself to be judged by my readers.

The gallant heroes of the new regime had coined several epithets for the ousted or soon to be ousted officers: Nabagrahas that included Swain and Astaratna excluding him. The Nabagrahas were N Swain sent as IG CRP Eastern sector, BK Panigrahi to Saha Commission Delhi as IG, PC Ratho (1956) as DIG CISF Rourkela, Somnath Mishra (1957) as Chief Security Officer SE Railways Calcutta, me to MHA DCPC, Balasbramanium (1963) to Railway Board as Deputy Director Vigilance, BB Nandy (1964), VApparao (1964), NR Pattnaik (1965) to IB. Since PK Mishra (1960) came later he did not figure in the infamous list of nine.

Here I will cite a significant fact about Chief Minister Nilamani Routray's knowledge about police and police officers. Since I knew him I paid him a courtesy call on the eve of my departure from Orissa. He saw me and asked me why I was going out on deputation when I had nothing to do with emergency and if I wanted to stay, he would immediately cancel my central deputation. I thanked him for his kind words and told him that I very much wanted to go to Centre apart from the fact that my continuance in Orissa would create an uncomfortable work-environment for me as I was branded a close associate of N Swain.

I will make one statement which the readers may interpret as one of bravado. Be that as it may, the officers kicked out were by far among the best in Orissa cadre of IPS which was echoed by BK Roy. During one of his visits to Delhi, he said, "How can I function when all the good officers have gone?"

Thus came to an end a very satisfying and fulfilling part of my career when I was proactively and directly involved in the crucial areas of police modernization, upgradation and welfare of Orissa Police.

Part-5

Government of India

- DCPC: Tech Upgrade
- IPS Association and a Renegade

Chapter-20

DCPC: Tech Upgrade

We left Cuttack on the same day, by the same train, BB Nandy and me. There used to be only one direct train from Puri to Delhi—Kalinga/Utkal Express—running alternatively on different routes without any AC coach. Now there are nearly eight trains running between Puri/Bhubaneswar and Delhi. In Delhi, we stayed in the annexe of Orissa Bhavan in Lodhi Estate and shared a room for several days. I joined the Directorate of Coordination Police Computers (DCPC) in the MHA in July 1977 as Assistant Director under T Ananthachari, who was the Director with office located in RK Puram. Apart from the Director, the Directorate had three Assistant Directors, me the senior-most in charge of operation and administration, MM Agarwal, on deputation from BSF and AD in charge of training, and YN Reddy in charge of system development on deputation from BPR&D.

In fact, all the staff of DCPC were on deputation from different police organisations like BSF, CRPF, IB, BPR&D as the cadre rules of DCPC were yet to be finalized. Police computerisation project, one of the earliest in government departments, was the brain child KF Rustomjee, who as the first Director General of Border Security Force (BSF), had raised the force after the 1965 India-Pakistan war and later became Special Secretary MHA.

A thinker, a visionary, he used to bubble with ideas relating to police mordernization, its professional upgradation and matters relating to internal security. BSF was perhaps the first government and police organization which took steps in introducing computer as management information system. A regular cell was opened in BSF under Ananthachari, who formulated the national police computerisation project in all the states with linkages to the computer at the national level and network up to the district level through a dedicated communication line. The project was approved by MHA and DCPC came into existence in 1976. Rustomjee's another brainchild was creation of the Coast Guards. I remember when I was AIG police receiving his famous tour notes on various issues relating to national security and other related matters. His project for a Coast Guards organization saw the light of the day in the late seventies.

Those were the days of main frame computers, massive hardware in the shape of a central processing unit (CPU), tape drives and printers housed inside a big air-conditioned hall. In DCPC it was getting ready and nearing completion.

The basic purpose of the project was to computerize crime, criminal and finger print data and store them in the magnetic tapes and process them in the CPU for matching results in case of crime or a detected or suspected criminal. This would replace the voluminous paper work, in the shape of registers, forms and documents and act as a tool for the police officers in criminal investigation. Collection of data at the grassroots level in police station was crucial for the success of the scheme, this data used to be collected in computer friendly forms devised in shape of zeroes and ones on a uniform format for all police stations in the country, all of which along with districts and provinces were coded for access to computer. While the format for collection for data on crime and criminals was easier, converting fingerprints was started on an ad hoc basis by devising a 10-digit formula for each finger, which was not a very satisfactory arrangement. Later I would be visiting the Japanese Police and the FBI in Washington to study their automated fingerprint system.

For online access to the computer from the district to state, state to state and from state to the national computer, the biggest hurdle was communication channel. Most of the internal communications in the state and outside were through telegraph and wireless system, the latter at the national level coordinated by the Directorate of Coordination Police Wireless (DCPW), headed by one of the most dedicated and committed officers I have seen—CP Joshi from Uttar Pradesh.

Although a technical man he had a dream and a vision for police communication which he was translating to action through determined footsteps. The plan envisaged by Joshi was to take a dedicated line for the police from P and T and implement the network. It was a slow process, but Joshi was marching ahead. Later, the satellites were launched and with that miracles were achieved not only in communication, but also in computers—nothing and no area was left which was not on line. By then Tamil Nadu was the only state which had established communication down to the police station level through a dedicated UHF channel, a project Delhi Police was contemplating to implement in Delhi. Tamil Nadu was ahead because of the dedication of one man -- Krishnaswamy (1948), a man with a vision who was bypassed for the post of police chief for political reasons.

The main frame computers chosen for all the states were manufactured by the Electronics Corporation of India, Hyderabad. A software engineer, SK Tandon, was exclusively earmarked for the police project and there was constant interaction and dialogue between ECIL and DCPC on system software, hardware configuration, supply schedule, etc. The DCPC computer system was inaugurated by Charan Singh, who was the Home Minister with all police bigwigs present in the function.

With a new political formation in power, known as Janata government, there was major shakeup in bureaucracy. Mathur (1948) of Punjab was Director IB while CV Narsimhan (1948) from Tamil Nadu became Director CBI, replacing the dreaded D Sen who worked under Mrs Gandhi. Having come to power riding the waves of emergency excesses, which meant police brutalities, the Janata government announced constitution of two commissions, the Saha Commission headed by Justice Saha to look into emergency excesses and the National Police Commission, headed by renowned ICS officer Dharmavira to suggest police reforms.

Like Mrs Gandhi, the Janata leaders started their campaign of vendetta targeting the lady, which backfired both in short and long terms. Criminal cases were instituted against her by CBI and one evening NK Singh, SP CBI, reached her residence to arrest her. She came out without offering resistance and while she was being taken to her place of detention, presumably outside the jurisdiction of the magistrate, she wanted to stop for a moment after the vehicle crossed the jurisdiction, came out of the vehicle and then refused to move. The CBI team was in a quandary, so were the bosses in Delhi including the Prime Minister and Home Minister. Mrs Gandhi was persuaded to spend the night in the police lines Delhi to be produced next morning before the magistrate. On production, the magistrate wanted to see the records of investigation. CBI failed to produce any as except the FIR no investigation had been done.

The magistrate expressing his displeasure discharged Mrs Gandhi, saying there was no case. Mrs Gandhi returned home triumphant leaving CBI and the political bosses red-faced. A cornered and ruffled Charan Singh shifted Narsingham from CBI and made him member secretary of the Police Commission.

The major areas in DCPC, system software development and training, were looked after by Reddy and Agarwal. That way my workload was light, in effect it turned out to be unusually heavy as I had to master all areas of computer to facilitate proper coordination. To that end I underwent all courses conducted by DCPC, basics of computer, programming, system development including specific software applications like crime, criminal system, fingerprint system, traffic, personnel management, computer security, hardware, etc. I also attended courses conducted by the Indian Institute of Public Administration, Administrative Staff College, Hyderabad and various seminars to upgrade my knowledge in this totally alien field.

Chari wanted me to become an able trainer in DCPC, which initially appeared to me to be a tall order. Within six months of my joining, Chari asked me to take a class on basics of computer in a training course that the DCPC was conducting for Intelligence Bureau. Although a good speaker in college, I was a little nervous but with Chari's encouragement I gave my first talk on computer to the IB officers which Chari said was more than what he expected. Then there was no looking back.

Apart from giving lectures in all the DCPC conducted courses, I became a much sought-after speaker in all other organizations like IIPA, Institute of Criminology and Forensic Science, Institute of Telecommunication, Army, Income Tax and in ASCI Hyderabad, IIT Mumbai and IIM

Ahmedabad. Every month I used to visit a state and conduct courses for senior and junior police officers in the project. My take home salary, which was in terms of hundreds, was augmented at least by Rs 300 to Rs 400 per month from the lectures I delivered outside DCPC and in those days it was quite substantial. We decided that we would spend this additional income by exploring the star hotels, well-known restaurants, seeing theatre, art shows and the like. I remember paying Rs 40 per head for a sumptuous buffet lunch at Hotel Ashok.

At a personal level, I had to find accommodation and bring my family from Orissa. The process of settling down in Delhi for an IAS and IPS officer invariably becomes highly unsettling with the delay and difficulties in getting residential accommodation and getting children admitted to school, all by own self which was a contrast to the cozy comforts of Orissa. Residential accommodation was allotted on the basis of pay drawn and the list used to be updated every month. My position would always be two or three for D2 type accommodation. Pending that we got hostel accommodation in Minto Road where my family joined me.

We admitted our elder daughter Padmini in the Lady Irwin School after running from pillar to post, and younger daughter Anuradha in a small school opened by Frank Anthony in Connaught place. After a few months, we shifted to Asia house on Curzon Road where we stayed till the end of my deputation.

I was offered accommodation in RK Puram and then in Vinay Marg but I refused, angered by one incident. When my position in one month was No 1 and I was looking forward to the allotment order, I found my very close friend BB Nandy, who used to remain below me, overtaking me by getting an out-of-turn accommodation on the basis of a letter from IB that became handy for the Director of Estates I Choudhry, an IAS officer of West Bengal cadre, his college days friend, to bypass me.

Asia House proved advantageous for us as the Lady Irwin School was behind and the Bharatiya Vidya Bhavan, where my younger daughter had shifted, was just in front.

Towards the end of the year, there was an Interpol conference in Paris on IT application in police and global networking. As Chari's mother had expired, he sent the name of YN Reddy to represent India in Paris. When the file came back, the MHA order was to depute me to Paris instead. All this was unknown to me till the file came back which showed that the decision to send me was based on the observations of CG Somiah, an IAS officer of 1953 batch of Orissa, then Additional Secretary, Expenditure in the Ministry of Finance. Somiah was one of the most brilliant, outstanding and positive minded bureaucrats I came across. Later, he became the Union Home Secretary and after retirement the Central Vigilance Commissioner. When the file was sent to the department of expenditure for clearance, he noted that since I had been brought to be groomed to take over as Director, I should go. He was soon to play a very crucial role in the IPS Association affairs which I shall describe in the next chapter.

I made quick preparation to obtain the passport and visa and proceeded to Paris, my first foreign visit to Interpol conference in 1977. With Ashok Mubai, one of my friends in IAS (1963) of Orissa cadre, in the personal staff of Atal Bihari Vajpayee, then External Affairs Minister, my reception including stay and transport in Paris was more than taken care of. There was some diffidence in me with my limited knowledge in the sector, but in the conference I found that the majority of the countries were way behind India and, in presentation, apart from those who were full computer professionals from some countries, I was as good, or even better than the other police officers in charge of the project in their countries.

For two days, morning to evening, the conference gave me no time for sightseeing. One evening I went to Pigalle area on foot and was fooled into seeing a nude show with an entry fee of 5 francs only. I purchased a ticket and entered the hall to be accosted by a nearly nude lady of African origin who demanded a drink which I was not in a position to afford. She then insisted on Coca Cola and the bill came to 80 francs, almost a day's allowance. I became nervous and quietly slipped off to the warm comforts of my hotel room. On the third morning I saw the famous Louvre Museum.

The return journey was eventful. In the afternoon I took an Air India flight which took off and after sometime landed at the Frankfurt airport because, as it was announced, the engine had developed a snag. We were asked to wait in the lounge. At that time several terrorist groups were active in Europe, prominent being the Red Brigade in Italy and IRA in UK. Airports were a target. When it was announced that we have to stay overnight, I saw a lady tall and beautiful, all fire and brimstone, going to the Air India counter and demanding immediate trans-shipment to Kuwait, a stopover en route. When the Air India official expressed helplessness, she burst out saying, "Do you know who I am? I am the sister of the famous terrorist Leila Khalid." The official looked at her with shock. I had to intervene, telling her that if that was how she wanted to flaunt her identity, we would not be able to reach our destination. She was pacified and we went to the hotel and I had dinner in the company of the sister of Leila Khalid of the Palestinian Liberation Organization, who was infamous for hijacking planes.

Early 1978, I received intimation about my placement in the National Police College, Bramshill, UK, and started preparations for my departure. Luckily, my father-in-law came over to Delhi to stay with my wife and daughters. I sold my Fiat car, a mistake I realized after my return from UK, for in Delhi it was difficult to manage without a car. I then purchased the Fiat from SC Mishra (1959, Orissa), who from R&AW went to Dhaka on an assignment.

I went to London in a British Airways Flight, collected my allowance from YMCA hostel and proceeded to Reading by train for overnight stay. In the transit guesthouse, I met an officer from Assam, SK Das (1955), and some officers from African countries. Next morning, after breakfast we all proceeded to Bramshill in a college van. The police college compound covered a vast area of 250 acres around the college building, a 17th century Jacobean mansion which housed the library, the administrative block, convention hall and director's residence. New buildings had been constructed for the academic block, mess and hostel where I settled in a single room. It was a real pleasure taking long walks in the sylvan surroundings on the campus with its sparkling lake where one preferred the bliss of solitude to the humdrum of urban life.

The British, meticulous in everything, had planned our course very carefully – we were kept busy from 9 am to 5 pm, with a brief lunch break. Computers were yet to become an integral part of teaching; study and the courses were conducted mainly through lectures and exercises. Lectures delivered on the professional side of police, mostly by the regular staff of the college, to me were nothing extraordinary, but the lectures delivered by eminent guest speakers on subjects such as History, Sociology and Economics were highly interesting, instructive and helpful, an area of deficiency in our training courses in the IPS and other services in India.

Many of these lectures were delivered by exhibiting models that accentuated the thematic content of a subject. This was more pronounced in History when talking about the great ancient civilizations of the world, mainly the Egyptian, Greek, Roman, Babylonian, Indian and Chinese. The speakers would dwell on their underlying intercourse and commonalities through trade, commerce, cultural exchanges, wars, conquests and bloodshed.

Such classes would be meant for all the trainees in the college and not confined to overseas officers. In the large gatherings, with the modern representatives of the only ancient civilisation, i.e. India, in their midst, their dominant role was a foregone conclusion. Neither SK Das nor I failed to excel in those deliberations. Unfortunately, Das fell ill and had to be sent back to India.

IRA terrorism had raised its ugly head in the UK. Their credo was violence. Like Naxalite violence in India, major incidents of killing, arson, looting were frequent happenings. During my stay, the IRA terrorists blew one restaurant in London, killing all the guests. Lord Mountbatten was killed when he was going out on his sail boat. Other countries in Europe were getting affected.

In the Middle-east, the PLO was active; soon Iran would be taken over by Muslim fundamentalists by overthrowing royalty and Jehadi terrorism would find its root and flourish in the Middle-east, Africa, Afghanistan and Pakistan. India was already having her share of woes in Kashmir, Northeast and with the emerging Naxalites.

A very useful part of our training was field exercises on anti-terrorism measures. We spent one full day at the Heathrow airport where the emphasis was on anti-hijacking measures. We spent one day each at British Oxygen, Barclay Bank head office, Sandhurst Military Academy where the historic Indian footprint impressed me, and in the city of Coventry which was bombed during the World War II.

Sadly, no exercise could be arranged in London Police which the Director, a county police officer, jokingly ascribed to the arrogance of the Met Police (Metropolitan Police). There was always a healthy rivalry between the Met Police and County Police, the former claiming superiority during friendly banters.

We had two superintendents — one Met and one County — in charge of the conduct of the daily programmes. Our Course Director was Mr Grey, a World War II veteran who had spent considerable time in South-east Asia. Each officer had to write a dissertation under the guidance of a tutor. My tutor was a fiery beauty, Irene Wilson, with a brain to match. Coming from the Welsh land, she was ever jovial, warm-hearted and had a vibrant personality. Since a Police Commission had been set up at home, I chose the topic "Reforms in Police", a subject on which we used to have many heated discussions. In course of time, I felt we dearly cherished each other's company with mutual respect.

We were hosted by each instructor, mostly for dinner in their residences. During these evenings I was touched by the gesture shown to me by the hosts. The evening we went to Mr Grey's house, we saw a large cut-out of an Air India hostess with a sign of namaste and Mrs Grey welcoming us in Indian style. She had laid out for us a sumptuous rice and curry dinner.

Irene hosted us in a cozy corner room of the castle. I saw her clad in a gorgeous blue saree with a welcome namaste. She was the connoisseur of all eyes that evening. During our field visits, we would be accompanied by an instructor. On one such visit, Irene was our guide. By the time we returned to college it was past midnight. Everybody in the bus was having a hilarious time. Irene's presence added to the gaiety. From among us, somebody coined a phrase and there was a chorus, "Irene we love you, don't leave us tonight."

The playful Irene's pleadings were ignored and she looked at me for help. I suggested that she should come to my room where we all would gather to while away the rest of the night, drinking wine and singing songs. So all came trooping into my room and soon it was packed.

I was keeping my fingers crossed, for virtually, I had

taken over the responsibility for her safety and anything not to her liking or approval would have been a black mark on me. We chatted till the early hours of the morning, then put Irene in her car and bade her good bye.

I became a bit of a mini celebrity in Bramshill. At that time, a racist MP was vomiting poison against immigrants, including Indians. Whenever I got an opportunity, I would retort with vehemence at the attitude shown by the British. One day I got a call from BBC in London for an interview on the racial utterances of the chauvinists. I agreed, a letter of request came which I put up to the Director for permission. He was in a dilemma and went in for the softer option of referring it to Home Office.

The permission came and I went to the London BBC office. After the interview, I joined some journalists over drinks in their club, where they debunked the then Prime Minister Morarji Desai's claim that all members of his Cabinet were teetotallers, citing the just concluded visit of Atal Bihari Vajpayee, the Foreign Minister, who loved his drinks and made no secret of it.

I had my one week field attachment with the Birmingham Police. Handsworth, a predominantly Asian colony, was an area of tension and I was hounded by the BBC for my views which I gave in good measure. A police inspector who was attached to us did us the favour of taking us to a nude show without any payment and making me sit very close to the disrobing girls. I thought, are police everywhere the same?

In the last month of the course I was the mess president. The last dinner was a gala yet a highly formal one, with all the British etiquette and table manners on full display. I was quite familiar with all that during my training at Mt Abu, but the Inspector, who escorted me like a shadow, giving me several instructions about the evening, was perhaps not sure of my ability.

In the evening we all gathered in the main hall of the castle where I put on the President's medallion and started the proceedings of the evening. The bar was open. I helped myself with one peg of whisky, the Inspector got jittery, and when I took a second one, it was enough to prompt the Inspector to whisper words of caution into my ears: "The evening has just started, Mr. Tripathy."

Amused, I took a third one. By then the Inspector was convinced that I would be bungling the entire evening. The gong sounded and the procession started, led by me and the Director's wife, followed by the Chief Guest and the Director, then the others, all in twos.

I sat at the main table, flanked by the Chief Guest and the Director's wife. The priest said, "Amen", and dinner started. The most delicate part of the dinner was proposing a toast to the Queen and Heads of States. The wine glass would circle, beginning from me at the head table and its counterpart at the end of the hall, quite faraway. At both the tables, the glass had to come back to me at the head table and the VIP at the opposite table at the same time, after which I would propose the toast.

By sheer luck the timing was perfect and a sense of relief filled me. We then all went back to the hall for a coffee session and speechification, where, as president, I delivered my speech to the thunderous applause of the audience; next I was on the dance floor, a place where I was simply naive, but allowed myself to be dragged by Irene to a merry Welsh tune.

The training over, I went to London for attachment to the Scotland Yard for which MHA had issued a separate order to study the police computerization project in UK. I studied their crime, criminal data system, evolving fingerprint system and the national registry of motor vehicles.

By early 1979 Chari's term was coming to an end and he

was repatriated to Orissa. I was promoted to the rank of DIG and posted as Director DCPC in March 1979. Interestingly, I was the first of the 1962 batch IPS in Centre to get promotion which was infradig for the IB as its officers traditionally were first to be promoted. But my friend Narendra Prasad, Director Police ensured that it did not happen. My IB friends took copy of my notification and got their cases processed for promotion.

The post of Director held tantalizing challenges in implementing a project dedicated to the latest technology of the world. By then police was at the forefront in introducing computers and with a national network there was the larger vision of the DCPC growing to be the National Crime Record Bureau. As I was bracing myself for those new challenges, I was faced with one of the most formidable challenges of my life, losing which, would have marred my standing and reputation for all times at Delhi.

Soon after I took over I learnt that the Bureau of Police Research and Development, a major central police organisation, was planning to grab DCPC. Chari with his wide contacts and support had created an independent police organisation. Now BPR&D felt that with a Director with no clout like me, DCPC was up for grabs. The Director of BPR&D was a 1948 IPS officer, 14 years my senior and for him I was a kid.

He prevailed on SS Jog (1953), Joint Secretary Police, who also agreed to the proposal to my shock. When I met Jog, he gave me the impression that a decision had been taken to merge DCPC with BPR&D. I was at my wit's end. This is where an IAS officer came to my rescue. He was Laxminarayan, an IAS officer of 1954 batch, who was then Additional Secretary Home. When I met him I found to my relief and pleasant surprise that he was opposed to the proposal on the simple principle that there was no overriding consideration for such a step when only two to three years earlier the MHA had created a separate department for the project. He assured me that authorities higher above would agree to his views. Here was an example of an IPS officer, that too very senior, showing a lack of vision which an IAS officer displayed. Success of the police computerization scheme depended, apart from evolving technology, on collection of computer-compatible data at the grassroot level in the police station and the attitude of the police chiefs of the states. By the time I became the Director, I had attended quite a few meetings with the police chiefs at the national, regional and state levels. While by and large they did show a positive attitude, there was also a note of scepticism about its success. Funds were not much of a problem as the scheme was financed out of the modernization grant. Recurring expenses were, however, to be met by state governments.

The project in each state was in charge of a DIG and here again the positive attitude of the police chiefs was eclipsed by their scepticism, for the posting became a sidelined placement in most of the states. Officers generally out of favour of the political establishment came to man the project. Many officers were outstanding but they also came with some amount of cynicism. The leading state, Tamil Nadu, had Krishnaswamy (1948) in charge, who did yeoman's service in the area of police modernization not only in Tamil Nadu, but also at the national level and was reconciled with the idea that he would not be the police chief. He was succeeded by the brilliant and erudite Laxminarayan (1951) who was Additional Director CBI and was repatriated after the fiasco of Indira Gandhi's arrest.

Gujarat had a 1948 officer, West Bengal a 1952 officer, Bihar, Madhya Pradesh and Andhra Pradesh had 1956 officers, Uttar Pradesh had Prakash Singh (1959) so on and so forth. So by the time I became Director, my counterparts in various states were senior to me by years, varying from three to 14. I had to balance my relations with them as I could ill-afford to displease them by being seen as the big boss from Centre. In a short span, I was able to strike excellent equations with all of them and this facilitated my work in the states.

Three areas were of crucial importance in the scheme. First was the collection of basic data at the police station level for which extensive training programmes were designed at DCPC and in the states. Some training programmes were a dynamic affair and for that I had to tour all parts of India extensively. The programmes were so packed that sometimes I used to fly to a distant state capital by the early morning flight, conduct a course and return home at night. Our second thrust area was upgrading technology and its applications.I was not satisfied with the 10-digit formula for fingerprint automation and was in search for technology for instant lifting and digitization. The third area was national networking on which the irrepressible C P Joshi, Director Coordination Police Communication, later a Padmashree awardee, was at work and with whom day-to-day coordination was necessary.

Against the post vacated by me, NC Padhi (1966) who later became Special Director IB and DG Police Orissa, joined and after undergoing various courses proved to be of invaluable help to me deputising me in many meetings and conferences and carrying ahead the goal of DCPC after he succeeded me as the Director.

In 1979, politics was in ferment. The Janata experiment which started with a bang was ending in a whimper, thanks to the love, lust and craze for power amongst the senior politicians who had taken oath in Gandhi's Samadhi for Sampurna Kranti in India only two years earlier. JP was bedridden; at any rate he had become irrelevant to the power crazy politicians. Morarji in sheer disgust resigned and Charan Singh realized his ambition of becoming the Prime Minister, at least a caretaker one, as he failed to prove his majority on the floor of Parliament. There was a resurgent

Indira Gandhi with an ocean of sympathy from her country people for the witchhunting indulged in by the government against her. Elections to the Lok Sabha were held in January 1980. Indira came with a thumping majority and formed the government.

Without indulging in any kind of vendetta which the Janata government did, she repeated every other act committed by the previous regime. State elections were declared that would result in Congress victory in many states. Governors were sacked and there was massive overhauling in bureaucracy, which saw changes of many CPO chiefs and other key police functionaries. T V Rajeswar, who later became a key figure in the other area of my activities i.e. IPS association affairs, taking over as Director IB was a foregone conclusion.

SMH Burney, an IAS officer of 1948 batch who was Secretary Information and Broadcasting during the emergency days and was hounded out by the Janata government and later repatriated to Orissa where Chief Minister Nilamani Routray had posted him as Chief Secretary, was brought back to Delhi as Secretary MHA. RN Kao, former R&AW chief, was appointed as her advisor enjoying unprecedented clout. Like 1977 there was a kaleidoscopic turn of events to which we were witness till things started settling down.

DCPC, my small organization, was nowhere in the scheme of the Prime Minister. I had assumed that she was not even aware of its existence till I received a phone call from V S Tripathi, an IAS officer of 1961 batch, then Joint Secretary to the PMO to meet him. Mrs Gandhi desired that police computer should generate the latest crime statistics for her perusal. At that time we were nowhere near generating the crime figures in the computer which was being done manually by a separate division in the BPR&D.

I explained this to him and the larger issue of a National Crime Record Bureau with an all India network. He asked me to submit a note telling me that he would send it to the Prime Minister suggesting merger of the crime statistics division of the BPR&D with DCPC. Tables had turned in less than a year when I was facing the crisis of loss of the identity of DCPC with its proposed merger with BPR&D and now I was in a position to take away a very important wing of BPR&D and bring it under my control. I told him that I would send a note, but piecemeal orders would not serve the purpose.

It was decided that the Asian Games would be held in Delhi in 1982 and Mrs Gandhi desired that the immigration data in all the international airports should be computerized before the games, to start with at the Palam Airport. This was duly communicated to me by PMO. For me it was a tall order for implementation of this time-bound project which needed the participation of three ministries—the Customs in the Ministry of Finance, the External Affairs Ministry, and the Home Ministry.

A committee was set up by the MHA with representatives of all the ministries, with me as Member Secretary. YN Reddy, my Assistant Director in charge of System Software, did all the ground work. We had rounds of discussions, deliberations, several meetings, interactions with the airport authority and prepared our report and submitted in stipulated time and I felt happy to note that it was implemented in Palam Airport as per schedule and later extended to Mumbai, Kolkata and Chennai.

With IPS officers years senior to me, I had many interesting experiences in some states. I had gone to Kolkata to review the progress of the project. The DIG, a 1952 officer, with his ideas (and idiosyncracies) had only problems to point out and not the solution. The SP a1963 officer SP Bhandari, had arranged a meeting with Chief Minister to sort out the bottlenecks.

In effect it turned out to be a regular meeting in the Rotunda at the Writers Buildings where Chief Minister Jyoti Basu, the Chief Secretary, senior IAS and IPS officers were present. So I had to educate them on computer before talking about the problems. I was indeed surprised to see the keen interest Jyoti Basu evinced in the subject. He was present throughout and during tea asked me about the points for discussion and asked the Chief Secretary, then his most trusted IAS officer, to sort them out.

At SPs' level there were some very enthusiastic officers. Pillai (1963) from Gujarat was one and he had the full support of the IG in charge of the project Hari Singh, a special recruit of 1948. He took keen interest and was instrumental in operationalising it in the scheduled time. Similarly, the SP in Mumbai Wankhade was equally devoted to the implementation of the project. One visit to Chennai remains etched in my memory. The redoubtable Stracy, our Deputy Commandant at Mt. Abu, was Director General of Tamil Nadu Police. I sent my card to him and when ushered into his office, he half turned his chair, looked at me, surveyed me with a smiling face and said: "You are Trips?" I said, "Yes sir". "You are the last batch I tackled." Again I said, "Yes sir." Then he offered me a chair and we had a pleasant chat.

As far as the central police organizations were concerned, BSF was first to use the DCPC computer on a time-sharing basis, followed by CRPF. The Intelligence Bureau was developing a system on name indexing. The CBI and BPR&D who should have started the preliminaries were clearly lagging behind. The Income Tax department took the help of DCPC in computerization of data but there was stiff resistance from within as a result, they had to slow down. And what a change in 30 years—without computers, nothing moves.

In the army there was Brigadier Balasubramanium, a keen proponent of the project. Army started the personnel information system and I was associated with the selection of hardware for the army.

Since computer usage was mostly confined to main frame

computers, at that time third generation ones, the fourth generation was in offing, that would be followed by mini computers in early nineties, number of computer users both in private and government sectors was limited. There was an umbrella society called Computer Society of India in which computer users were members. DCPC's presence was not insignificant, because apart from DCPC, the state computer set ups also had become members.

The CSI used to hold an annual session in different parts of India to discuss various issues, relating to hardware technology, development of system and application software, communication network, etc. Apart from general session there were technical and professional sessions also. Similarly at the Asian level, there was an organization holding its convention in different countries. It was in 1980 or 1981 that I received a request from the organizers of the conference scheduled to be held in Manila to present a paper on "use of computer in enforcement of law in India". I sent the paper which was accepted, but could not make it to the convention.

A very interesting incident took place in the annual CBI conference of 1980. In the CPOs medals are awarded to the recipients on the conference day by the VVIPs. Mrs Gandhi was the chief guest and after the welcome address by Director JS Bawa, a perfect gentleman, Mrs Gandhi was to decorate the officers. I was in the invitees gallery. We saw PS Bhinder, Commissioner of Police, who was closely linked with the emergency days, going to the dais and whispering something to Mrs Gandhi. She looked at something, perhaps the list of the awardees, got up and left the conference in a huff, leaving the Director and others on the dais shocked and dazed and the audience puzzled.

Officers on the dais ran after her, but she went to the exit gate, got into her car and left Vigyan Bhavan, the venue. Then we went to the lounge for tea and learnt that Bhinder told Mrs Gandhi that she would be rewarding the CBI officers who had caused all sorts of harassment to her during the Janata regime. Bawa was visibly crestfallen.

In my case, award of the meritorious service medal was going by default as there was nobody to propose my name. My junior, Manabesh, had got it on the recommendation of state government. In Centre, the CPO chiefs send their recommendations to the MHA. In my case I was my own head of department and as such was not in a position to send my own name to the ministry. When Narendra Prasad learnt about it, he sounded Jog, Joint Secretary Police who rang me and asked for my brief bio-data which I sent. He was gracious enough to recommend my name and I was awarded the medal in 1979.

In 1981-82, I along with SK Tandon, the project in charge of ECIL Hyderabad visited Japan and USA to study traffic control system and automatic fingerprinting system. We went to Tokyo and while driving from airport to the hotel got a feel of traffic control by computer, the signalling, warning, forecasts, etc. We visited the impressive police headquarters of Tokyo and after interaction with officials were taken around the city to study the system.

I took the opportunity of studying the Japanese police system by devoting a day to it. From Tokyo we flew over the Pacific to Los Angeles where we visited the Silicon Valley, San Francisco for a day and flew to New York to study the traffic control system managed and manned by wardens functioning under the control of the city mayor, not New York police. Then we visited Washington and studied the fingerprint system in the hallowed FBI building.

By mid-1982 my five years tenure was coming to an end. A six-month extension came in a routine manner. I had an open mind on the issue of deputation as I was not particular in sticking to Delhi. After six months another extension was inevitable as there was nobody to take over from me. NC Padhi was yet to be empanelled. This also suited me as the educational session of my daughters came to an end by March/April 1983. The other important mission in which I was involved as Secretary of the IPS Central Association had also been achieved. Time had come to say goodbye to Delhi. I sent proposal to MHA to promote NC Padhi and post him as Director DCPC. I shall describe my last days of deputation in Delhi in next chapter.

I had reasons for satisfaction about my tenure in DCPC. It was eventful and pleasant. I had built up a very dedicated team who extended their unquestioned loyalty and devotion to me, their leader. The cadre rules of DCPC had been finalised and I had drafted officers and men from BSF, CRPF and ITBP who were absorbed as DCPC employees. I was indeed touched by their farewell to me and the sentiments expressed by them.

Chapter-21

IPS Association and a Renegade

My involvement in IPS Association activities started pretty early in my career, from the days I was SDPO Bhubaneswar. At that time the agenda of the association was mainly the issue of delay in promotion of the IPS officers to super time scale, removal of the discrepancy in the pay scales between two All India Services and the general apathy of the government to police and the welfare of its personnel while it depended on police in all crises. My involvement took the form of activism while I was SP Keonjhar, rooted in an overbearing sense of being wronged by the government with two successive adverse confidential remarks.

Time had come for me to ponder over the future. Was I to continue for the rest of my life as an underdog, a chronic dissenter and condemned to a state of obscurity as had happened to some, or rise above that gloom and shine both professionally and intellectually and make myself as 'whole a person' as possible? Keonjhar, the place where I had spent my carefree student days, now posed this very serious and crucial choice and I opted for the latter.

As a person acting on the dictates of my heart rather than mind, I had to hear several acerbic remarks. Police chief BB Mishra labelled me a pathological case, a renegade. Later, in the early eighties when I was Hon. Secretary of the IPS (central) Association in Delhi, TN Chaturvedi, then Union Home Secretary, seeing me frequenting the corridors of North Block and fully aware of the reasons, once called me to his office and told me: "You are behaving like a trade union leader."

In Orissa, the senior most AIG was traditionally the Hon. Secretary of the IPS Association while at the Centre it was usually the prerogative of an Intelligence Bureau officer. When I began my service SS Padhi (1951), AIG 1, was the Secretary. A highly amiable and affectionate person, he used to think very highly of me because of my interest in service matters and in all association meetings he would encourage me to speak out and also endorse my views.

There was an abiding bond between me and SS Padhi which lasted till his retirement excepting for one incident in which I differed with him when he was DG Police, that too on service matters, clouding our relationship which I tried my very best to clear as this avoidable misunderstanding arose purely out of my impulsive nature. Following that tradition RN Das (1955) and S Mishra (1956) acted as Hon. Secretaries. It was in 1975 that I was chosen to become the Hon. Secretary in which capacity I stayed till 1977 when I went to Delhi on deputation.

As far as the constitution of the Association is concerned, there was only the Central IPS Association with branches in all states. All IPS officers were ipso facto members of the Association. Very often I came across criticisms, mainly from senior officers, of inaction and inertia on the part of the Association, not only in Orissa but also in other states and at the Centre. I also noticed there is a lot of truth in this as the Associations, whether at the Centre or in the states, did not function on a dynamic basis.

It was entirely up to the Hon. Secretary and the executive committee to keep up the tempo of the association activities. In spite of all these handicaps, the fact remains that right after independence, particularly from the Second Pay Commission onwards, the IPS Association with the help of the state branches had played a key role in improving the service conditions of the IPS, a service that was intellectually and professionally considered inferior to its counterpart, the ICS and IAS. Thus, the comfortable situation in which the IPS officers are placed in the 21st century came through long drawn and sustained struggles. This appreciation will be more pronounced if we briefly go into the genesis of the service.

IP, the Imperial Police, started in the early nineties of the 19th century, was the prerogative of English boys. After the 1861 Police Act, senior posts in police were manned by Army officers as would be evident from the fact that a Superintendent of Police in North India was generally known as the ' Kaptan Sahib' with three stars. After police training colleges came up, the IP recruits were sent to India for training in the Indian Police colleges. In contrast, entrants to the Indian Civil Service were trained in universities like Oxford and Cambridge apart from other institutions.

IP was opened to Indians only in 1920 after the Montagu-Chelmsford reforms and the first Indian to be drafted to IP was AK Sinha of Bihar and Orissa cadre in 1920. He was already a directly recruited Deputy SP and by the time he joined IP he had served as SP of more than one district. He was also SP Sambalpur in Orissa. He was the first Indian IP officer to be appointed as IG Police serving as police chief of Bihar. For the Indians joining the IP, minimum qualification was graduation and bright Indian students joined IP, thereby raising its intellectual calibre. It will be unfair to say that British officers were not academically endowed as the Indian officers. Some had high college education and demonstrated understanding of a very high degree of the Indian conditions. The pay scale of the IG Police at Rs 2,750–Rs 3,000 was lower than a Member Board of Revenue whose equivalent is now the Revenue Divisional Commissioner. The Board of Revenue had a chairman at the capital with a fixed salary of Rs 4,000 while a Member posted in the field had a scale of Rs 3,500. The DIG's scale was less than the optimum of the senior scale of ICS which did not have a selection grade.

After independence, the recruitment to IPS was started through a combined competitive examination for all civil and central services. While the starting salary of a probationer was kept uniform at Rs 350, discrepancy, that too very wide, was introduced in the senior scale: Rs 800 for IAS and Rs 600 for IPS. Selection grade of IAS remained higher than the DIG's scale. Provision of keeping two optional papers for IPS entrants as against five for IAS and three for central services reflected the thinking and mindset of the government in putting the IPS at a substantially lower pedestal than the IAS. By the time the Second Pay Commission was constituted in the 60s, awareness had crept in about the wide disparities. IPS officers had become senior by then and had the forum of an association both at the central and state levels to articulate their feelings.

After the Second Pay Commission, senior scale of IPS was fixed at Rs 740–Rs 40 higher than the central services whereas senior scale of IAS was fixed at Rs 900, continuing the wide disparity. DIG's scale was at Rs 1,600 to Rs 1,800 where as IAS selection grade was Rs 1,800 to Rs 2,000. IG's scale was same as that of a Commissioner at Rs 2,500 to Rs 2,750.

It was the Third Pay Commission which recognized the need for improving the pay scale of IPS in view of its job content. While the Commission gave uniform starting salary of Rs 700 and senior scale of Rs 1200 discrepancy set in with IPS senior scale at Rs 1,200 to Rs 1,700 and IAS at Rs 1,200 to Rs 2,000. In selection grade, IPS pay was Rs 1,800 while for IAS it was Rs 2,000 to Rs 2,250 which became the DIG's scale. The scale of Addl IG police was Rs 2,250 to Rs 2,500 which was the level two of senior administrative grade of central services with a level one grade at Rs 2,500 to Rs to 2,750, which was equivalent to the pay scale of an IG police and Commissioner in IAS.

Thus, while the Third Pay Commission recognized the importance of IPS, its recommendations to improve the pay scale of IPS were confined to equalization at junior scale and equal starting at senior scale. From selection grade upwards IPS remained at disadvantage vis-à-vis IAS and central services. Yet another disadvantage the IPS was suffering from was its equation with the armed services that would put up stiff resistance to any improvement in IPS pay scales. They insisted on an edge in Brigadier's scale over the DIG's scale. As a result, the Brigadier's scale was kept at Rs 2,000 to Rs 2,400 as against the DIG's Rs 2,000 to 2,250. This rank in the police was the worst affected, sandwiched between the IAS and the Army. On the other hand, the central services got substantial benefits in the senior administrative grade at Rs 2,250 to Rs 2,500 for level two and Rs 2,500 to Rs 2,750 for level one.

Among the various committees set up by the government to bring about reforms in the examination systems, two are notable–the Kothari Committee set up in 1979 that introduced uniform system of examination for all All India and Central Services and the Satish Chandran Committee set up in 1989 to examine the proposal for a separate examination for IPS officers which recommended the existing system to continue on the ground that IPS should be treated as a civil service which was also our stand and which received the support of P C Hota, who was Secretary of UPSC. I prepared a paper for P C Ratho, then DG Police, to present our views in person before the committee. I was IG CID Crime then.

Improving the status and pay of the police chief was one issue the Association was pursuing at the central level. As a result the government sanctioned a charge allowance of Rs 250 for the IGP in charge of a state so that a state IG after reaching Rs 2,750 could get Rs 3,000 which was the pay scale of Addl Chief Secretary. In the 70s, the IAS secured a major gain by upgrading the pay scale of Chief Secretary to the scale of a Secretary at the Centre, which was Rs 3,500—a scale allowed to only one IPS officer in the country, the Director, Intelligence Bureau. CPO chiefs of CBI, BSF and CRPF were placed at Rs 3,250.

Another area of darkness was the bleak promotion prospects of IPS officers. With limited number of posts in the super time scale and non-availability of ex-cadre posts, there was a clear difference of 8 to 10 years between IAS and IPS to reach the scale of Rs 2,500–Rs 2,750. While in some states the situation was better, Orissa was way behind the Centre and some other states in giving promotion to IPS officers to the rank of IGP.

It came mostly after completing 25 to 26 years of service by which time IPS officers at present are comfortably placed in the rank of Additional DG Police. Why IG Police, even for promotion to the rank of DIG, some batches had taken nearly 19 to 20 years to get to that grade. This had a highly demoralizing effect on the morale of the officers. Some states, particularly the southern ones, had started inducting IPS officers to ex-cadre posts with Andhra Pradesh taking the lead followed by Kerala, Karnataka and Tamil Nadu.

This was the scenario when I went to Delhi in 1977. After the change of the Indira Gandhi led government, the entire bureaucracy was in a state of flux with impending departures of several officers particularly from the IB, perceived close to the political powers during emergency days. Ravindran of IB, who was Hon. Secretary, was being repatriated and a meeting was convened in the FICCI auditorium to elect a new Hon. Secretary and discuss the service matters. I accompanied Chari to the meeting.

During discussion there was a suggestion to pass a resolution to condemn the excesses committed by the police in different states and send a copy to the new political executive. Somehow or other I did not like the idea. Some of our well-known and highly reputed IP/IPS officers were associated with the emergency and at any rate it was we who committed excesses at the behest of politicians. So whom were we condemning, us? Because we did not have the courage to withstand the political dictates? It was a highly hypothetical question because police as the instrument of the government had to be utilised to implement the measures.

A resolution was passed which would have highly detrimental effect on the Association in 1980 after the return of Indira Gandhi to power. Ramachandran (1956) of Maharashtra who had joined as IG in the National Police Commission was elected as the Hon Secretary and Chari as Jt Secretary.

Ramachandran's election as the Hon. Secretary was a sound decision as at that time the central and state associations had the formidable task of steering the proceedings of the Police Commission in an atmosphere that should be congenial and conducive to police.

The six-member National Police Commission set up in 1977 had Dharamvira, member of ICS, former Cabinet Secretary and Governor of West Bengal, as chairman. The other members were Justice NK Reddy, Sarvashree KF Rustomjee, NS Saxena, both members of IP, Prof MS Gore, well-known social scientist, and CV Narsimhan (1948 IPS) as Secretary. Ramachandran was a dynamic officer and he kept in touch with IPS officers and kept up an atmosphere of exchange of thoughts and ideas, discussions and interactions. His role as Hon. Secretary of the IPS Central Association helped matters.

The state associations were required to organize discussions and seminars on the need for police reforms and send views of the public and the enlightened citizens to the NPC. They also had the crucial responsibility of motivating the political executive to send favourable views to the NPC. Many state associations did commendable job in this regard. I was a frequent visitor to Ramachandran's room with Chari initially, and then alone after Chari's departure, and would interact with him from time to time.

When Mrs Gandhi returned to power in 1980, the Commission was still functioning. Narsingham who was Director CBI when Mrs Gandhi was arrested in 1977 was packed off to his cadre. The NPC, however, finalized its recommendations and submitted its reports in six volumes, dealing exhaustively with all aspects of police and policing right from the grassroot level. By all standards their work and output were commendable. Presence of an ICS officer and a judge only added to the credibility of the reports of the NPC.

With Mrs Gandhi back in power, there were misgivings about the fate of the reports. KF Rustomjee met her and discussed the subject of implementation of the reports. He was advised to meet Home Minister Gyani Zail Singh who it seems did not show much interest. How far Mrs Gandhi's predilections were responsible for non-implementation of the reports is very much a debatable point. The reports were fresh and in government it takes years to implement if at all a decision is taken.

All that I know, Mrs Gandhi appointed her powerful Director CBI D Sen during emergency to process the recommendations. Sen's OSD Pratap Mukhopadhya, a 1964 batch IAS officer from Orissa, put me across to Sen who to my surprise gave me several chapters to process and submit them to him with my views and as I used to learn from Pratap, Sen endorsed whatever I wrote. The pity is successive governments dithered over this issue, as a result, as of now the implementation of NPC recommendations to my perception has been derailed.

If NPC was the brainchild of the Janata government, its later avatar, the NDA, did precious little to implement the reports. In 2006 after a writ petition was filed by Prakash Singh in the Supreme Court, there was a revival of the issue, and we are still harping on the non-implementation of the Supreme Court judgment. But to my mind the Supreme Court judgment did more damage to the essence of the recommendations of the NPC which rightly stressed the need for a uniform police system in the entire country through enactment of a uniform Police Act.

The Supreme Court had left it to the states to formulate their own Police Acts and the Acts so far enacted by some states do not bear any testimony to improvement by way of reforms. It is old wine in new bottle. The Soli Sorabjee committee which had IPS officers to draft a model Police Act was of the view that a Central Act is not a tenable proposition as police is a state subject coming in list 1 in the seventh schedule in the constitution. Nobody disputes that but in my view the committee should have explored the possibility of a Central Act under Articles 252 and 263 and the feasibility of bringing police reform to the concurrent list.

Now all that we can do is to cry hoarse over the Prakash Singh judgment. I have raised this fundamental issue in some forums, but people have just glossed over it. To me it is a typical police syndrome, to have in our hand something to complain about to cover up our inadequacies. I personally feel very sad at the turn of events as I was a great enthusiast in the NPC. I also notice that those who used to be active and enthusiastic about NPC are generally silent realizing perhaps the futility of it.

The NPC was wound up after submission of reports and the officers were repatriated. Ramachandran went back to his state leaving no successor and all papers with Manabesh Mukherjee. Return of Mrs Gandhi to power put the Association in a state of quandary. TV Rajeswar on taking over as Director IB issued direction to all IB officers to dissociate themselves from the Association.

This was a clear rebuff to the Association which had passed a resolution condemning excesses committed by the police during emergency. The Association virtually came to a standstill as the bulk of the members were from the IB and its Director as the primus interpares amongst the CPO chiefs with his clout with the Prime Minister and Home Minister was in a position to further the interests of the service but now would not.

Some IB officers went to the extent of sending letters to the Hon. Secretary in obedience to the Director's directive. It was urgently necessary to sort out this impasse. We decided to call a meeting of the executive committee, and states' representatives in Delhi and some of those who were visible in the Association activities. In the meeting it was felt that the time was too sensitive to call a meeting of the general body which at any rate would be witness to the absence of IB officers. It was decided that the executive body would evolve a consensus in choosing the Hon. Secretary and Jt. Secretary.

The choice fell on me and sensing that, I had sounded Gautam Kaul (1965) to become Jt Secretary which he was gracious enough to agree. There were important items in the agenda of the Association, most important being creation of the post of Director General of Police in the states and rationalization and improvement of pay scales at senior levels.

Gautam proved to be of invaluable help to me in the activities of the Association. He had the advantage of contacts in Delhi which helped us carry forward our programme.

I don't frankly remember the names of all members of the executive body, but members who were devoting time to Association matters were HP Bhatnagar (1956), DyDirector BSF, whose room in the North Block was our meeting place; AP Mukherjee WB (1956); Nikhil Kumar UT (1963). Anantha Chari, whenever it was possible for him to come from Orissa, used to join the group. Natarajan, Joint Secretary Police, and Narendra Prasad, my batch mate, Director Police in MHA, who were committed to our agenda were of tremendous help. Quite a few IB officers who did not take part directly were keen to extend whatever assistance we needed. In particular I remember DC Nath (1960) and MK Dhar (1964) who rendered positive help to us.

The biggest challenge before us was to win over the Director IB, because we knew he would be associated with the decision-making process and we had to see that he would extend his support to our cause. I called on TV Rajeswar and told him about my new role as Hon. Secretary of the Association. He talked to me in a very friendly and cordial manner, and told me that it would not be possible for him to withdraw the letter he had written to the IPS officers in IB. But he assured me of all support in his capacity as Director IB.

An incident brought me closer to Rajeswar who, willy-nilly, had to attend a meeting of the IPS Association. It was the death of a famous IP officer GK Handoo who was with Pandit Nehru for several years. When we were planning to pass a condolence resolution I got a call from Rajeswar asking me to see him. When I met him he told me that a regular meeting of the Association should be held to pass the resolution and he assured me that the North Block conference hall would be made available to us. He also asked me to draft a condolence resolution which would be vetted by BN Mullick.

I attempted a draft, took it to MK Narayan, then Jt Director, who later became Director IB, NSA and then

Governor of West Bengal. We both went to Rajeswar who added his own and asked me to take the draft to BN Mullick for his approval. I went to the residence of Mullick who took a quick glance at the draft and asked me to collect it next morning. When I went to collect the draft next day, I found it totally altered and longer than the previous one. I came to my office, got it typed. Between Gautam and me we had contacted as many retired and serving officers as possible and in the afternoon when I went to North Block conference hall it was overflowing. The ice had been broken.

We needed to identify the priorities of the issues which the Association would take up. Obviously, the subject that demanded top priority was creation of the post of Director General of Police which was a legitimate demand of the IPS officers, more so when the posts of state Chief Secretaries had been upgraded to a Secretary's scale. The next issue was the rationalization and improvement of the pay scales of senior ranks like selection grade and DIG's scale and abolition of the post of Additional. IGP.

For creation of the post of Director General of Police, the players were Home Secretary, Finance Secretary, Cabinet Secretary, Home Minister, Finance Minister and Prime Minister. Support of Director IB TV Rajeswar and RN Kao, former R&AW chief who had joined as chief advisor to Mrs Gandhi with unprecedented clout, was crucial to our mission.

We were also sure of a positive response from Cabinet Secretary Krishnaswamy Rao Saheb. We, the core group, needed to meet frequently to devise our strategy and decide on follow up actions. We had to meet Home Minister Gyani Zail Singh and Finance Minister Pranab Mukherjee. We knew Home Secretary TN Chaturvedi would not go out of the way to support the proposal. Expenditure Secretary CG Somiah, whom I met, assured that Finance Ministry would clear the proposal. We met the Home Secretary in a delegation led by AP Mukherjee and got a non-committal response.

On the advice of my colleagues, I met RK Dhawan, the powerful Private Secretary to Mrs Gandhi. I had a talk with him in a friendly atmosphere, he listened to me patiently and said it would not be necessary to meet the Prime Minister, all that we should do was to get the file moving from minister to minister which meant that Home Minister, should mark the file to Finance Minister who in turn should mark it to PM.

We arranged a meeting with Home Minister Gyani Zail Singh through a batch mate of mine in Punjab and met him in a delegation. IJS Bindra, an IAS officer of 1964, was his Special Assistant. An astute politician that he was, Zail Singh sent him out and then told us in Hindi, "Now we can talk freely." After listening to us he asked, "What do you want me to do?" We told him to mark the file to Finance Minister by name. He handed over the file to me and told me, "You write down what you want and I will put my signature." We left his room with the Home Ministry file in my hand. Next day was a holiday. I had asked my PA to come to office to take dictation. I went to my office, dictated the needful and next day handed over the file to Zail Singh's PS, explaining what was to be done.

We secured a meeting with Finance Minister Pranab Mukherjee, most likely through DC Nath, met him in a delegation and explained our case. He also agreed to send the file to Prime Minister. I kept RK Dhawan informed of the development. The file came back with the approval of the PM for creation of a post of Director General in principle. In normal case, meeting the ministers was not difficult but our strategy was that they should be properly briefed before our formal meeting. Hence we had to take the help of IPS officers who were known to Gyani Zail Singh and Pranab Mukherjee.

Then the next exercise, the bureaucratic process of clearance by Secretaries committee, began. By then Gyani Zail Singh had become President of India and PC Sethi was the Home Minister. We met PC Sethi, and updated him on our efforts on the proposal and were assured of his support. Clearance by the Secretaries Committee was of critical importance as the finer details of the proposal would be worked out for preparing the cabinet memorandum. The committee headed by the Cabinet Secretary had Secretaries Home, Finance and Personnel as members. We had met Cabinet Secretary Rao Saheb through RN Kao and received a favourable response. Somiah advised me to get the Director IB co-opted to the committee. This was a ticklish situation and we decided to take the help of RN Kao. He was sitting in South Block next to the room of Cabinet Secretary. His OSD Ratnakar Rao, an IPS officer of 1961 batch, fixed the appointment.

We met Kao and requested him to talk to Rao Saheb to induct Director IB to the Secretaries Committee. He rang up Rao Saheb in our presence and passed on the request which was readily acceded to. Then it was my turn to meet Director IB and brief him about the pros and cons of the proposal. In the meeting next day the Secretaries Committee cleared the proposal.

We thought we were at the end of the tunnel. A message would go to all the state governments to convey their concurrence after which notification would be issued creating the post. Then came another hurdle. The Home Secretary wanted the clearance of the Law department before sending messages to the states and, as expected, the Law Department suggested amendment to the Police Act of 1861 to replace the words 'Inspector General' with 'Director General'.

I was in my office when Narendra Prasad rang me, told me about the development and asked me to come to Natarajan's room immediately. I rushed to North Block. If the Act was to be amended, there would be indefinite delay and this process at any cost had to be bypassed. When I reached NP's room I found that there was a convergence of our thought processes.

Why not designate the post 'Director General and Inspector General of Police' and meet the requirement of law.

We went to Natarajan's room, broached our idea and Natarajan without sending the file to Home Secretary dashed off a wireless message to all Chief Secretaries informing them of the decision of the Government of India to create a cadre post of Director General and Inspector General of police and requesting them to send the concurrence of the state governments within a stipulated period for issue of notification. Then at our level, Gautam and I contacted as many state associations/police chiefs as possible to expedite the concurrence of states. Within the stipulated period majority of the states responded, perhaps with the exception of Kerala and J&K, and notification was issued creating a cadre post of Director General and Inspector General of Police in 1982. That was the saga of the post of the upgraded police chief.

During those hectic days I was often seen in the corridors of North Block in pursuit of the proposals. This did not escape the notice of TN Chaturvedi who called me one day and told me: "Your office is in RK Puram. I often see you in North Block." I gave a meek and unconvincing reply that it was in pursuit of the proposals of DCPC. Then he said: "You are behaving like a trade union leader." While it was a reprimand I took it as a compliment.

Our next mission was rationalization and upgradation in the Selection Grade and DIG's scale which had assumed importance with the Fourth Pay Commission in the offing. In our memorandum to the government, we had demanded a fixed scale of Rs 3,250 for DG Police, Rs 2,750–Rs 3,000 for IGP, Rs 2,250–Rs 2,750 for DIG that was equivalent to level one and level two Commissioners scale in the central services, abolition of the post of Addl IGP at Rs 2,250–Rs 2500 and Rs 2,000–Rs 2250 for selection grade. With the DG's scale fixed at Rs 3,000 we had to take a relook. When I met

Somiah, Secretary Expenditure, he gave me very practical suggestions.

He said neither the IAS nor the Defence Services would agree to a scale of Rs 2,250–Rs 2,750 for DIG which would be higher than a Brigadier's scale of Rs 2000–Rs 2,400 and equivalent to a Commissioner's scale traditionally at par with the IG's scale. He suggested a running scale of Rs 1,800 to Rs 2,000 in selection grade and a running scale of Rs 2,000–Rs 2,500 for DIG. In fact, this was what we were thinking aloud in our internal discussions. It would break the hither to framework of giving a fixed scale in selection grade to IPS, take the maximum of the DIG's scale to the starting scale of an IAS Commissioner and a running scale for DIG whose maximum would be higher than a Brigadier's scale.

The proposal was processed in the MHA. Concurrence of Finance was not a problem. But when the proposal was cleared by the Secretaries Committee in early 1983 a minor alteration was made. The selection grade for the first time became a running scale of Rs 1,800–Rs 2,000. Post of Additional. IGP was abolished allowing the existing posts to wither away and in DIG's scale two levels were created, 50 per cent at Rs 2,000–2,250 and 50 per cent at Rs 2,250–2500. Taking the scenario prevailing then into consideration it was undoubtedly the best leverage IPS got after independence.

My days in Delhi were getting numbered. I was happy that some historic developments had taken place during my tenure as the Hon. Secretary of the IPS Central Association. For this mission my hats are off to Gautam Kaul who gave his unstinted support. Gautam shared my burden in a way that should be exemplary to all IPS officers. And how can I forget the core group of my colleagues who were always around me to share my burden, AP Mukherjee, HP Bhatnagar, Natarajan, Narendra Prasad, Ananthachari and Nikhil Kumar. I am mentioning all these details so that the present and future generations of IPS officers know that their predecessors had suffered and fought in the sixties and seventies, so that a foundation was built, over which the bricks are being laid in the subsequent years.

Now at the administrative level the equation between the Collector and SP is something which was unthinkable in our days. The SPs are prominent; they are being approached, talked to on issues relating to public safety which was a prerogative of the Collector during our time. With the upgradation of the post of police chief, there is near parity and by all accounts he is perceived to be the most important functionary in the state administration, next only to the Chief Secretary. With the abolition of the post of Additional. IGP and creation of the post of DGP, Additional. DG posts were only logical. And now IPS officers are getting into that scale in their 24th, 25th year of service, years we were taking to become IG Police.

In September 1982 my mother expired at Sambalpur. Due to heavy rain there was disruption of road communication in Orissa. I got the news of my mother's illness from Chari and reached Sambalpur through a circuitous route from Delhi to Kolkata, then to Ranchi from where I took a flight to Rourkela and then I drove to Sambalpur to see my mother's dead body. After all rituals, we returned to Delhi with my father leaving my sick sister with my brother Akshya at Sambalpur where he and his wife were serving as lecturers in local government colleges.

I will conclude this chapter by narrating three experiences in Delhi. I was visiting my friends and colleagues to say goodbye. I went to see Home Secretary TN Chaturvedi and told him that I was going back to my state. He looked at me and asked me, "I hope you have not come for an extension." I said, "No sir", it was a farewell call. My visit to TV Rajeswar was highly touching. He asked me why I was not keen to continue in Delhi. This was one idea that never weighed heavily on me for I was mentally prepared to go back. I thanked him for his help to our Association to which Rajeshwar's words which have been etched in my memory were: "Tripathy, you have done great service to the IPS. IPS should be grateful to you."

It did not occur to me that I should call on R N Kao, which was a grave omission on my part. One morning, when I was packing my luggage, Ratnakar Rao, his OSD, rang me and told me that Kao wanted to see me and whether I could come. I said yes and drove to Kao's office. I was somewhat shabbily dressed because of the packing I was doing at home. Kao dressed in his immaculate white was walking up and down in his room.

When I entered I begged to be excused for not being properly dressed. He asked me, "You are going back to your state." I said, "Yes sir." He told me he would get a post created either in the Home Ministry or the Cabinet Secretariat if I wished to stay. I was nonplussed, an offer coming from a legendary IP officer. I thanked him profusely, expressed my gratitude and told him we have already made arrangements for our departure. He wished me good luck and said, "Tripathy, you have done yeoman's service to IPS." I was overwhelmed.

Part-6

Return to Orissa

- Inspector General of Prisons: A Time of Reforms
- Orissa Tourism: Unutilised Potential
- Back to Police: State CID Crime Branch
- Road Transport: Running on Whims and Fancies
- State Vigilance Chief: Razor's Edge
- State Police Chief: A High, A Scandal, and Denouement

Chapter-22

Inspector General of Prisons: A Time of Reforms

After I returned to Orissa, I had to wait beyond the expiry of my joining time as there was a conflict in the proposals of the DG Police and the Home Secretary. N Swain, who was DG Police, had sent a proposal for my posting as DIG (Administration) in the police headquarters. That was the first time when the government had taken a decision to post an IPS officer as IG Prisons which till then was headed by a doctor from Orissa Health Service.

Mismanagement of prisons growing out of maladministration had created near chaotic conditions in the department. In fact that was a feature in all prisons throughout India. Some states had started posting IPS officers to head the department. Home Secretary R N Das wanted that I should join as IG Prisons. For me either post was welcome. Swain, whose proposal showed his unflinching faith in me, was to retire in August, but he would not budge an inch. Chief Minister J B Patnaik also did not like to override Swain's proposal. I decided to meet Swain to request him not to insist on his proposal in view of his impending retirement to which he agreed and I was notified to join as IG Prisons.

After taking charge, I discovered to my utter discomfiture that I was most unwelcome in the department. In the head office most of the staff were sullen as if they were conveying their disapproval to the entry of an intruder into their territory. Accustomed to an atmosphere of laxity they were apprehensive of hard days with instant reprisals if they remissed. Various associations in the prison service had earlier passed resolutions opposing posting of an IPS officer as IG Prisons. They had even instigated a PIL in the Orissa High Court, which to my horror, I found was filed by one of my class mates and very good friend, who of course was unaware of my posting, citing the infamous strictures on police by Justice AN Mulla of the Allahabad High Court. The medical fraternity had opposed the posting of an IPS officer in place of a doctor.

Several self-styled champions of human rights had given statements that it would take away that touch of humanism and empathy so vital for the suffering prisoners. This was not only amusing but also sad for it reflected public perception of an IPS officer. I had literally landed myself in soup, forsaking the certain comforts of my posting in police.

But this was a challenge I could not have run away from and decided to make myself not only acceptable but win their unstinted loyalty. In the first few days, as I was examining the working of the department, I found the department, although one of the oldest in the country, had staggering deficiencies that had a crippling effect on its working. First and foremost was the lack of pride amongst the Prison officials in their profession. Hamstrung by neglect and indifference from government and absence of a chief who would fight for them, they were wallowing in self pity.

For the administrative department in government, the Home Ministry, Prisons was of no priority, it was in the sunshadow area, all the light being stolen by Police. Kept at a much lower pedestal than the police in terms of pay, rank and other facilities the prison officials were not even treated like second cousins.

Although they were required to discharge their duties in uniform there was no training facility for the staff. Except the district jails, which had full-time jail officials as superintendents, all the sub divisional jails had sub divisional medical officers as superintendents. Lack of training, laxity of supervision led to indiscipline, corruption and other malpractices.

Inside the prisons, overcrowded with convicts and under trial prisoners, similar anarchy prevailed. A shoestring budget that failed to take care of the annual food bill, clothing and medical needs of the prisoners aggravated the situation. The department, one of the oldest, was yet to formulate cadre rules for its various ranks causing disaffection amongst the staff. The probation and correctional wing of the department was in a dysfunctional state, with no vision of prison reforms in place.

There were twin formidable challenges ahead: one, streamlining the internal administration and, two, prison reforms. While both tasks could go hand in hand, I decided to keep the former as the foremost item in my agenda as I was sure improvement was possible only in a disciplined atmosphere, through motivated staff. It was necessary to augment the resources of the department to a satisfactory level so that the reform programmes would not falter.

A meeting of the superintendents was convened. The gathering, predominated by doctors who were in charge of sub divisional jails, hardly was encouraging for sheer lack of interest and ideas. The hardcore jail staff were uncertain of a new dispensation. I encouraged and reassured them of a promising future and tried to break the ice. After the meeting, I was convinced that my first task would be to have fulltime superintendents in all the jails, a proposal I pursued with government and succeeded in getting sanction thereby providing a windfall for the jail staff much to their astonishment and joy. Full-time jail officers as superintendents necessitated creation and upgradation of posts, which inevitably called for an overdue rationalization of cadre rules.

Since the circle jail superintendents were the senior most officers in junior grade one of the state service, limiting promotion prospects to only four posts and in the absence of avenues to go higher which in other departments was routine, it was necessary to provide scope for the jail officers to go to the rank of DIG/ Additional IG of prisons and corresponding avenues for the Probation and Correctional staff.

Absence of training very often made the jail staff look comic in uniform. I saw a dozen ways of coming to attention and saluting. I had a very able DIG in the person of A K Dalua, a senior officer of the state civil service, who not only had ideas but also the will to pursue the proposals in the secretariat. We explored the possibility of starting a training school within available resources. At Berhampur, which had a circle jail, some newly constructed buildings were vacant. Government approval was obtained to get some instructors from police for outdoor training. Indoor teaching staff was provided from the department, and a Jail Training School was formally inaugurated by the Governor.

Another grievance of the jail staff was the disparity in the pay scales compared to the police. Initially I had reservations on the issue of parity, but was convinced of the justification for parity as the officers and men were exposed to considerable risk in the discharge of their duties functioning in an environment of outlaws.

One scheme that provided great satisfaction to the prison staff was the constitution of a jail employees' relief and welfare fund in the line of police. The government agreed to provide an annual grant-in-aid which was supplemented by a monthly contribution by prison staff.

Overcrowding in Orissa jails was an acute problem. The congested and unhygienic living conditions aggravated indiscipline amongst prisoners. The seventh and eighth Finance Commissions had given grants for construction of new jails and dormitories in the existing jails. The biggest and oldest jail at Cuttack was to be shifted. This was done on a priority basis by selecting a site at Charbatia near the ARC and as many as 11 new jails were constructed. The practice of visiting jails had gone by default, a factor responsible for malpractices and indiscipline in the jails. I started visiting the 67 jails and covered almost all of them in course of two years.

The next task that was taken up was to attain a fair degree of self-sufficiency in the budgetary provisions which were utterly inadequate. In fact, this was the darkest area of the prison department which languished in the backwaters of Home with police taking the biggest chunk. When I looked at the provision for diet for prisoners in 1983–84, I found that huge arrears were pending from the previous year that would take away a large portion of the funds. The diet scale prescribed in the outdated Jail Manual needed to be revised.

We sent a proposal on revised scale to the government which was approved giving us teeth to force the government to provide funds for the prisoners and by the end of the next financial year, there was no arrear bill and this made a big difference in the level of prisoners' satisfaction. The revised diet scale at that time was one of the best in India as I would find from my visits to Maharashtra, Karnataka and Tamil Nadu.

Similarly, the scale of prisoners' clothes was revised and additional cleaning materials like soap, washing powder, etc. were added.

Having started a regular training school it was necessary to update the scale of uniform of the guarding staff and the officers. The scale was brought at par with police and the step uplifted the morale of the staff considerably.

Having returned from Delhi, I could appreciate the importance of exposure of officers to various training courses at the national level. This was yet another dark spot in the already darker domain of prisons. Now BPR&D is conducting courses for prison officers in different states. At that time it was not there. I turned to Dr Hira Singh, who was the Director of National Institute of Social Defence in New Delhi. He used to visit Bhubaneswar for the implementation of the Children, Act. We struck a chord instantly and he agreed to conduct refreshers' courses in Bhubaneswar. We had faculty from NISD, police, judiciary and the university and the courses brought a qualitative change in the mind of the officers.

I agreed to the implementation of children's Act although it was the responsibility of the state social welfare department which I knew would not be able to do in the absence of provision of funds. That was our problem also, but I decided to give it a try. The urgency was punctuated by a PIL filed by the fiery activist Sheila Barse from Mumbai in the Supreme Court where appearing personally she had the guts to take on Justice Ranganath Mishra.

A committee was formed to see the condition of children in the jails in the country and in that connection she visited Orissa and we developed an instant rapport. We had some buildings in Berhampur and Rourkela which could be spared for starting the observation homes to which the children would be shifted. I also agreed to empower the probation officers as superintendents of the homes and moved government for creation of Children's Courts to try the cases. All this was done in record time that earned me great admiration from Dr Hira Singh in particular and the Ministry of Social Welfare in general. I was inducted as a member of the Central Advisory Committee on Social Defence.

In 1985, the United Nations organized a three-day convention in Delhi on "New Dimensions of Criminality and Crime prevention". I was invited to act as an observer along with K F Rustomjee, Upendra Buxi, who was Vice-Chancellor of Delhi University and an academician from National Institute of Social Sciences, Mumbai. This convention was attended by many acting and former heads of states and eminent persons from the fields of criminology, social defence and other related human faculties. The underlying theme of the convention was that it is not only poverty that breeds crime and criminality, but also development that creates new types of crime, many sophisticated like group terrorism, cartels and mafia for which the nations should be adequately prepared and equipped both in terms of human resource and technology.

By the end of the second year of my stay, many measures initiated had been implemented and the department was in a position to command positive response from the government and public that boosted the morale of the staff considerably.

In most of the measures, prison reform was inbuilt, like upgrading the scale of prisoner's diet and uniform to their level of satisfaction, steps taken for decongestion in living, implementing the Children Act, provision of better health and sanitary facilities, expeditious grant of parole—a complaint I faced in the district jails from the convicts.

Incidentally, when I talked to the prison welfare officers who were to monitor police enquiry before grant of parole, I was told that the thana officers in routine manner would object to the release of a convict on the ground that he would be unsafe for the community where he and his family lived. It was evident prison reform was interlinked with change of attitude in the other two related and crucial departments, police and judiciary– in the larger context, the criminal justice system, in which a holistic approach is yet to be taken to reform the system. We talk and discuss about reforms in isolation, in police, in judiciary and in prisons, but have not taken any worthwhile measures in reforming the whole.

I took up the matter with the DG Police BK Panigrahi who immediately issued a circular, but it was only an ad hoc step. Judiciary being the holy cow was beyond access. The District Judges who were visitors to the jails were required to deal with the overcrowding of undertrial prisoners, delay in production and issues relating to trial, but their notes invariably avoided this sensitive area and dealt with the prison conditions which were the responsibility of the IG Prisons or the District Magistrate. I did bring this matter to the notice of the administrative judge of the High Court, but to no effect. I asked the superintendents to send letters to the ADM (Judicial), citing instances of inordinate delay in trial. They were unsure for they thought it would amount to contempt of court till I convinced them that correspondence with the ADM Judicial would not be tantamount to contempt of court.

Some states had started open-air jails to provide freedom of movement to the prisoners, the long serving convicts and employment opportunities. This was no doubt a great leap in the domain of prison reforms. We decided to initiate measures to start one in Orissa. I was of the considered view that the proposed facility should be near the capital for better and more effective supervision by the head office. We selected two sites near Khurda-Chandaka road.

I could not, however, witness the fruition of my proposal till I left due to dearth of funds. Several years later the open-air jail came up and I was filled with satisfaction when I visited it.

One scheme which brought universal satisfaction for the prisoners was the introduction of incentive in the form of wages for their labour in the jail. Most of the district jails had some industrial activities, some moribund, some dead. Textile items produced in jails such as bed sheets, covers, towels, dhoti, durry (rugs) and blankets were popular. Durries produced in Baripada and Keonjhar jails were very much in demand. Baripada circle jail was famous for manufacturing sofa sets with sabai grass, a locally grown wild grass.

Similarly, Bhubaneswar jail was manufacturing blankets which were mostly supplied to the prisoners. There were stitching units, pickle and other home products units managed by the female prisoners. It was necessary to activate these industries, boost production and be self-sufficient. Payment of wages would no doubt provide incentive to the prisoners. Accordingly, a scheme was prepared, which categorized payment to two categories of prisoners – skilled and unskilled, the former getting marginally higher wage than the latter. Income from labour would be kept in individual account to be opened in the name of each prisoner. There was great enthusiasm amongst the prisoners at the launch of the scheme in Cuttack jail by Chief Minister JB Patnaik.

For providing better facilities for the women convicts and strengthening vocational activities, the idea of a separate female jail was mooted. We had vacant buildings outside the jail campus in Sambalpur with spacious accommodation. A proposal was sent to the government for starting an exclusive female prison in Sambalpur, which was sanctioned and long-serving female convicts were housed there. But this was an experiment that did not elicit enthusiastic response from the convicts as they were unwilling to be shifted to

Sambalpur from distant places where they were able to meet their kith and kin more frequently.

Years later, Kiran Bedi, the first lady IPS officer of the country, a highly dedicated and dynamic officer, received Magsaysay award for bringing out prison reforms in Tihar jail when she was IG Prisons in Delhi. Everything she did was picked by the print and electronic media, leading to wide national coverage, an advantage a Delhi-based officer enjoys and a disadvantage, a provincial officer suffers from. A friend of mine in IPS quipped in the web: "If an IPS officer wants to be a Governor, he should belong to the Union Territory Cadre." That is why I call myself a country cousin.

After three years of stay I expected a shift, for it was time for me to go back to my parent department. There was no indication, my continuance as IG Prisons eminently suited the Home Department and the Chief Minister. The DG Police also wrote for my reversion to the police but to no effect. Another one and half years passed and when there was no indication of my transfer, I met the Chief Minister and requested him to give me a posting in police from where I was out for nearly a decade. I briefed Nilamadhab Mohanty, my batch mate in IAS, and his Secretary. It seemed the Chief Minister had something else in his mind.

Till my return to Orissa in 1983, there was no initiative on the part of the government to introduce computers in other departments. S B. Mishra, an IAS officer of 1965 batch, who was Secretary to CM and his most trusted bureaucrat, called me to discuss this matter. We agreed that a setup should be started to take up the project in government departments and it should be a registered society with a governing body so that the usual bureaucratic red tape could be avoided. He asked me to prepare a project report which I did and a society was formed with us as founder members.

At that time I was also following a proposal of the Government of India for providing a building for starting a branch of National Informatics headed by Dr Seshagiri with whom I had worked in Delhi.

SB Mishra arranged an orientation workshop which was attended by Chief Minister JB Patnaik, all the cabinet ministers, chief secretary Gyanchand and secretaries to Government. Dr Seshagiri came from Delhi. I was virtually the main speaker followed by Dr Seshagiri and Srinivasan, a very senior IAS officer who had became a computer buff. It was a resounding success and a beaming JB Patnaik announced the scheme in Orissa, its potential for employment and the decision of the Government of India to develop Bhubaneswar as one of the four software cities, the other three being Bangalore, Pune and Chandigarh.

It was another matter that Orissa failed to capitalize on the prospects of a booming IT industry and remained in the backwaters showing signs of life of late. When it came to selection of a chief executive, I suggested the name of NC Padhi whose repatriation to Orissa was due and it was approved. I remained in the governing body for quite some time in course of which NC Padhi's term ended and again on my suggestion Pujari from Kerala University was appointed as CEO.

One day I received a call from Nilamadhab who was in Delhi with the Chief Minister telling me that I should be prepared to join as the Managing Director of the Electronic Development Corporation. My immediate reaction was one of resentment. He, however, explained that the Chief Minister had decided to change the incumbent MD against whom allegations had come to his notice. After their return to Bhubaneswar, the Home department issued notification posting me as MD Electronics Development Corporation. Its administrative department was Industry where SB Mishra had joined as Secretary. Niranjan Patnaik, relative of JB Patnaik known closely to me since my Keonjhar days, was the minister.

The administrative department had to issue the enabling notification on the strength of which I could join. But it seemed the minister and his secretary were more comfortable with the incumbent MD and were unwilling to spare him. I think J B Patnaik must have realized that he had committed a mistake by ignoring his trusted minister and bureaucrat. SB Mishra, however, went out of his way to mollify my wounded feelings, showering embarrassing praise on me and assuring me that a suitable posting would be decided.

I was not interested in any suitable posting and requested him to use his good offices with the Chief Minister to send me back to police. But that was not to be and I was posted as Managing Director of the Orissa Tourism Development Corporation. I had overstayed my joining time which was regularized and I joined the post and became part of Orissa Tourism in mid-1988.

Thus came to an end an eventful and satisfying chapter of my life. The prison staff had given me iconic status and for long considered me to be their saviour and mentor. Even now when the associations of officers and guarding staff take up issues with the government they come to me for my moral support.

Chapter-23

Orissa Tourism: Unutilised Potential

Tourism in Orissa presented several paradoxes, high on talk and low in action. JB Patnaik was, and perhaps has been, the only Chief Minister who took keen personal interest in the development of the two areas, what were called the sunshine sectors—Information Technology and Tourism—where the environment is clean, state intervention much less than in heavy industries, where one of the biggest problems was land acquisition, apart from water and power supply. Fortuitously, I happened to be associated with both the sectors.

When I joined the Corporation, I was already an open critic of Orissa tourism for what I saw in Orissa after my return from the Centre in 1983. I saw the picture of Lord Jagannath displayed as posters everywhere—on the walls, light posts, luggage boots of cars, bus bodies. Such obscene display of the deity hurt my sensibilities.

Then, I learnt that Lord Jagannath had been officially adopted as the mascot of Orissa Tourism to make Orissa the hub of foreign and domestic tourists. With my limited perception, I failed to realise how a picture of the deity could attract tourists to the state and how JB Patnaik, who was a great devotee of Lord Jagannath, could agree to such an obnoxious proposal.

In the end, Lord Jagannath had failed to attract tourists to Orissa. After returning to Orissa I started writing articles on contemporary issues in the Oriya dailies. My intial articles dealt with the above subject and neglect of heritage monuments of the state. But the mandarins would not concede; they had to paint a rosy picture. The result: doling out bluffs through fabricated figures and cooked up statistics.

In 1988 it was said the footfalls of foreign tourists to Orissa had risen from a mere 2,000 in 1980 to 25,000 in 1987 and internal tourists exceeded 15 lakhs. When I went deeper into the matter, I found that as regards the foreign tourists, in the absence of any method to collect data about their arrivals and departures, the tourist officers were collecting figures from the hotels in Bhubaneswar and Puri which were the two main destinations of the foreign visitors.

This resulted in duplicating the arrival figures as the tourists invariably after visiting Bhubaneswar would visit Puri. In essence, the actual arrivals did not exceed 12,000 to 13,000. As regards the internal tourists, arrival figures in the many bus stands of the state would be added up to show the tourist arrivals.

When I discussed the figures with the Tourism Minister who had a lot of respect for me, he literally begged me not to press for a scrutiny. What was strange was that during the eighties successive directors of tourism preferred to shut their eyes to such fabrication of figures.

In the hype that was being allowed, many basics were being forgotten. Nobody had taken any initiative to tap the central government employees who were entitled to visit any part of India once in four years. Tourists from outside the state came mainly from West Bengal, the traditional devotees of Lord Jagannath, on pilgrimage.

We established contact with the tour operators in Delhi, the main source of LTC tourism, and signed agreements with some agencies to bring tourists to Orissa on package tour. There was a lot of talk on promoting various types of tourism in Orissa such as beach tourism, leisure tourism, adventure tourism, ethnic tourism. Thirty years later, as of now, these talks remain just that—empty talk and speeches.

The Puri-Konark beach was an ideal site for promotion of beach tourism that could include water sports, leisure, ethnic lifestyle and cultural extravaganza. When my friend RK Bhujabal came as Tourism Secretary, he immediately agreed to survey the area. I, along with others, identified about 1000 acres of land on the beach for the purpose.

I prepared a project report where I suggested that the Orissa Tourism Development Corporation would act as the nodal agency for implementing the project. The objective was to cut through the red tape and political interference, but red tape and roadblocks were precisely what happened and the scheme went in limbo, with powerful people including politicians eager to grab the land. Now, when I drive down the same roads, I see how dreams die.

Barring a few hotels coming up in a haphazard manner, there is no trace of an integrated tourism complex which we conceived in 1989. As I write this, I feel particularly sad as having just returned from Bali, the only Hindu island state of Indonesia with a population of nearly four million, a land which the Oriya historians claim was frequented by the brave Oriya sailors in the days gone by, teeming with foreign tourists from all over the world.

In 1969, the international airport at Denpasar, the

capital of Bali, was opened by President Suharto. Since then, there has been no looking back. In 2012, the island had attracted 2.6 million tourists, the majority from Australia, Japan and China. In contrast, Orissa, which was touted as the "destination 21st century" by the mandarins and the political bosses, had taken a grand leap from 25,000 in the 80s to 40,000 in 2012– not even ½ per cent of the total number of foreign visitors to India.

Orissa is an example where, when the basics are not addressed and bluffs rule the roost, the result is a ballooning disaster. Kerala and Goa, which were on the same footing as Orissa, have taken remarkable strides in tourism, taking away a major chunk of tourist arrivals in India.

Another dark area was the hotels run and maintained by OTDC called Panthanivas. Located in different places of the state, they presented a sordid picture of mismanagement – occupancy was poor even at Bhubaneswar, rooms and toilets shabby, and restaurants running at a loss.

A primary factor for this state of affairs was the absence of professional staff in the hotels. The managers, coming mostly on deputation from the tourism department, had no background or training in hotel management. They were political appointees, spending more time in keeping the politicians and officers in good humour than in running the hotels.

When I took the decision to recruit professional managers, opposition to the proposal was predictable. Fortunately, I had the support of Minister Sarat Rout and Chief Minister JB Patnaik. We recruited trainees from the Government of India run Institute of Hotel Management and Catering.

In the initial enthusiasm to promote tourism in the state, several projects had been started and rightly so. I found that many were lying incomplete due to non-availability of funds. There was a hotel project in Puri in collaboration with the Ashoka Group of ITDC. It was lying incomplete as the state share had not been paid. This was taken up with the IPICOL, the financing institution. Funds were released, work was completed and Hotel Neelachal Ashok was opened by Shivraj Patil, the then Union Minister for Tourism. Similarly, hotel projects in Rourkela and Similipal sanctuary were completed and inaugurated by Chief Minister JB Patnaik.

One of the reasons why Orissa was not on the itinerary of foreign tourists was the fact that the state did not figure in the popular tourist circuits, which were mostly organized by the tour operators based in Delhi. The most popular circuit was the golden triangle covering Delhi, Agra and Jaipur with a spill over to Varanasi and Khajuraho. The other two popular destinations were Kashmir and Goa with Kerala fast catching up. Terrorist activities in Jammu and Kashmir had brought down the arrival figures by the early nineties. The other states, which were making sure and steady progress, were Tamil Nadu, Karnataka, Maharashtra, Andhra Pradesh and Himachal Pradesh. We organised Orissa nights in Delhi, Mumbai, Chennai, Srinagar and interacted with the tour operators. The predictable response was lack of infrastructure in the state. Without improving the state infrastructure, we had started blaming the Centre for lack of air connectivity to important cities in the country.

By the end of the century, all the state capitals and important places in the country were connected by rail to Bhubaneswar and by the middle of the last decade, many important cities such as Delhi, Kolkata, Mumbai, Chennai, Hyderabad, Bangalore and Lucknow were connected by air. Yet tourist arrivals have not recorded the desired target. Now Bhubaneswar has been declared an international airport. It remains to be seen if this will improve the tourist arrivals.

According to me, three factors ail Orissa tourism: lack of professionalism, poor infrastructure and lack of aggressive marketing. After the initiative shown in the early eighties, no effort has been made to improve and strengthen the above areas other than waxing eloquent on Orissa's tourism potential.

A memorable event that took place was signing of an accord with the erstwhile USSR to encourage Russian tourists to visit India. The agreement was signed in Taskhent by both the governments. The delegation to Taskhent included the state Tourism Secretary SM Patnaik and me. We visited USSR and were witness to the sure and indisputable effect of glasnost and perestroika, which would soon swamp the country leading virtually to the opening up of Russia and the disintegration of the artificial Russian federation.

The friendship treaty was signed with much fanfare in Taskhent, followed by Indo-Soviet cultural extravaganza and endless feasting and drinking. There I saw what I had heard and read—popularity of Indian films and their stars, particularly Raj Kapoor and Nargis. Songs of the film Awara were heard in the market places; there was a spontaneous sense of warmth shown by the people to Indians.

We made an overnight train journey to Samarkand, the birth place of Chengiz Khan, and saw the massive mausoleum. From there we flew to Moscow for the specific task of expediting the sculpture of Indira Gandhi that was being built by a famous Russian sculptor and was later installed in front of the state secretariat. We visited his house, a luxury dacha in the suburb of Moscow and were treated to lavish dinner and costly wines. This gave us an inkling of how, in the "all equal" state and society of Communism, the rich and privileged were living in a rarefied atmosphere.

This was in contrast to what we saw in the streets of Moscow. That year there was food scarcity in Russia and we saw long lines of men, women and children before the departmental stores to take their share of bread and potato, the staple diet in the country. With the country on the threshold of opening up, American goodies were in great demand, so was the American currency, dollars in exchange of roubles which were becoming waste papers. The hotel corridors were crowded with beautiful girls, not cheap looking street walkers, ready to bestow their favour in exchange of dollars.

My friend SM Patnaik, a pious and religious man, was shocked when I braved some adventurism by entering into a dialogue with these people, warning me that the KGB watching us would report everything to the Indian embassy.

We met Ambassador TN Kaul, a Russia lover, and had useful interaction with him. Tarai, an Oriya IFS officer, was a junior functionary. Our liaison was, however, done by the effusive Nandini, a young IFS lady. The various sights in Moscow highly intrigued me. The wide roads were spotlessly clean, metro was superb. Housing, healthcare and primary education were within reach of all citizens. But that obviously did not satisfy the people, the shops selling Russian goods were empty, American goods, overcrowded and the departmental stores overflowing to sell the basic food items to the people. Within the next two to three years the Russian federation collapsed and Communism became passé.

Towards the end of 1988, my promotion to the rank of Inspector General was in the offing. I represented to the government that I should be sent back to police in the interest of my career. In the event of my continuance in OTDC I should function as Chairman-cum-Managing Director. I found that JB Patnaik was not in a mood to spare me. I talked to DGP PC Ratho, who also wrote for my repatriation to police. One day, I decided to meet JB Patnaik. When I went to his office, NK Panda, a 1954 IAS officer who was Chief Secretary, was already in his room. He asked me not to insist on going back to police and function as Vice Chairman-cum-MD as it would be embarrassing to ask the Tourism Minister to demit the office of Chairman. I was non-committal. Finally, the DG's proposal and the pressure of a journalist friend of mine who was very close to JB Patnaik worked and I was posted as Inspector General of Police, CID (crime), Cuttack where the police headquarters is located.

Chapter-24

Back to Police: State CID Crime Branch

By the time I joined the State Crime Branch as Inspector General of Police, it was June 1989, back to real police work after about 12 years, if my tenure in MHA from 1977 to 1983 is taken into account. I was happy. We shifted to a house on the Cantonment Road where I stayed till my retirement. I had P C Ratho, my well-wisher, as DG Police. My DIG was Amaranand Patnaik, a very dedicated, honest and committed officer. He later became DG Police of the state.

During my time, the Crime Branch apart from its investigative wings had may other establishments under it: the State Forensic Science Laboratory, the State Crime Records Bureau, the Railway Police and the Human Rights Protection Cell, some of which have now become separate agencies. In fact being the oldest wing of the police, the CID covering the Crime Branch, Special Branch and Railway Police was created soon after 1902 on the basis of the Police Commission report. The DIG CID and Railways as the incumbent was then called was next in importance to the police chief and one of the most important functionaries in the state government. In 1964, Special Branch was separated with the creation of a post of DIG Intelligence, the remaining agencies functioning under the DIG CID Crime which was later upgraded to the rank of IGP.

My nearly three-year tenure in the Crime Branch saw lightning developments in the state politics and the fate of the police chief, being inextricably linked to the political developments, witnessed five DGs. The JB Patnaik government was getting increasingly unpopular with allegations of corruption, nepotism and impropriety running thick. Basant Kumar Biswal, who was a minister in the first cabinet of JB from 1980-85, had been dropped in the second term and had turned against him. And for many reasons, Prime Minister Rajiv Gandhi was not happy with JB who had to step down and as a stopgap arrangement Hemanand Biswal, a tribal leader from western Orissa who had been dismissed from JB's cabinet in 1986, became Chief Minister in December 1989, only three months ahead of the state elections. Hemanand's first job was to change DGP PC Ratho, who was perceived to be very close to JB and bring SN Sinha (1956) in his place.

Assembly elections took place in February 1990 and the results were a foregone conclusion. Biju Patnaik, then leader of Janata Dal, came to power with a massive majority, winning 123 of the 147 seats and reducing the Congress to only 10 seats. With Biju as Chief Minister, SN Sinha's days were numbered. By then DN Singh of 1957 batch, who had become close to the Janata politicians during 1977–80 playing the JP card, was waiting for his order of appointment as DG Police.

Singh was appointed as police chief in May 1990 although only for seven months. He was, however, confident that he would get an extension which he would loudly announce in every gathering. That was not to be, only because this bravado had reached Biju's ears and had irked him. Somnath Mishra his batchmate became DG in January 1991 only to last till July when PC Ratho staged a comeback.

I was drawn to the vortex of a serious conflict with D N Singh that made my stay in Crime Branch uncomfortable keeping me in a state of suspense on a day-to-day basis. In the beginning of my career, I was very close to DN who I thought was a rebel for a cause. But over a period of time I noticed that, he was not a rebel but a dissenter for the sake of it. He would fall out with all police chiefs, including his greatest benefactor RK Padhi, without any cause or principle. So over a period of time the distance between us increased. My proximity with successive police chiefs only heightened his negative feelings towards me. Thus when he took over as DG Police his reservations about me and my continuance as IG Crime were only logical. But he dared not try to shift me as my close friend Pyari Mohan Mohapatra was the Secretary to Biju Patnaik. On my side I had no intention to join issues with him and was mentally preparing myself for the end of his brief tenure.

The situation, however, changed by mid-1990 when the anti-Mandal agitations broke out and engulfed the entire country. There was widespread violence in Orissa with police opening fire at several places without any provocation. There was a reason for the reckless police firing. Biju Patnaik with his usual bravado made some infamous statements which attracted considerable media attention, like police hathare goli (bullets in the hands of police to fire), castrate the rapist, handcuff the saas and and chain the sister-in-law of the victim in a dowry death case, assault the officer who is not doing his duty among others. These populist slogans, going against the tenets of rule of law and giving power to people and police to deliver instant justice, were raising eyebrows.

One such incident happened when I was in charge during the anti-Mandal agitations. Students agitating in front of the Cuttack railway station started pelting stones. There was lathi charge and they were dispersed. While the situation was getting under control and I had gone to one end of the station, the armed police, at the other end, fired at the crowd, some citing Biju Patnaik's statement in support of their action. A well-known journalist was injured, I rushed to the spot and sent him to medical college in a police vehicle where he got prompt medical attention and his life was saved. The statement of Biju Patnaik, which was treated as an authorisation to police to open fire, just boomeranged and apart from the station, police opened fire in front of Ravenshaw College and Chandi Mandir crossing which only aggravated the situation.

DN had sent RN Mohapatra (1959), special IG Administration, to remain in charge of Chandi Chowk where a huge crowd had assembled. There was firing and one person died. This only worsened the already tense situation at Cuttack and DN Singh was visibly alarmed at the turn of events. But he was trying to keep up a bold face. From the station I went to DGP's office and found DN Singh surrounded by his officers, the Revenue Divisional Commissioner and the local minister. I gave a brief report about the incident at the station and on my way to my office dropped in the room of Spl. IG (Admn) where I found a despondent RN Mohapatra sitting with a gloomy face. I gave him my moral support and went to my office.

Near the staircase I found my DIG BM Patnaik, who was a college days friend of mine, rushing to DGP's office. I asked him the reason; he told me that DN Singh had entrusted him with the task of disposal of the dead body. I asked him why the Crime Branch should be involved in the disposal of the body when it was the job of the district police. He had no answer. I advised him to be careful before involving Crime Branch in the matter.

At midnight I got a call from Justice RC Pattnaik, a sitting judge of the High Court who later became a judge in the Supreme Court. He gave me horrifying details of the incident of firing at Chandi Mandir crossing and sought my help. The parents of the deceased boy went to district police to take the body, and the district police passed them on to Crime Branch. They approached BM Patnaik, who evaded the issue and after post mortem, the body was taken to a faraway place and burnt. Justice Patnaik tried several times to talk to DN Singh over phone, but the DGP would not respond, that was the reason he rang me up to intervene. I told him that whatever I heard from him was news to me and the matter was beyond me for any fruitful intervention.

Next morning from various accounts I received, the firing was avoidable and DN Singh in a state of panic or ill-advised took the decision to dispose of the body without taking the parents into confidence.

There was huge public consternation over the appalling events of the previous evening, particularly the surreptitious manner in which the dead body was disposed of. DN Singh's conduct came in for severe criticism. Biju Patnaik, whose temper was running high, announced a commission of inquiry to look into all incidents of police excesses during the anti-Mandal agitation. The commission was headed by Justice GB Patnaik, a sitting judge. I was appointed as the nodal officer and Biren Patnaik, Bar-at-Law, a famous lawyer and friend of Biju, the state counsel.

A new responsibility was thrust on me to defend the indefensible.

Alarmed at these developments, DN Singh's next ill-advised strategy was to get rid of me from Crime Branch and get DPS Chouhan, a 1963 officer, in my place. Because of mishandling of the situation at Cuttack, the SP had to be transferred. BM Patnaik was asked to go to Rourkela as DIG Western range. On the pleas of these transfers, he included my name for posting as Special Secretary Home and obtained CM's order to that effect. I doubt if Biju Patnaik with frayed temper cared to read the proposals. That was October 26, 1990.

Pyari Mohan could know about it only after the CM cleared the file. He rang me and told me of the developments and advised me to meet the CM next morning, which I did. I told Biju about the order he had signed on the previous day, posting me as Special Secretary Home, and also reminded him that he had appointed me as the nodal officer to the commission of inquiry. He flared up and asked me how it happened. When I told him that it was the DG's proposal, he picked the phone and gave DN Singh a mouthful, stating that Tripathy would remain in Crime Branch and hold additional charge of Special Secretary Home.

DN Singh at the other end must have been shocked at the rebuff. The notification was cancelled on October 27. I had to set up the basic infrastructure to start work as the nodal officer. The budget for the commission prepared by me was readily approved and funds sanctioned. .

For the next six months it was a taxing time for me. Day time I used to be in the Crime Branch, and then I would proceed to the residence of advocate Biren Patnaik to prepare records for the commission of inquiry and return home not before 10 pm or 11 pm. Two to three times a week I used to go to Bhubaneswar to dispose of files in the Home department. The surcharged atmosphere had become explosive following a report of DN Singh that Congress goondas under the leadership of JB Patnaik were responsible for the violence in Cuttack. That was a sweeping report setting the Congress in a course of confrontation with the government.

The Congress leaders, after the Chandi Chowk firing and disposal of the dead body in a hush-hush manner, were baying for the blood of DN Singh, RN Mohapatra and BM

Patnaik. In this murky atmosphere and, for me, the busy and hectic schedule, the only silver lining was the company of Biren Patnaik. Friendly, warm, affectionate, erudite, professionally brilliant, Biren Babu with a flourishing practice was much sought after in the social life of Cuttack and Bhubaneswar. He had an air of muted flamboyance, loved the good things of life and believed in the dictum of "work and enjoy". His yearning for good life had cost him dearly in his early life—his wife was staying separately with their children—a fact which prevented his elevation to the Bench. Many judges of the High Court were his juniors and had great respect for him.

Biren Babu had taken the setbacks in his life philosophically and was staying alone in his sprawling house. He was a friend of all senior politicians—Biju, JB, and Nilamani Routray. In fact, he was not confined to the lawyers circle but had friends who apart from politicians were bureaucrats. police officers, academicians and doctors. Once he liked a person the dye was cast. He would go to any length to help him out. I happened to be one of them.

For me, his house was open and vice versa. A lover of good but simple food he would drop in our house at any hour of the day and ask my wife to prepare the item of his choice. Age difference did not matter to him. While he was the contemporary of officers of the rank of DIG when I started my police life, I became one of his trusted friends during my stay in Cuttack.

Justice Gopal Ballav Patnaik, who later became the Chief Justice of India, was goal and work oriented. He wanted to complete the work within the stipulated time, a contrast to the prevailing commissions of inquiry some of which have not finished their job even after 8–10 years. But being holy cows they are beyond question. One commission set up in 2007 to examine the feasibility of establishing High Court branches in other parts of Orissa has just submitted its report without any recommendation. Two commissions of inquiry were set up in the aftermath of the riots at Phulbani where several persons belonging to a minority community were killed. One retired justice died, the other took up from where the deceased left and nearly eight years have passed and the report remains elusive.

In this case I was determined to facilitate the inquiry within the stipulated period. Work for the commission used to start in the evening. District Magistrates, SPs and concerned officers of the affected districts came with their draft affidavits with supporting records. Biren Babu used to correct, often rewrite the entire text and ensure that supporting records were in place. I have mentioned earlier, we had to defend the indefensible. We decided that our sole aim would be to place records before the commission, justifying the incidents of firing and use of force.

Congress had decided to intervene and their counsel was Bibhudendra Mishra, another highly reputed lawyer, a former minister in Nehru's cabinet and JB's friend. His brief was simple, counter the stand of the state counsel and he had enough ammunition to fire. It was a highly tricky situation. In the midst of all these goings on, I was a witness to or a party to several events which called for abundant caution.

RN Mohapatra with whom I had an excellent equation came one day to my house and requested me to see that no stricture was passed against him as his promotion was due. One day my journalist friend, who was close to JB, rang me up to say that JB wanted to meet me at a neutral place. He persuaded me to meet JB at his residence late at night. I drove to Bhubaneswar and met JB who was seething in anger over the reports of DN Singh and he wanted that no cover up job should be done on the incident of disposal of the dead body. I had been appointed as the nodal officer because Biju Patnaik had reposed faith in me which was not to the liking of DN Singh as he did not trust me. Thus, the aim of each party ran counter to the other and I had to tread the path with utmost caution lest I faltered.

The proceedings of the commission went smoothly and with remarkable promptness. The commission issued notice to DN Singh to appear but he avoided complying with it. One day, the commission told me to advise DN Singh to appear and depose failing which he would face severe consequences. I went to the residence of DN Singh and persuaded him to appear before the commission which he finally did. The commission gave a very balanced and considered report. There was no adverse remark against RN Mohapatra, who thereafter forgot to convey a word of gratitude to Biren Babu who had gone out of his way to help him. He conveyed his anguish and sadness at the fragility of human relationship.

There were many uncomfortable moments with DN Singh who would not miss an opportunity to embarrass me. He started commenting on my tour diaries knowing very well that I was discharging three responsibilities, one of which was based in Bhubaneswar and involved my trip to Bhubaneswar every other day. He topped it with taking a very irrational and ill-advised step by sending draft charges against me to the government for going to Delhi without taking his permission. This was the reward for good work done.

A Garuda statue stolen from Puri, which had created a sensation in the state, was recovered by the CBI and had to be transferred to Crime Branch. In that connection I went to Delhi keeping the DGP and Home department not only informed but also requesting for sanction for journey beyond the state. On the plea that he had not been informed, he sent draft charges without even calling for my explanation. I knew that the draft charges would be trashed in the Home department which in fact they were but the DG chose to remain silent instead of asserting his authority over his subordinates.

My elder daughter Padmini (Baby) was married to Visva Pavan Pati, an officer of the Indian Postal Service on February 21, 1992. For us, me and my wife, it was a poignant occasion in which there were spontaneous and uncontrollable tears of joy and happiness. Her welfare had been our prime and obsessive concern right from her childhood and the happy occasion had kept us, particularly my wife, busy in the preceding months. By the beginning of February 1992, my shift from Crime Branch was imminent.

Transport Minister Bhagbat Behera, who was a year junior to me in Ravenshaw College, was putting pressure on me to take over as the CMD of the Orissa State Road Transport Corporation (OSRTC) as the Chief Minister wanted a new incumbent. I was avoiding it, but had to yield to his pressure. I joined the OSRTC as Chairman-cum-Managing Director in early April 1992.

Chapter-25

Road Transport: Running on Whims and Fancies

When I joined OSRTC, I had no illusion about its future. Road transport in Orissa broadly fell into two sectors. One covered the southern districts, which was run by a company called Orissa Road Transport Company with its headquarters in Berhampur, the remaining part of Orissa was covered by the government-controlled Road Transport Department which was usually headed by an IPS officer in the rank of DIG designated as Transport Controller and then Director Transport. In effect, it had become the dumping ground for a police chief who for various reasons was not wanted by the political executive.

As a result JC Ghosh, an IP officer, was posted as Transport Controller after he was shifted from the post of police chief. Before him, the senior most IP officer MA Khan held the post. After J C Ghosh, RK Padhi, another IP officer, was also adjusted here after he was shifted from the post of police chief in 1968. Narayan Chand, the senior most DIG, was posted here before going as Addl IG Vigilance.

It was during RK Padhi's tenure in the late 60s that a Corporation was formed with Padhi as Chairman. Subsequently, the post of Chairman was held by a politician with an IPS officer as Managing Director. At one point in time, the department/corporation was running more than 1,600 buses. But mismanagement, malpractices and corruption gradually eroded the base of the Corporation and it began to shrink, with the IPS officers reduced to becoming helpless spectators.

Political interference, trade unionism and lack of accountability were the order of the day. Printing and selling of tickets was spurious, in fact it was liquid cash going to the pockets of the conductors and drivers at the end of the day. Per kilometre expenditure was high, ratio of employees per bus, one of the highest in India thanks to the political patronage, and level of maintenance, abysmally poor in spite of two big workshops in Cuttack and Sambalpur.

The profitability of the Corporation received a body blow when a scheme called 'Banner Scheme' was flaunted in the early 80s. By then many private operators had come to the field and the government took a decision that the private buses would ply under the banner of OSTRC. They would pay a fixed sum to the OSRTC for the benefit of the banner. The experiment proved disastrous. The private operators got assured routes and reaped profit, but being relatives of politicians or politicians themselves they did not care to honour the terms and conditions of the scheme. With their influence and clout, they showed their thumb to OSRTC. The scheme was subsequently scrapped but by then the Corporation had incurred losses to the tune of several crores of rupees.

The ORT Company in Berhampur, in charge of a General Manager, was no better. When it started in the 50s, it was a profitable organization but over the years lost its stature and became a loss-making venture. Later, the company was elevated to a Corporation with Prafulla Mishra, an IPS officer of 1970 batch, as Chairman-cum-Managing Director. The next experiment was to merge both the Corporations ostensibly for better management and profitability. When Biju Patnaik became Chief Minister in 1990, his Transport Minister Bhagabat Behera hastened the process.

Both the Corporations were merged and Prafulla Mishra, who was very close to Bhagabat, became the CMD of the newly formed OSRTC in the rank of DIG. Both the organizations between them were running more than 2,000 buses in the 1960s, covering more than 70 per cent of the total routes. By the time I took over in April 1992, the fleet strength had been reduced to 700 and went up to about 900 when I left a year later covering only 30 per cent of the total routes.

Another experiment in the beginning of the nineties depleted the resources of the OSRTC further. It was introduction of small buses, ostensibly for twin-city services in Cuttack and Bhubaneswar. In effect, they were diverted to Koraput, Kalahandi, Phulbani, Balangir, Sundargarh and Mayurbhanj, all hilly areas. The newly manufactured Eicher, Toyota and Swaraj Mazda buses were introduced in a terrain that was highly unsuitable leading to frequent breakdowns and delay in repair due to lack of expertise. As a result, when I took over I found most of these buses lying sick in the bus stands.

This had irked Biju Patnaik who conveyed his displeasure to Bhagabat. By then OSRTC was a top loss-making Corporation and the Finance department would not consider any proposal in a positive manner. When I met Biju Patnaik, he told me point blank to wind up the Corporation. I came to believe, Bhagabat Behera insisted on my coming as CMD so that I would act as a cushion between Biju's wrath and him. For all his shortcomings, Bhagabat was an emotional and impulsive person and tended to be swayed by events. Being one year my junior in Ravenshaw College and a firebrand student leader, he did enjoy my affection. But this arrangement did not help him.

Biju in his typical manner in a cabinet reshuffle divested him of Transport portfolio and Bhagabat fuming and fretting submitted his resignation. Harish Chandra Buxipatra, senior to me in college, a well known Communist leader in his student days, became the Transport Minister. He was a perfect gentleman. PK Dey, my batchmate in IAS, was the Transport Secretary and SC Hota, an IAS officer of 1968 batch, with a positive mindset was the Transport Commissioner. It was a good team.

The preceding scenario would explain that OSRTC had become virtually a deserted child of the government. Against this backdrop I could have just sat pretty, marking my time to walk out. I studied the financial health of the Corporation at length and got convinced that given a chance and with a little backing of the government it would be possible to make it self-sufficient. Corporation being a public sector undertaking had certain advantages which if properly utilised would bring dividends for the organization and I decided to (a) place the facts relating to the financial position of the Corporation and the likely prospects before the government and (b) to initiate some concrete measures on an experimental basis to prove their viability.

The Central Institute of Road Transport based in Pune was requested to form a working group to examine the above premises and submit its report. The Director of the institute, a dynamic and resourceful man, readily responded, and after a great deal of deliberations we formulated the following basic parameters for future operations by OSRTC.

1. With private operation mushrooming in the coastal region, OSRTC should withdraw its operations from the area and operate in the districts of Koraput, Kalahandi, Phulbani, Balangir, Sundargarh and

Sambalpur, comparatively backward areas in western and southern Orissa.

2. The Corporation which would be given preferential treatment on the nationalised routes should operate exclusively on the Cuttack-Berhampur, Cuttack-Sambalpur and Cuttack-Rourkela corridors.
3. The Inter-state routes to West Bengal, Madhya Pradesh and Andhra Pradesh should be exclusively operated by OSRTC.

I sent the report to the Transport Minister who immediately sent it to Chief Minister for discussion in a Cabinet meeting. The Cabinet discussed the report and formed a Cabinet Sub Committee to formulate a transport policy. I was the convenor of the committee. Now I had to see that the proceedings of the Cabinet Sub Committee were conducted with utmost dispatch. I ensured that all the meetings were held in my office chamber in Bhubaneswar and after four to five sittings the consensus views which were mostly the same as the recommendations of the study group were formulated and I drafted the report which was signed by the ministers.

Pending consideration of the report by the government, it became imperative to show some result on an experimental basis. Transport Commissioner SC Hota was more than willing to help. We decided to take over the Cuttack-Berhampur corridor where the private operators were running on temporary permits. Hota did not renew the permits and handed over the route to OSRTC by issuing 50 permits. We ran a bus from Bhubaneswar to Cuttack and vice versa every half an hour. A monitoring group was located midway at Balugaon to ensure that the buses were plying as per schedule. The Transport Commissioner also put an enforcement team to check unauthorised operation by private operators.

To say the least, the experiment was a huge success. Cash was flowing to the coffers of OSRTC every day. What was remarkable was the performance of the motivated OSRTC staff. Corruption, embezzlement, malpractice, the tag of notoriety which the staff had carried on their shoulders was washed off.

I did not remain to pursue the recommendations of the Cabinet Sub Committee to their logical end. RM Patnaik, who was heading the State Vigilance, developed cardiac trouble and had to take leave and rest. In his absence, Amulya Patnaik (1964) was in charge. I was posted as IG Vigilance in June 1993 and Amulya came to OSRTC.

My one year tenure in the OSRTC was physically and mentally very taxing. You name a problem and it was staring at you in OSRTC—financial crisis, human resource, trade unionism, corruption. It was marching from one problem to another. As a result, my blood pressure shot up. Earlier, in 1988, it suddenly went up with a bleeding nose when I was in Nepal with my wife, Bhujabal, and his wife on a visit. Then it had become normal. Now I started taking medicines to keep my BP under control.

Chapter-26

State Vigilance Chief: Razor's Edge

I joined Vigilance as its chief in the rank of IG in mid-1993 and soon thereafter was promoted to the rank of Additional DG. In April 1994, I was promoted to the rank of DG Police and continued in the Vigilance organization. PC Ratho the DG Police retired in October 1992 and was succeeded by SC Misra, a 1959-batch officer bypassing his senior batchmate RN Mohapatra although the latter had the backing of some senior and powerful ministers in the Cabinet.

As I climbed the ladder in the police hierarchy, one unedifying and disconcerting phenomenon I noticed was the widening gulf in interpersonal relationship. People with whom you were friends in the early days, spending hours in the ambience of sundowners, start becoming formal, aloof, cautious, distant and, in some cases, hostile. Spontaneity gives in to artificiality, frankness to make believe and in some cases undercutting. This is the tragedy of the services and I felt it was more marked in IPS. One of the reasons could be non-availability of the so-called good and prestigious posts leading the incumbents of other posts to feel neglected and ignored.

There are many areas in police like communication, armed wing, crime records bureau, human rights which provide crucial support to the police and the duties of the incumbent chiefs of these areas in no way can be treated as marginal. Similarly, outside the police, when the IPS officers demand ex- cadre jobs, an officer posted there must take it as a challenge and prove his worth. My time spent as IG Prisons, Managing Director of the Tourism Corporation and CMD of the Road Transport Corporation never made me feel unwanted. In fact it was the other way around. Every job I took as a challenge and performed my duties with a determination to succeed.

When I joined Vigilance it was hotspot. In Crissa there was virtually a tradition of a succeeding government instituting Vigilance/CBI cases or Commissions of Inquiry against the previous regime, the outgoing Chief Minister being the main target. As a result almost all Chief Ministers after independence, barring Nabakrushna Choudhury, Binayak Acharya and Nilamani Routray, had become accused in criminal cases of corruption or faced strictures from Commissions of Inquiry.

First Chief Minister Dr HK Mahatab faced a CBI case on the affairs of Sirajuddin Mines, Biju Patnaik, Biren Mitra, RN Singh Deo faced Commissions of Inquiry and Nandini Satpathy was an accused in a Vigilance case of disproportionate assets. Now when Biju Patnaik came to power, Vigilance was faced with an avalanche of allegations against JB Patnaik, previous Chief Minister for 10 years, and several ministers.

What was strange and inexplicable was the way Biju started the process that violated the basic norms of a vigilance inquiry, which usually starts with a preliminary enquiry, followed by institution of a criminal case. Biju, the showman that he was, with his promise to root out corruption, announced a house committee in the Assembly that would look into allegations of corruption against Congress politicians and senior officers. The committee was a toothless tiger as it had no power to inquire. It was a gimmick and Biju knew it. The next unconventional step he took was to issue signed orders to Director Vigilance to start criminal cases against JB Patnaik, six of his ministers and several senior officers whom he named.

Frankly speaking, I don't know how I would have reacted to these orders. RM Patnaik, a man of reticence and rectitude, would surely have felt indignant at this. But he had no alternative but to register cases after some sham inquiries and obtained warrants for searching the houses of the accused persons. This was big news as never in the history of Orissa such massive so-called anti-corruption drive had been launched.

Initially, it was all bouquets, but later when the pace of investigation slowed down and the real motive of Biju became known, brickbats started pouring in. The media, which sensationalised the news, had become critical. JB Patnaik went to High Court, first for quashing the FIR and then for further investigation into the case on sound facts. All these developments must have taken their toll on RM who by end of 1992 was not in his best of mind and health.

In the above background, when I joined the Vigilance in mid-1993 things were on a boiling pot. Investigations were still continuing three years after registration of FIR and it was necessary that they were taken to their logical end. It was necessary to prepare a report indicating the progress of investigation into each case and put up the same before the Chief Minister for his information.

For me particularly, it was very important as I had friends and well-wishers both in Janata and Congress and there was every possibility of being misunderstood by either camp. By then Home and Vigilance, which were with Biju, were looked after by two ministers on an informal basis. That was again typical of Biju. Impatient of the nitty gritty of Home and Vigilance, he entrusted two of his trusted aides, Water Resources Minister Bijoy Mohapatra to look after Home and Law Minister Narasingh Mishra to look after Vigilance. They would be consulted in all matters relating to their organizations by the police and vigilance chiefs, but their stamp would not be there in the files.

This arrangement suited me fine as Narasingh was a personal friend of mine and acted as a buffer while finalising the cases which were in their penultimate stages and thus on a tricky and sensitive course. One case that created a lot of tension was the one instituted against JB Patnaik. For reasons not clear, the vigilance had not taken into account the income of his wife Jayanti Patnaik, a former MP, while calculating their income and expenditure and had drafted the final report pegging his assets at more than 10 per cent of his income.

The general norm in disproportionate assets cases was to ignore a case if the assets are less than 10 per cent. In this case, a chargesheet could be filed as the assets had exceeded 10per cent. He filed a petition in the Orissa High Court pointing finger at the Vigilance Department and also government for not taking the income of his wife into account. In the High Court, Vigilance was on the defensive and the court ordered that before submitting final form, Jayanti Patnaik's income must be taken into account.

This amounted to a fresh investigation and we had to move the Lok Sabha Secretariat to get the details of her income. This was quite a difficult task. Uma Sankar Mishra (1968), who later became Director CBI, was the chief security officer in Parliament. He he!ped a lot in obtaining the information and when her income was added, the disproportionate assets fell down to 5 to 6 per cent which was negligible. JB, the main target of the Janata government, was going scot-free and it was my enviable task to prepare the report. A bureaucrat thus lands in extremely delicate situation which needs to be very finely balanced. He gets involved in the currents and crosscurrents of politics in spite of himself.

When JB Patnaik was Chief Minister, he liked me, and it was purely for my performance in various jobs that I held. Now a report with my signature exonerating him was susceptible to various interpretations by interested political groups. In this tricky situation, Narsingh Mishra's presence was of great help. A bitter critic of JB, he was very keen that JB Patnaik faced the court. When I took the report, he read it carefully and realized that nothing could be done and knew Biju would explode. He, however, took the responsibility of conveying the result of further investigation to Biju after which I would take the file.

One day he rang me up to say that Biju wanted to discuss the file. I took the file and went to Biju's office with Narsingh. Biju looked at me and said, "So you have decided to let off Janaki (JB)." I told him, "Sir, this is the finding after further investigation taken up on the basis of the High Court order." He glanced through the report and just signed it.

By mid-1994, another development that kept the attention of the police in general and IPS in particular glued was the change of DGP. SC Misra was being appointed as the Chairman of the State Service Selection Commission and speculation ran wild about his successor. RN Mohapatra, his senior, was the natural aspirant, but there was a strong undercurrent of opinion in my favour. I never looked forward to becoming DG Police by bypassing an officer three years senior to me. There virtually emerged three groups in support of three candidates.

The powerful group of ministers in Biju's Cabinet led by Bijoy Mohapatra with whom RN Mohapatra had established a good rapport took up his case. Pyarimohan, the powerful Secretary to Chief Minister, had persuaded Biju to select me and Biju was very much inclined in my favour. RN Das, the Chief Secretary while not very enthusiastic about RN Mohapatra, would not back me, because of Pyari and wanted to strike a via media by taking up the case of RM Patnaik, one year my senior.

I found that apart from political factors, the other factors that were weighing heavily were the personal likes and dislikes of the people who had a role in decision making .One day, RN Das called me and spelt out his mind, RM Patnaik DGP with me as special DGP virtually in command. Being the junior most of the three, I had no intention of jumping into the fray, moreover I was holding the post of vigilance chief in the state. I told RN Das that I was happy where I was. The lobby of the group of ministers finally prevailed and RN Mohapatra succeeded SC Misra as DGP and this was undoubtedly the right step.

As I have mentioned earlier, the higher you go, the lonelier you become and friendships fall apart. RN Mohapatra, with whom I had very good relation and for whom I went out of my way during the deliberations of the GB Patnaik Commission, had suddenly turned his back on me and during the developments which culminated in his becoming DGP, he totally switched me off. Obviously, he saw in me a potential threat. But that day was not far off. Biju, who came to power with a massive mandate, was losing ground although he took some bold decisions to improve the lot of the people. By one stroke of pen he increased the number of districts from 13 to 30 for providing better and easier accessability for people to the district administration. This well-intentioned scheme could not be implemented properly due to scarcity of funds for building infrastructure and dearth of human resource. Suddenly, there was a crisis in IAS and IPS. It was not possible to find junior- and middle-level officers to become Collectors and SPs.

Yet another decision that signified his foresight was empowerment of women. He ordered 33 ½ per cent reservation for women in all services including police and 50 per cent reservation in all panchayat bodies. His obsession with heavy industries, particularly steel plants, proved counterproductive. While the two sectors in IT and Tourism in which Orissa had promise and potential and were rightly highlighted by J B Patnaik in the early eighties remained neglected, his all-out efforts to start a second mega steel plant at Jajpur with much fanfare ended in a whimper. His desire to be a key player in national politics kept him busy in Delhi with Orissa Bhavan becoming the hub of all confabulations in the then quicksand of national politics.

Elections were held in March 1995. Biju was very hopeful of a comeback, but got a drubbing in the elections. Of the 147 assembly seats, Congress, which had won only 10 in 1990, won 80 seats and staged a comeback. Then choosing the Chief Minister became a tough task for the party high command which had decided to keep JB Patnaik out. He did not even contest the elections. The favoured candidate was Giridhari Gamang, a former Union minister. But Basant Biswal, who was close to JB in the eighties and then fell out with him, was a formidable aspirant. He had huge money power, but was not acceptable to all sections of the Congress because of his high and mighty behaviour.

JB, the deft politician that he was, struck a deal with Basant Biswal in which the five-year term would be equally held by both as Chief Minister, keeping Gamang out of the reckoning. Biswal agreed and JB was elected leader of the Legislature Party. He was sworn in as Chief Minister with two Deputy Chief Ministers—Basant Biswal and Hemanand Biswal from Western Orissa. Later JB forgot the commitment, raising the pitch of hostility between him and Basant Biswal to a new high.

In the new dispensation with JB as my political boss,

I was perhaps holding the most sensitive job in the state as the vigilance chief. He and some ministers were accused in vigilance cases instituted in 1990 at the behest of Biju. JB could have just changed me and brought some one of his choice. I was mentally prepared for that. It would in fact have saved me from a lot of mental tension which was looming large on the horizon. When he decided not to disturb me, I had to prepare myself for the next course of development—would he take arbitrary decisions in respect of cases pending and follow the Biju method of instituting criminal cases against his political rivals. I was determined to see that no fresh case would be instituted on the basis of signed orders of the Chief Minister as it had happened in 1990. The first step of JB was to sign an order employing Indrajit Ray, his most trusted man, as Advocate General, a step which cost him dearly later.

Indrajit who started his political career in the seventies when Nandini was Chief Minister was sharp, intelligent and resourceful. From being close to Nandini he had travelled a long way in the Congress party and had become very close to JB. As a lawyer, he was doing fairly well. By the time he became AG, he had become a good friend of mine. My acquaintance with him started through my brother-in-law who was his contemporary and friend. He used to address my wife as Nani (didi) and show respect to me. His engagement as AG I thought was alright without knowing his vaulting ambition. Being very close to JB, he started exercising his influence over various wings of the administration. He took an official accommodation behind my house in Cuttack and the place was crowded with favour seekers.

Usually, the power exercised by the Secretary to Chief Minister as it had happened with Nandini, JB and Biju was exercised by Indrajit. Thus apart from being a constitutional authority as AG, he became the focus of extra constitutional authority, taking crucial decisions in many spheres of the government.

In the above backdrop, yet another angle was the role of Basant Biswal, the Deputy Chief Minister who thought JB had become Chief Minister due to his help. There was no love lost between them, and he would challenge the authority of the CM quite openly, often talking about JB in derisive terms. He had a group of administrators who were loyal to him and wanted to have his finger in all the pies, including top appointments in the state. He was loud mouthed, and would unleash his anger openly. In contrast to such indiscretions of Basant Biswal, JB was suave, cunning, articulate and measured in his reactions. He would never openly criticise Basant Biswal and would keep the weaknesses, indiscretions of his opponents as ammunition to fire as and when the opportunity came.

One of the hottest rumours after JB became Chief Minister was the change of DGP and of course the natural choice was me. But that did not happen. Soon I learnt that RN Mohapatra had developed good equations with Basant Biswal who might have blocked the change. One or two IPS officers who had access to JB had also become close to RN and they might have also played some role. But the overwhelming majority were looking forward to a change.

Following the policy of tit-for-tat, JB, Indrajit and Basant Biswal wanted registration of criminal cases against Biju and the Janata ministers as it was done in 1990. This was a challenging moment for me. I went to JB and explained to him the implications of registering vigilance cases and persuaded him to constitute a cell under the supervision of a senior IPS officer to scrutinise files of various departments, which were under the charge of ministers whose integrity was questionable and start cases on the basis of evidence. He agreed and put BP Saha (1963), who was IG Prisons, in charge of the cell. BP Saha's integrity and absence of political leanings were unquestionable.

A room was allotted to me in the Secretariat and the Chief Secretary issued directives to all Secretaries to make the required files available to the cell. Althrough Indrajit had reservations about such an arrangement, he had to remain silent. Meanwhile he wanted an official status in the vigilance organization. Vigilance traditionally had a retired High Court judge as Advisor to give views on investigation of cases referred to him by the Director Vigilance. Justice Gopal Swamy, a retired judge of the High Court, was the Legal Advisor. One day, I received a note from the Chief Minister that his services should be terminated. I was a bit puzzled as I could not comprehend the reason of such an order. Justice Gopal Swamy, a perfect gentleman, had another three or four months to go and I told JB to wait till then. But he was insistent.

I went to the residence of Justice Gopal Swamy, forewarned him and casually suggested whether he would resign in the line of an AG resigning in the wake of a change of government. But he declined. Then I decided to delay the termination as long as possible and in due course sent a proposal to the government for the appointment of a successor to Gopal Swamy. I suggested the name of Amiya Padhi, a retired lady judge of the High Court. The file came back promptly, keeping Indrajit Ray in charge of the job of the Vigilance Advisor until further orders. When I told the CM's Secretary, MM Panda, that it would be a departure from the practice hitherto followed in vigilance, he gave me a lame excuse that it was only a temporary arrangement. Later after I left, he became the Chief Prosecutor of Vigilance cases, thus wielding enormous unquestioned authority over the organization.

The cell under BP Saha was doing an admirable job. Each report on a suspect politician was taken by me to JB with whom I had discussion before taking his order for registration of a criminal case. As a result of the scrutiny by the cell, some important targets like Biju, Narasingh Mishra and Dilip Ray were getting out of the net. Biju had enough assets that rendered registration of a criminal case unlikely. There was one case of irregularity. He had encroached upon some government land while building his house, `Navin Niwas', near the airport. But when he became Chief Minister, it had been regularized with payment of penalty charges. We both agreed it would be an insignificant incident to start a criminal case against a former Chief Minister. But soon thereafter, Vigilance hit jackpot when a bank account of Biju was located with cash inflow up to Rs 18 crore. Although the account was in the name of Janata Party president Ashok Das, he had not transacted a single pie leaving the transactions to Biju who was not in a position to explain the sources of the funds, simply attributing them to contribution from Janata. We made enquiries in the Income Tax department, Delhi as to whether the party had shown the funds in its return and found that no return was submitted by the party. There was no other way but to register a criminal case.

After scrutiny of files, criminal cases were registered against some former ministers and the process of investigation started. Biju, with his flamboyance, took every opportunity to attract media attention. One morning, a rumour was circulated from his residence that vigilance was going to arrest him. The media in Bhubaneswar became inquisitive and started fishing out news. When I reached office, Biju rang me and told me, "Tripathy, I am waiting to be arrested by your people." I was surprised and told him, "There is no move to arrest you." However, I had to cross check with the Chief Minister who also expressed his surprise.

Talk of change of DGP never abated. Frequent telephone calls on the subject became an irritant to me. By then I was convinced it was Basant Biswal who had blocked the change. Left to him, JB would have signed the order much earlier. He had brought RK Bhujabal (1963 IAS) who had fallen out of favour in Biju's regime and gone to Delhi as Special Secretary, Agriculture, as Chief Secretary. Biswal did not object.

From people who were close to Basant Biswal and were my friends and well-wishers, I came to know the factors that were going against me in becoming the police chief. They were (1) my closeness to Pyari Mohan, the powerful secretary of Biju Patnaik who would know all secrets from me (2) my lack of experience in police as I had not held the charge of a range as DIG and did not have Intelligence background necessary for a police chief and (3) my drinking. Each had an element of truth, spiced up with malicious lies.

I told Pyari, he was the albatross round my neck in a lighter vein. Earlier I have mentioned that my prolonged absence from mainstream Police for which JB Patnaik was responsible in good measure and my good work in non-police posts I held were now going against me. As regards drinking, I was only a social drinker, never have I taken drinks at home alone. I could know that Basant Biswal was briefed in the above line by some police officers who I knew were jealous of me. My well-wishers persuaded me to meet JB and lay bare the truth. I met JB and raised all the points held against me, reminding him that he was responsible for giving me two non-police assignments and the sheer bluffs the malicious propaganda contained.

Since, I knew his mind I did not expect an answer. One fine morning, Bhujabal rang me to say that he had received a note from the Chief Minister for issue of government order appointing me as the Director General of Police, marking the beginning of the end of my police career.

Chapter-27

State Police Chief: A High, A Scandal, and Denouement

I joined as Director General of Police, Orissa on November 16, 1995. My wife was away in Delhi with my elder daughter Padmini whose husband was serving there. My younger daughter Anuradha was pursuing her PG course in the Delhi School of Economics.

I took over my assignment with tremendous goodwill from all ranks of police, politicians, administration and discerning public. When I joined as DG, JB Patnaik was not enjoying unfettered powers as he was in the eighties. With Basant Biswal as the alternative focal point and with a mind to rundown JB, the political atmosphere had changed drastically. Biswal managed to get two key portfolios, Finance and Water Resources. While with one he could pull the purse strings of all departments, the other with its largest budget was flowing with money. He would not hesitate to prick JB at the slightest opportunity. Seeing the cold war between the titans, the other Deputy Chief Minister, Hemanand Biswal, wanted to make his presence felt by joining issue with JB once in a while.

My predecessor had provided excessive security to Biswal which he was not entitled to, ignoring the other Deputy Chief Minister. Within a few days of my joining, Hemanand demanded the same scale of security as the other Deputy CM. He rang me up several times till I told him to obtain government order for what he wanted.

Basant Biswal wanted that officers from all departments should pay court to him in his residence. He expected the same from me. I paid him a courtesy call and did not repeat my rounds to his residence which was next to the CM's residence. This only added to his anger. I was advised by my colleagues to keep him in good humour which I was not prepared to do by visiting him now and then and listening to his ranting against JB. I had to devise other methods to get funds from Finance.

Then of course there was Indrajit, the powerful Advocate General with tremendous clout in the affairs of the state. He had managed to ingratiate himself with Basant Biswal who earlier used to fume and fret at his sight. Indrajit made no secret of his proximity to JB and vice versa. In fact, JB during his visits to Cuttack used to drop in his house occasionally when I would also be called, some time for official discussion. JB, who was averse to drinking, would not mind our imbibing a few drinks. JB's powerful Secretary in the eighties S B Mishra now was the Additional Chief Secretary, still JB's trusted man in administration. In the above backdrop of different actors in position I started functioning as DGP.

After I left vigilance, the post of vigilance chief was downgraded and Uma Sankar Mishra (1968) was appointed as IG and Director. As he was out of the state during change of police chief, I remained in additional charge for a few days. It was either on November 18 or 19 when I was sitting in my old office in vigilance clearing files that I received a call from my Spl. IG Administration Anadi Sahu informing me that firing had taken place in Puri during JB's visit, killing three people. The crowd was on the rampage, attacking the Town Police Station on the main road and destroying property, setting fire to shops. The first acid test for a so-called "inexperienced" DGP was mockingly before me.

I asked Anadi to proceed to Puri immediately with additional force, telling him that I would soon be joining him. I came to my residence, changed to my uniform and proceeded to Puri. By the time I reached Puri, the town presented a ghostly look. Anadi had taken charge of the situation, posted pickets in strategic places and people were being warned over mike against hooliganism. The police station was surrounded by people in spite of promulgation of Sec 144 CrPC demanding suspension of the SP whom they blamed squarely for the unfortunate events.

JB had returned to Bhubaneswar and was in touch with me. He was also a bit worked up as the Assembly was in session and next day he would face fireworks. After talking with Anadi and the Collector, I suggested to JB to announce liberal financial help for the victims' families and institution of a Commission of Inquiry to bring down the heat. On SP's suspension I evaded the issue, for suspending him in my first encounter with a law and order situation was something I was not prepared for.

By the time I returned to Cuttack, it was well past midnight. JB, still awake, rang me and asked me to come to his residence before 10 am with a report so that he would make a statement in the Assembly. Report writing was completed early next morning and I proceeded to JB's residence to brief him. He had to take on a furious Opposition who disrupted the proceedings of the House. The impasse continued in the afternoon. By that time, several Janata MLAs had decided to proceed to Puri under the leadership of Biju Patnaik to fish in troubled waters.

After lunch, I went to the assembly and when I was going to JB's chamber, I saw Biju coming from the opposite direction. I could have avoided him, but I did not. When we came face to face and I wished him, he told me, "Tripathy this is your first contribution to the people of Orissa on becoming DG." That left me speechless. He did not stop to listen to me and walked away. This was Biju, who, when I called on him three days earlier, an act most serving DGs would think twice before doing, keeping of course JB informed, had wished me good luck, who a little over a year earlier had almost made up his mind to appoint me as DGP and had made light of the situation by telling me in a lighter vein: "You look too young to be DG Police." But this was also politics and in the changed scenario, he was certainly right. My detractors, who had also become prophets of doom, got a great opportunity at baiting me.

A popular Oriya proverb whose meaning is "before entering the house the head has hit the door" circulated in the rumour mill. I entered the house and there was no other incident of firing till I exited two years later.

My first task on becoming DGP was to get adequate funds from the government to fill the gap in crucial areas of district police administration. The previous ministry somehow or other had not taken due care as a result of which there were deficiencies in all areas. Due to non-availability of fuel police vehicles in districts, and police stations had come to a standstill, telephone connections were cut off due to non-payment of bills, supply of uniform to police personnel was inadequate, even stationery was not available in the police stations. In such circumstances, how do we expect the police to deliver, to be responsive and proactive.

Pending major areas, we decided to make police self-sufficient in the flow of funds for basic housekeeping and running the establishment. I was lucky to have SC Hota (1968 IAS), a positive-minded officer as Home Secretary. He had implicit trust in me and that was mutual. I had the added advantage of having RK Bhujabal, my classmate, as Chief Secretary. The Chief Minister was of course fully supportive. Thus it was possible, to a great extent, to counter the negative mindset of the Finance Department. By the end of the financial year, we ensured that in all the crucial areas of logistics, self-sufficiency was attained. In fact, there was so much of money for motor vehicles, fuel, telephone and miscellaneous charges that SPs either surrendered funds or gave advance for the next financial year.

A police chief has to decide his style and strategy of functioning. If he is office bound and takes all decisions by himself he is most likely to falter. That would mean there is trust deficit between him and his subordinate staff and, bogged down to office, he is not in a position to play a role in the larger police perspective. It can be argued that police being one of the oldest regulatory departments, it functions within well-defined parameters and there is not much scope to go beyond, and all that police needs to do is to enforce rule of law.

This core value of police remains and will remain unquestionable. But we have to admit that the concept of rule of law is becoming wider and more extensive, in tune with the pace of development. And it is the duty of police leaders to see that the police, apart from being known as a regulatory department, also becomes a development department through a process of evolving. This was the theme of a UNESCO seminar held in Delhi in the eighties, where I was invited as an observer, where there was no second opinion that the tempo of development can be kept up when there is peace in the area, which is the responsibility of the law enforcements agencies, mainly police. For enforcing rule of law, the instruments have become sophisticated and if we neglect this area of modernizing our logistics police will continue to languish.

Then comes the crucial issue, who will enforce, policemen, without housing, without proper educational facilities for their children, without healthcare and facilities that a man looks forward to? Managing these human resources is a tough task and a challenge that the police chief will have to face by having the courage and conviction to articulate the feelings and aspirations of his men before authorities. Right from the early days of my career, I was lucky to have developed the attitude of a welfare-oriented policeman. My participation in various police welfare schemes while I was in police headquarters had strengthened the resolve to put police welfare on the top of my agenda.

After discussing with my staff officers, we decided to call a press conference and put the picture of police in Orissa in proper perspective. It was not to be a forum to complain against the government though I feared such a perception. I called a press conference and, along with my staff officers and others, gave an outline of the complex job before the police and the need to augment our human and logistic resources.

It was perhaps a first-of-its-kind press conference although police chiefs have held many press meets on specific issues earlier. The press conference hit the headlines next day in all newspapers, and with the exception of one Engilsh and an Oriya daily, all the papers presented the news in a positive perspective. The correspondent of Hindustan Times wrote: "Bureaucrats in the Secretariat are taking serious view of the press conference held by DGP." To say the least, this was wildly off the mark. As apprehended, Basant Biswal took exception to the press meet and asked me what authority I had in speaking what I spoke. I said, as the police chief I had full authority to meet the press to highlight the issues and there was no sense of complaint against the government but to make political authorities aware of our problems.

The Chief Minister said nothing to me, in fact he announced a slew of measures that included: a) augmentation of PS staff by four constables in two phases; b) sanction of 10,000 Gram Rakshis at the rate of 2,000 a year; c) sanction of one additional platoon of armed police in each district; d) sanction of eighth battalion armed Police in Berhampur; e) Raising the grant in aid to Police Welfare Fund from Rs 3.50 lakh to Rs 10 lakh a year. I had mentioned in the press meet that Orissa Police had one of the lowest budgets in the country and in all fairness it should be at par with states like Kerala and Haryana where the annual police budget was Rs 250 crore. Budget of Orissa Police in 1995-96 at Rs 177 crore became Rs 240 crore in 1997-98

There were several associations in police, each with its own agenda. The constables, sepoys of armed wing and havildars had an association with substantial clout with government. Officers of the ranks of ASI, SI, and Inspector had Orissa Police Association with equal measure of influence. The OPS Association had Deputy Superintendents and Additional Superintendents as members. Then there was IPS Association. Leaving aside pay, other demands of the constables, sepoys and havildars association on hike of duty allowance, transport allowance, standard in uniform, healthcare, etc were acceded to by the Chief Minister. After the bonanza, they put me on a high pedestal.

The OP Association which was indebted to Biju Patnaik for conferring gazetted status on the Inspectors was somewhat discomfited with JB. It is this Association whose members form the bulwark of policing, investigation of cases, collection of intelligence and maintenance of law and order and who make or mar the image of police

It was known that I would not turn my eyes away from

acts of misdemeanour. Their president, who was close to my predecessor, had become a critic of mine. But in the face of the avalanche of goodwill, his criticism did not cut any ice. In fact, nobody took notice of it. One major issue of tension between the OP Association and police headquarters was direct recruitment of DySP, which was discontinued in 1977. It was purely a populist measure whose consequences the police leaders ignored knowingly and which had started weighing heavily on us. Successive DGs did send proposal to the government to reintroduce the system, but again bowing to populism, did not follow it up. It was only BK Panigrahi, who had written very strongly to the government urging restoration of the practice.

I was an open advocate of direct recruitment of DySP and followed it with the government in a determined manner. Instead of taking any unilateral decision, I started a process of dialogue which was conducted by BB Mishra, Special IG admn and Gopal Nanda, DIG. We had to take care of the stagnation in the rank of SIs, which became one of the causes of non-induction of these officers to IPS. It was proposed to allow the SIs up to a particular age to compete for recruitment to the rank of DySP.

After detailed discussion with the Association, a proposal was formulated which contained a mix of induction from outside and rank of SI. After several rounds of deliberation, the government approved the scheme and order was issued for direct recruitment to the rank of DySP. I had just retired and the OP Association emboldened in my absence ensured that the GO was not implemented.

It was while I was DGP that the last directly recruited DySP was promoted to IPS in 1997 by a promotion board and I told the member UPSC and others that the crisis in supervisory rank of Orissa Police had begun. Now 16 years later, the system is yet to be resumed, all the posts in promotion quota (59) are lying vacant and the vacuum is unlikely to be filled up in the coming decade. In recent past, due to efforts of successive DGs, the government decided to go in for direct recruitment and although orders were issued, the state Public Service Commission is yet to start the process. This is a standing testimony of how a populist political decision under pressure from an Association could virtually paralyse the senior hierarchy in police.

The biggest challenge ahead of me was the Nabakalebar festival, coterminus with the annual Rath Yatra in Puri. This festival comes in the year in which there are two Asadhas (Hindu month). It was last held 1977 and was due to be held in 1996 after 19 years. During the festival the wooden bigrahas (idols) of Lord Jagannath, Balabhadra and Devi Subhadra are changed by new ones made of a particular timber located at a particular spot that would be indicated by the chief priest (Daitapati). This ritual starts on a specified date and three teams leave Puri in three different directions to locate the timber and the statues are made ready before car festival when the Darubramha (essence) of the Lords is brought from the navel and installed in the new deities.

While during the normal car festivals the strength of the crowd varies between six and eight lakh, it was expected to be double during the Nabakalebar in 1996 calling for police arrangements on a much larger scale. Related issues like road, sanitation, healthcare and accommodation needed similar attention. In 1977 the wheels of the chariots cracked, leading to chaos and confusion during the festival. A commission of inquiry was set up to look into the lapses in the arrangements. In fact there was a history of some mishap in every Nabakalebara in the 20th century and this was the last, with me as DGP. I was keeping my fingers crossed. Basant Biswal got an opportunity to suggest to the Chief Minister that in view of the enormity of the situation I should be changed, if not permanently, temporarily and a more experienced officer posted as I would not be able to manage. JB, of course, did not listen.

With Anadi Sahu as Spl IG administration, preliminary arrangements had been started for the festival. He took voluntary retirement, joined Congress to contest the parliamentary elections to be held in May 1996. He was succeeded by BB Mishra (1967), a dedicated officer, methodical and systematic in his approach. The other IG post was filled up by Prafulla Mishra (1970) on promotion. Both the officers in my office proved to be invaluable assets to me in the ensuing days. Puri had a competent Collector in Suresh Mohapatra, SP SK Pradhan was equally competent.

Successful conduct of the Rath Yatra depends to a very great extent on the cooperation the administration receives from the priests, who can do and undo things. In one of the previous Yatras, the idol of Lord Jagannath just refused to move, which people ascribed to divine anger. Biju Patnaik who was Chief Minister prostrated before the Lord begging him to move. So did DGP. In fact it was sheer mischief on the part of the sebayats.

One good thing was the excellent equation JB had with many sebayats. So was Prafulla who knew many priests personally and brought them closer to me which would help us avoid any confrontation with them. It is they who would ensure timely performance of the numerous rituals preceding the installation of the new deities and car festival. Several items required for the rituals are brought from predetermined places and sources. And it is here that the temple administration falters, failing to coordinate the various activities relating to the rituals of the Lords. After discussion with the CM, we decided that an officer of DIG rank would take up this responsibility and act in close cooperation with the temple administration and the priests.

There is now only one king in India, i.e. at Puri. He is called Gajpati who presides over all activities of the temple. He is also the chairman of the temple administration. Historically, it was the Gajapati who had ruled Orissa and carved out a huge kingdom, stretching from the border of Bengal to Andhra Pradesh. After the British occupied Orissa in the beginning of the 19th century, they allowed the Gajapati to continue as the spiritual head of the temple. There is much folklore concerning the Gajapati, a famous one being his role as a sweeper. Although he was the king of a large kingdom, he has to sweep the platforms of all the three chariots on the day of Rath Yatra.

Apart from crowd control, which meant regulating the crowd by maintaining a continuous flow, the challenging task was regulating traffic on the Cuttack–Puri Road. The endless stream of vehicles would include the cars of VVIPs, some of whom would throw tantrums at the police demanding priority in movement. For this tough and delicate task, we chose two brilliant officers, Gopal Nanda, DIG in overall charge of traffic, and Abhay, SP, in Puri town.

After several visits to Puri, numerous deliberations and discussions with the district and temple administration, priests and Chief Minister, who was personally involved, a document on police arrangements was drawn which I was told later remained as the model document for several years. Timber was brought from the designated places in ceremonial processions for making of the idols which had to be completed before the Rath Yatra, which fell in the third week of June.

Camp arrangements that included the management of the massive human resource needed careful attention. Accommodation, toilet facilities, food, including packet food for staff on duty, had to be planned carefully. For senior officers on duty, who were many, it was decided to start a mess in a separate building instead of depending on Puri Police. Many snide remarks were often heard about lavish camp arrangements for IPS officers and I was determined to avoid this at all costs. It was obligatory on the part of all senior officers to take food in the mess and drinks in the evening on payment.

Apart from relieving the local police of this burden, it created an ambience that gave a boost to team spirit. Sharing food with the DGP in an informal atmosphere with accompanied banters had magically lifted their morale and determination to make the event a grand success. Unlike the usual car festival, where their duties were limited to two or three days, this time it was much longer and to that extent was the spirit of bonhomie and togetherness. As for me, I truly enjoyed the friendly atmosphere.

While discussing the various items of the rituals and ceremonies, we had to face stiff resistance from the sebayats who would not agree to the scrapping of a particular "darshan" to avoid delay as this was one of the occasions for them to collect "Buxis" from the devotees, but, if allowed, would cause delay and upset the schedule. After discussion, the Chief Minister agreed to declare a grant for the sebayats subject to their acceptance of our condition. Then I persuaded Jaguni (Jagannath Swain Mahapatra), the head sebayat of Lord Jagannath, an influential man, to bring a delegation of the sebayats to Bhubaneswar to meet the CM. Jaguni by then had become a great fan of mine and readily agreed. The CM declared liberal compensation for the sebayats and the impasse was resolved.

All rituals and ceremonies relating to the Nabakalebar proceeded with clock like regularity. There was no hitch, no unpleasantness, and no hard feeling which, indeed, surprised me for when such massive arrangements are made slips are not uncommon. On the day preceding the car festival, the three chariots of the Lords, getting ready about 200 yards away from the temple, had to be dragged. This task is usually performed by the policemen on duty.

The IPS probationers from Hyderabad happened to be at Puri on that day and I asked them to drag the chariots to their position, which they did with gusto. We returned to the mess in the evening with a sense of suspense, jubilation and anxiety. For timely performance of the nocturnal rituals, DIG GK Das remained inside the Temple to chase, prod and pursue.

The day of the festival remains etched in my memory, with events flooding me one after another but not letting me down. We came to the Temple early in the morning. By that time, JB and his wife Jayanti Patnaik, a former MP, were already sitting on one of the 22 steps leading to the temple. The sanctum had been sanitised, allowing only a handful of privileged persons such as state ministers, High Court judges led by Ranganath Mishra, former Chief Justice of Supreme Court and some senior officers.

The procession of the deities to the chariots was scheduled at 9 am and I had my first brush with the VVIPs, the judges who wanted to go inside the temple, to obtain a darshan (sight) of the Lords. After discussion, we decided to take them in a single line inside the temple, but before this could be organized, the judges led by Ranganath Mishra broke the cordon and entered inside.

I was so furious that I shouted at the top of my voice, "You judges, this is the example you are setting!" But they were judges and could do what they liked. Prafulla, who was by my side, advised me to control my temper. After coming out Justice Chatterjee, the acting Chief Justice with whom I had developed a good equation, literally hugged me and said, "Brother, excuse us for the inconvenience. Once in a year we do it for the darshan of the Lords".

When I came out to the open, another incident was gathering cloud, and this time the VIP, predictably, was Dy CM Basant Biswal. He demanded right to passage that was reserved for the Governor and CM. He insisted on taking his car on that route to come to the nearest point of the rear boundary wall of the temple. But Abhay, who was on duty, would not allow. He talked to the SP in a threatening tone, but the young SP stood his ground.

His son, who was an MP, tried to bulldoze him by threatening to initiate a privilege motion; the threat too did not work. I was receiving all the information on my VHF set and remarked, "Well done." Basant Biswal walked the distance and entered the temple, fuming and fretting, only to see and hear the other ministers showering praises for the excellent police arrangements.

Two senior ministers pricked Basant Biswal further by heaping praises on the DGP. I quietly left the place and came out of the temple to the police control room. Sanjib Chandra Hota, the Home Secretary, became the object of wrath, fielding all abuses against the police. Then, not finding the DGP, he left the temple and went to the Circuit House from where he sent a message to me through the police wireless to meet him at the Circuit House.

Look at the ego of these politicians! Public service – highly emergent, critical and sensitive in nature—becomes subservient to their injured ego. I told the operator to send a message to the Dy CM that the DG was busy with the car festival duty and not in a position to leave the place.

Barring these two incidents, everything proceeded according to our plan and schedule. The procession of the Lords was completed in time; the Gajapati was awaited for sweeping the platforms of the chariots. The crowd at that time was perhaps at its peak. No untoward incident had taken place. The international and national media were present in full strength.

When they saw me by the side of the Chief Minister, they surrounded me to get a brief on the arrangements made for the smooth conduct of the festival. I thought it was the Chief Minister they were interested in. But they insisted on talking to me first, thereby landing me in a tricky situation.

There is a certain accepted method to estimate the size

of the crowd by dividing the area into various sectors and multiplying them with probable number of people a sector could hold. But over years, this has become subjective. Politicians do not bat an eyelid and blurt out exaggerated figures; IPS officers of late, I find, are also resorting to the same tactics.

Before I could talk to the press, JB signalled me to come near him and wanted to know the estimate of the crowd. By a reasonable estimate it was about 12 lakh. JB wanted me to say more than 15 lakh. I had to react quickly and when asked about the crowd, I said it would vary between 12 to 15 lakh.

The coming Nabakalebar, which will be held in 2015, it is said, will attract 50 lakh people. Nobody will dispute the numbers if the political executive doles out the the figure; the media will hype it, but objectivity will be lost.

After sweeping of the platforms by the Gajapati king, preparations started for the dragging of the chariots – Balabhadra (Taladhwaja), Subhadra (Debadalan) and Jagannath (Nandighosh), in that order. Light drizzle brought a lot of relief in the scorching sun. The three chariots are dragged to the temple of Gundicha Devi, mausi (aunt) of the Lords, where they stay for seven days after which they return to the main temple in their chariots.

Dragging started as scheduled and by evening the chariots were nearing the temple. JB was walking with us all the distance and by evening, when we broke for the day, he was beaming with joy, with immense satisfaction over the fact that the last Nabakalebara of the century had gone off without any incident.

He left for the Circuit House, asking me to meet him there with all my officers. After making necessary arrangements, I, along with my joyous teammates, went to Circuit House to meet JB. He paid handsome compliments to the police for the excellent arrangements done for all the rituals and ceremonies of the Nabakalebara. The prophets of doom were belied and I stood vindicated. We returned to the mess in great spirit and transited from the spiritual to the spirituous.

The remaining part of the journey of the Lords was completed next morning. By then, the swelling crowd of the previous day had vanished; policemen pulled the chariots to their destination. JB was so pleased that he wrote an article in the newspapers titled "Satabdira Sreshta Nabakalebara", highlighting how it was totally incident-free, unlike the previous ones of the century. He wrote a personal letter to me, conveying his great pleasure and requesting me to convey the same to the force. This was different from the usual commendations received from the government, in due course.

Apart from this epochal event, several others had marked my tenure during the preceding two to three months. Sometime in May, there was a confrontation between the lawyers of Bhubaneswar and the police, when the former wanted to gatecrash into the Secretariat. There was the inevitable scuffle which ruffled the feelings of the lawyers who demanded the immediate transfer of SP BK Sharma, a budding young officer.

Apart from the demand, they approached the Advocate General Indrajit Ray, basically a lawyer from Bhubaneswar, who assured them that the SP would be transferred. They also approached Deputy Chief Minister Basant Biswal who also promised that the SP would be transferred..

That evening, I was at a friend's place. In the absence of a mobile phone I was in the dark about these developments. Returning home at about 10 pm, I found several calls from Basant Biswal, Indrajit and the SP. I rang up the SP to update myself about the situation. Then Indrajit called and told me that the government had decided to shift the SP. I asked why and told him that I would talk to the CM.

Then came a call from the Deputy CM, telling me, "DG

saheb, BK Sharma has to be suspended". When I asked the reason he flared up and told me, "If not suspension, he must be shifted." I told him that an inquiry should be instituted and the SP, if found guilty, should be taken to task. This is certainly not what he wanted with all the assurances he had given to the lawyers to shift the SP.

Then he told me, "Do you know if you don't do this, we will shift you." I told him it was the pleasure of the government to take a decision and that I would talk to the CM. I rang up the CM, whom I got on the line luckily, and expressed my unwillingness to shift BK Sharma. This perhaps, I am not sure though, was what JB had in mind and asked me to convey this either to Basant Biswal or Indrajit. I then talked to Indrajit who was apparently not very happy.

Vijay Rama Rao, an IPS officer of the 1959 batch from Andhra Pradesh cadre, then Director CBI, with whom I had built up excellent rapport was due to retire. At that time, the Director CBI was basically a nominee of the Prime Minister unlike the present system of a committee preparing a panel of names for appointment to the post of Director with a fixed tenure of two years.

Rama Rao, an appointee of Prime Minister PV Narasimha Rao, was very keen that I should succeed him. He also told me that if Narasimha Rao won parliamentary elections, he would see to it that I become Director CBI.

Sometime in April or May, I went to Bangkok in a delegation headed by the Director CBI to attend an Interpol conference and he declared this before the members of the delegation. This was contrary to the proposal formulated by the department of personnel whose panel contained the names of officers of the 1961 batch. PC Hota, Secretary Personnel, told me that the 1962 batch was yet to be considered for posting as CPO chiefs. Rama Rao, on hearing this, was unperturbed and said the decision would be taken at the PM's level.

In the parliamentary elections, the Congress was defeated and a period of instability began at the Centre. HD Deve Gowda became Prime Minister and it was obvious that I was nowhere and it was also more or less clear who would become the Director. But speculation was rife and there was a news item in an English daily speculating on the possible names which included me. By then Biju Patnaik had become important in national politics with Orissa Bhavan as the centre for confabulations. It seems Biju read the news item and one evening I got a call from him in Delhi. He told me, "Tripathy, you are listed to be Director CBI." I said it was all speculation and there was no basis, particularly in the changed context. Then he told me, "We will see that you are not appointed as Director CBI." Hearing this I lost my control and told him, "Sir you should be happy if I get the post. But I find, you want to block it."

Srikanta Jena, his bête noire who was a minister, heard this and later in the night rang me and cursed Biju. I went to attend the annual DGPs' conference soon after the Rath Yatra and was congratulated by some on my possible appointment. When Deve Gowda came to address us, we saw Joginder Singh (1961) of Karnataka cadre closely following him. I told my friends, "Here is the new Director CBI", which he became although for a brief period. Next year when I went to attend the conference and also the annual general assembly of the Interpol which India was hosting R C Sharma of 1963 batch, an upright and dedicated officer, had taken over as Director.

I have often wondered why Biju, who was surely large-hearted, told me like this, that too on the basis of speculation in the media. Some Janata leaders told me, my position in the Centre would block his chances of becoming a union minister which he very much wanted. But sadly he could not get a berth in the union cabinet.

Elections for Parliament held in May 1996 passed off smoothly. I remember an interesting incident in those days.

MS Gill, the Election Commissioner, came to Orissa to discuss the arrangements and a meeting of all Collectors, SPs, RDCs and DIGs was held in the third floor conference hall of the Secretariat. When I reached there I saw the sitting arrangements on the main table where the Election Commissioner was flanked by the Chief Secretary and Development Commissioner after whom the DGP and Home Secretary were seated.

I did not occupy my seat; instead I took a seat along with my SPs and DIGs. Home Secretary Sanjiv Hota came and enquired about the DG and saw me sitting with the SPs. When he called me I told him that I would not occupy a secondary position on the main table in a meeting where the main topic of discussion was law and order.

In fact, Sanjiv was not aware of the seating arrangements and shouted at the Protocol Officer for the faux pas and immediately corrected the aberration with the Election Commissioner flanked by the Chief Secretary and DGP. These are the pinpricks IPS officers receive which they have to fight out. Earlier in different contexts, police chiefs RK Padhi and Narayan Chand had defied protocol. Lot of these pinpricks are caused by the minions in the Secretariat.

Biju's pet project, a second mega steel plant in Orissa, did not materialize when he was Chief Minister from 1990–1995. JB on becoming CM in 1995 wanted to show that he could do it. So, hectic activities started for selection of sites and other formalities. He wanted it to be a shore-based plant. Being a master tactician, he chose the coastal town of Gopalpur near Berhampur (Ganjam district), which was the parliamentary constituency of Prime Minister Narasimha Rao who agreed to lay the foundation stone. Tatas were roped in for the plant.

Land between Chhatrapur, the district headquarters, and Berhampur was chosen for the plant. There was considerable opposition to land acquisition which was handled by him very skillfully. He associated me right from the beginning with all the aspects of starting a steel plant and as a result I had to attend all top-level meetings. Muthuraman, the Managing Director of Tata Steel, a dynamic person, gave a boost to the project activities.

The foundation stone laying ceremony was to be a grand affair in Berhampur more so when it was the parliamentary constituency of the Prime Minister. The ceremony was combined with a public meeting at Berhampur and Parlakhemundi, a town bordering Andhra Pradesh and infested by Naxalites. Frenetic police arrangements were made as the visit was sensitive from security point of view. It was made worse when the PM decided to spend the night at the PWD IB in Berhampur, in the heart of the town and surrounded by buildings. His security in charge Shyamal Dutta, who later became Director IB, was keeping his fingers crossed, so were we.

I advised Shyamal to stop PM's interactions at a particular hour in the evening after which we would keep the IB fully sanitized. The foundation stone laying ceremony passed off smoothly. I was moved and impressed to see Ratan Tata instead of demanding a pride of place in the ceremony sitting quietly in a distant corner. That was true greatness. The meeting at Parlakhemundi also went off smoothly. So also the public meeting in Berhampur, except for an incident that took place, thanks to rival groups in the Congress professing loyalty to JB Patnaik and Basant Biswal.

The entry into the inner cordon was regulated by the SPG, which had allowed a specific number of people, majority of whom happened to be JB loyalists. At the last moment, Basant Biswal came with a group of supporters, demanding entry which the young SP Arun Sarangi refused at which Basant Biswal took umbrage. Giving vent to his anger, he was taking Arun Sarangi to task in front of other ministers who were thoroughly enjoying the scene.

By the time I reached the venue in the PM's carcade, I

saw Basant Biswal and Arun Sarangi locked in high pitched arguments. Niranjan Patnaik, a senior minister, told me, "DG saheb take care of the situation." I separated Arun from Biswal and after ascertaining what the Dy CM wanted, talked to Shyamal who instructed the SPG staff to allow a certain number of people.

After the meeting, I went to the PWD IB and with the help of Shyamal stopped the programme of the PM for the day. Giving a pat and instructions to Arun, I went to Gopalpur where I was staying and where my junior colleagues were waiting for me. While we were enjoying the evening ambience at Gopalpur came a call from JB who asked me to meet him in Berhampur. Obviously he wished to convey his happiness. Sensing my mood of reluctance, he asked me to instruct Arun Sarangi to meet him which I did. I knew that JB wold give him a pat.

After the retirement of RN Mahapatra, I became the senior-most IPS officer serving in Orissa. S N Tewari (1963) was promoted and was posted as DG Intelligence, by upgrading the post. BB Panda, who had the backing of Basant Biswal, was becoming impatient. There was a cadre post of DG Home Guards and Fire Services, but Basant Biswal wanted that Panda should be posted as DG Crime, an idea JB did not like, but had to accept because of political compulsions. Panda was promoted and posted as DG crime. I thought that I would be like a cat on the hot tin roof with two DGs under me, Shyam, my classmate, and Bana, one year senior in college, breathing down my neck. But nothing of that sort happened. There was neither any obstacle nor any impediment on my way. Shyam went out of his way to report to me everything, some of which the Director Intelligence had the privilege of withholding because of his direct access to the Chief Minister.

We decided to celebrate 60 years of Orissa Police, its Diamond Jubilee (1936–96), with focus on certain areas. An organizing committee was formed with BB Mishra, Spl IG (Admn), as Chairman which functioned through several sub committees each headed by a senior IPS officer. We decided to highlight three areas of policing: a) police-community relationship that would include a people-oriented police force; b) police welfare; and c) police mordernization. We obtained government approval in principle for the observation of Diamond Jubilee over a period of one year with different programmes spread over the year.

Seminars, symposia and meetings were held at Cuttack and Bhubaneswar and all district and range headquarters to highlight police-community relations with encouraging response from public. A police museum, one of the first in India, was started to store and exhibit historical documents, police uniforms, arms and ammunition and other weapons like sword, photographs and items of antiquity. This was one of my pet projects. Later, I was horrified to learn that the museum was turned into a store. I got the information from a newsman, and on verification I found it to be true. Ironically that was when I was in charge of the Indian National Trust for Art and Cultural Heritage (INTACH) in Orissa and had offered my organization's hand to streamline and improve the structure and inputs of the museum. An Industrial Training Institute was started for providing vocational education where children of the police families were given preference.

One subject that always bothered me was accommodation for our officers, both IPS and juniors, when they went on tour. So I mooted the idea of starting police messes in important places like Bhubaneswar, Puri, Berhampur, Rourkela and Sambalpur. There was tremendous response to this. Construction of a mess building started at Puri. Some young SPs took the initiative and started messes at Bhawanipatna, and Keonjhar. Steps were initiated to construct a building in Bhubaneswar and convert the Addl SP's house in Sambalpur into a mess. The momentum lasted for quite some time after my retirement. Similar facilities were initiated for the junior officers by finishing an incomplete building at Cuttack. For me, mess life was very important as it is the only way in which the police chief can establish rapport with his officers.

Mess life at Cuttack was revived with frequent gatherings that helped the IPS officers to unwind themselves. In my interactions with officers, I believed in pointing out the faults of a blundering officer directly on his face without mincing words and in the evening asking him to join me over a drink in the mess. Mess life remained vibrant which I had noticed during the tenures of RK Padhi, BB Mishra and Narsingh Swain.

Cash reward for medal winners had been introduced in some states and in Orissa that was a long standing demand of all the ranks. We persuaded the government to sanction cash rewards to the awardees of President's medal for distinguished services and police medals for meritorious services, an event that brought jubilation to all ranks. We also introduced a system of award by the Governor to deserving officers of all ranks.

It was decided to bring out a souvenir on the occasion of the Diamond Jubilee of the police. We had to depend upon the SPs to collect advertisements and every pie that came was kept in an account that was operated by officers whose integrity was unimpeachable. A quality souvenir edited by BB Mishra was published.

Police housing was always a dark area with the satisfaction level in Orissa one of the lowest in India. There was a Police Housing Corporation, but funding was a problem. We formulated a scheme to take loans at the rate of Rs 4 Crore a year from HUDCO for which the state government would provide guarantee. The government accepted our proposal but later this was not followed up as, perhaps in the 21st century, flow of central funds increased manifold, in fact so much that the department was not able to spend the money.

My activism in IPS Association activities should have come to an end after becoming DGP, who is not supposed to be its member. In 1996, after the annual senior police officers' conference, the IPS Association had its meeting and my junior colleagues successfully persuaded me to join the meeting. There were the usual criticisms of the government, which included the Chief Minister. All this was part of the game and had to be taken in proper spirit. But same night tales were carried to JB that the IPS officers, particularly some promising officers who have proved their mettle, were critical of the CM and the DG was a passive listener. This was a blatant example of trust betrayal. Next morning, JB rang me and asked if what he had heard was true. I told him that it was a thing that had to be taken in stride, only difference was, I as DGP was present in the meeting. I called two vocal officers and asked them to meet the CM and clarify the discussions.

Show of concern, some imaginative initiatives, surefooted action and a sense of empathy are the qualities which men look forward to in their leaders. In retrospect I think my colleagues were duly motivated and passed on their sense of pride to their officers and men down the line. As some officers told me later, the years proved to be euphoric to the force with something or other happening. In all these activities I was particular in associating all retired officers staying in Cuttack and Bhubaneswar. There was a pervasive feeling of isolation, of being left out of the police mainstream which I termed as the "predecessor syndrome". There is a tendency on the part of the police chiefs to say that things were terribly wrong during their predecessors' time and they had come to clean the Aegean stable. Some also suffer from a sense of being unequal to their predecessors and in the process choose to forget them. I felt that nothing could be a better gift than the blessings of my seniors.

My standing informal instruction to Prafulla, my IG

headquarters, was to contact all retired DGPs personally during any event and ensure their presence, if necessary by providing transport. The effect was salutary and our gatherings were enriched by the presence of retired officers.

The lady spouses of the senior officers complimented our police welfare programmes by organizing several activities in the fields of healthcare, education, building vocational capacity and art and culture.

There was another notable event when, like the Nabakalebara, my competence was questioned by none other than Basant Biswal. A world Muslim convention was held at Bramhabarada in Bhadrak district, where the Muslim population almost equalled that of the Hindus. Delegates from several countries, particularly the Middle-East and South-East Asia, had come and the fact that the situation was very sensitive was beyond doubt. We had taken all inputs from IB and Special Branch into account and drafted the police arrangements. Both my IGs, Bipin and Prafulla, were directly involved in the exercise. They visited Bramhabarada, had several rounds of discussions with the organizers who had made excellent arrangements as for them money was not a constraint and laid down several stipulations for smooth conduct of the three-day convention.

I personally visited the place and satisfied myself about the arrangements. But how could a DG without intelligence background handle such a super-sensitive event, thus spake my detractors to Dy CM Basant Biswal who was immediately taken in.

Two days before the event, in the late evening when I was sitting in my office and reviewing the arrangements, Basant Biswal rang me and, in his typical way, said, "DG Saheb, terrorists have started coming. Do you know? There will be bloodbath." I told him that we have taken into account all inputs from different intelligence agencies and have made adequate arrangements under direct supervision of two IGs.

But he was not satisfied and conveyed his "intelligence" to JB, who was in Delhi. JB rang me at night and told me what Biswal had told him.

I suggested to him that on his return to Bhubaneswar next day he should visit the place and satisfy himself, which he agreed. I decided not to go to Bramhabarada and sent my IGs, who explained the police arrangements made for the safe and smooth conduct of the convention. To say the least, JB was fully satisfied and to cut the story short the convention passed off smoothly.

Basant Biswal was getting bitter and frustrated as the compromise formula to share the CM's chair had been forgotten by JB. He most likely thought that I was one of the persons who was keeping JB's "gaddi" safe and would not miss any opportunity to run me down. Being JB's neighbour he would get all informatiom from JB'shousehold. One day he rang me up to say that JB had put him under surveillance and wanted an explanation from me. This was news to me as I was sure that no such surveillance was mounted on him. I told him he was wrong, but when he challenged I asked him to give me the identity and photographs of the people watching his house and he agreed.

I cross checked with SN Tewari, Director Intelligence, to make sure that Biswal's house was not being watched under the CM's order. Biswal never came back to me.

Then he got a stick to beat me with over an alleged statement of mine to the media in Puri. The souvenir fund amounting Rs 20 lakh had to be utilized for the welfare of the force. It was decided to earmark a portion for a mess in Puri, some for a Kalyan Mandap in Tulsipur Police Line in Cuttack -- a suggestion of the havildars and constables association – and some for a guesthouse for the junior police officers.

An opposition Janata MLA, raised a question in Assembly, alleging malpractice in the management of funds. I had gone to Puri to lay the foundation stone of the police mess when some media persons asked for my views on the Assembly question. My temper was running high at the baseless allegation and I strongly reacted, saying that while there were malpractices elsewhere, this one fund was managed by persons of unimpeachable integrity. My reply was distorted and next day some papers presented my reply in a way as if I was questioning the integrity of the MLA.

All hell broke loose, there was a privilege motion against me which was admitted by the Speaker and it was referred to the privilege committee chaired by Biswal. He was so excited that he rang up in the evening and told me, "DG Saheb, now you know what we can do to you." I asked "what". He said, "We can send you to jail." I retorted, "Sir please do that. If for doing good work and rendering good service, I am sent to jail, I will not mind." The privilege motion dragged on for more than two years after my retirement till it was dropped by the very same Biswal in circumstances in which I had become his darling. It is said that nemesis takes over. The honourable MLA is now neckdeep in allegations of land grabbing.

Time passed and I felt that the wheels of time during my DG tenure moved the fastest. I remained so busy that I hardly had any time to look into important matters of my family, which included the marriage of my younger daughter Anuradha. She had passed MA in Sociology from the Delhi School of Economics and had taken up some projects, mostly on women- and health-related issues. By early 1997, things started moving and her marriage was fixed. My son-in-law Subhasish had just qualified for the IAS. His father PC Panda is from the well-known Panda family of Berhampur. On July 10, they tied the knot.

Our two daughters, Padmini and Anuradha, our very own and very precious possessions, had become part of other families. Subhasish was allotted Himachal Pradesh cadre. My retirement age, which was 58 then, was a few months away, leaving behind 35 years of police life and waiting for the end in its 36th year.

It was on July 11 that an incident took place that completely destroyed my peace of mind for the rest of my tenure. On July 14, BB Mishra came to my office and told me whether I knew about the alleged molestation of one Anjana Mishra by Advocate General Indrajit Ray on the July 11. I was shocked and surprised as I had not heard of it till then. How Indrajit, who was close to me and who on July 10, was looking after my VVIP guests at my daughter's wedding reception, had not told me anything about it.

I rang up Indrajit in Bipin's presence and told him what I had heard, demanding to know how I was in dark. He did not deny the incident, told me it was a conspiracy hatched by his detractors to defame him and the Chief Minister had assured him that the situation was being taken care of by Surendra Swain, the DIG central range. I spoke to Swain, who confirmed what Indrajit said. The Anjana–Indrajit saga had begun, marking the beginning of the end for JB.

Anjana Mishra by then was a fairly well-known name in Orissa for her suffering in the family of her husband. A bright student in college she was married to an Indian Forest Service officer from Sundargarh. It seemed her in-laws tried to paint her as mentally challenged and sent her against her will to the mental asylum in Ranchi from where she wrote frantic letters to her family, her parents, in-laws, husband, NGOs and police to take her out. She was declared sound of mind by the hospital authorities. Since no family member responded to her call, police had to intervene. She was brought from Ranchi and put in an NGO shelter home called Vasundhara. After reaching Cuttack, she filed a complaint against her husband and in-laws and a criminal case was registered. With her background portrayed as a suffering, tortured and neglected woman, she was in the news. Several women's organizations had taken up her cause and her case was the talk of the town.

What intrigued me was the unusual interest shown by

DIG Surendra Swain who went to the extent of taking over the investigation of the case. He had to be instructed to act as a supervisory officer which was only proper. Surendra, who had direct access to JB, did not heed the instructions and JB did not foresee what was waiting for him for giving indulgence to the DIG.

July 11 was a holiday and it seems Indrajit called Anjana over phone to see him at his residence to discuss the case and, according to Anjana, she in good faith went there. She obviously went there after talking to people who were helping her. She was taken to the bedroom where she was allegedly molested. Shocked and surprised she returned to Vasundhara. The reasons for her not going to the police station to lodge FIR were unclear.

By the time I came to know on July 14, she had already contacted the Chief Minister demanding justice and not getting any response she had also contacted Nandini Satpathy, former CM, who told me later that she talked to JB advising him to obtain the resignation of Indrajit, but to no effect. In view of all these backdoor activities and confabulations, I preferred to remain silent for I thought that it would be foolish on my part to talk to JB who had not talked to me on the subject, smug on the assumption that Surendra would sort out the issue. Indrajit was so confident that he proceeded to Delhi on July 16 on way to London which was prescheduled.

On July 18, Samaj, a premier Oriya daily, published the news without naming Indrajit. One week of whispers and murmurs had opened up, and the next day, there was a public outcry. Indrajit talked to me from Delhi on July 18 and I advised him to cancel his trip to London and return to Orissa. But he would not. On July 19 late evening, I got a call from Akshya, SP Cuttack, informing me that Anjana in the company of DIG Surendra Swain, women activists and a host of supporters came to Cantonment Police Station to lodge FIR against Indrajit. He wanted my instructions and the simple instruction I gave him was to register FIR if her complaint revealed a cognizable offence. Having said this I thought that it was time I talked to JB. Luckily, he was at home.

I informed JB of the developments, telling Anjana was right there at the police station filing her complaint. That was the first and last time JB lost his usual cool and told me, "You are not able to manage things," By then, I was sufficiently worked up and shot back by telling him that eight days had passed and it was not brought to my notice and now Anjana in the company of the range DIG was filing her complaint in the PS and in such a scenario what could I do. He was surprised to know that the DIG, whom he had entrusted to manage the situation, was at the police station asking the staff to register the FIR.

Properly briefed, Anjana insisted that the FIR had to be registered as 354/376/511 IPC i.e. molestation and attempt to rape. Indrajit rang me from Delhi to see if the sections could be diluted, but that question did not arise. The drama at the police station continued till midnight and the July 20 edition of papers had a field day lapping up the news. In the arena of electronic media, OTV was the only regional channel but there were the national news channels which covered the incident extensively because of the VVIPs involved.

When I next went to Bhubaneswar and met JB, he was on the defensive. I suggested that if Indrajit resigned, all the commotion would subside and the CM would not be targeted for defending him. But he would not listen. Opposition was mounting by the day in the shape of road blockades, dharnas and gheraos in Cuttack, demanding Indrajit's resignation and arrest. Anticipating what was lying ahead for the police, I asked the SP to see that the investigation was conducted in a fair manner. But with JB as Chief Minister and Home Minister, the public would never believe it. There was a PIL in the High Court for transfer of the case to CBI and the bench was headed by the Chief Justice.

I had good rapport with Chief Justice S N Phukan of the Orissa High Court, who was from Assam. Having gone up from judicial service he appreciated the problems police faced. One day he rang me and asked me to meet him in his chambers which I did. He wanted my frank views about the transfer of the case to CBI. It was informal and unofficial, so I told him that as DGP I would file my objection to the transfer. But my personal opinion would not be against it as that would save the local police from being dubbed as a plaything of the politicians. I also requested him to take a look at the up-to-date police report on investigation.

Justice Phukan in his judgment transferred the case to CBI and at the same time expressed his satisfaction over the investigation done by police till date. That put an end to the public demonstrations and agitations, but the demand for resignation continued.

I heaved a sigh of relief, but it was virtually impossible for me to cut myself off. Within a few days, JB called me to meet him at his private residence in Bhubaneswar. When I went to his residence, Indrajit was there. JB asked me to meet Trinath Mishra, then Director CBI, and discuss the case. I refrained from explaining the futility of such a meeting in the presence of Indrajit, who was looking shaken. I went to Delhi, met Trinath Mishra, heard what I expected him to tell and duly reported to the CM.

The ghost of this case chased me for the next two years.

After CBI took up the investigation several attempts were made to thwart its process which I did not know. The FSL report on the torn apparel of Anjana was sought to be changed, in fact it was changed to suit the defence which I came to know only after my retirement. A Special Branch inquiry was ordered which was rather strange as the Special Branch had nothing to do with criminal investigation. Chief Secretary SB Mishra asked the DIG Intelligence for an inquiry about which the Director Intelligence was unaware. The SB report questioned the authenticity of Anjana's allegation which to say the least was unwarranted. A lady Inspector who was literally acting as Anjana's escort gave a statement that was meant to falsify Anjana's complaint and question her credibility. The CBI team headed by Loknath Behera, an Oriya from Kerala cadre, went ahead with the investigation.

Biju Patnaik died in April 1997 and that was one occasion when our police arrangements went completely awry. He had become ill and was staying in the residence of Union minister Dilip Ray instead of his house. Both his sons, Prem and Naveen, who then never dreamt of politics, were residing in Delhi. Biju's body was flown to Bhubaneswar for the last rites. Crowd was certainly expected, but not in the scale which actually turned up. I went to the airport to receive the body. JB was there. He gave me specific instructions to ensure that the funeral ceremony was conducted in accordance with whatever his family and party men desired. Police arrangements had been made to regulate the crowd at his residence which was just a stone's throw from the airport.

By the time the plane arrived, the crowd had swollen so much that there was not an inch of vacant space to take the vehicle carrying the body. Prafulla Mishra who was at Biju's residence sent me the alarming news that the residence was overflowing with people. We were simply keeping our fingers crossed and praying to God. I with my colleagues inched through the crowd and reached the residence, the body was kept on the verandah for darshan by public. The situation was getting tense with the crowd surging for a darshan.

Biju's eldest son Prem, losing his temper, asked me to disperse the crowd, if necessary by force. Infuriated at his remark, I told him, "You should be proud to see how the people loved your father and you are asking me to disperse them by force." Naveen, the sober one, called me aside and told me to conduct the affairs as we deemed fit. Since Dilip

Ray was in command of the situation, I persuaded him to hasten the journey to Puri where it was decided, the funeral would take place. Being a highly reasonable person, he agreed.

The volatile situation became worse when news came of a plane load of VVIPs, that included Atal Bihari Vajpayee, LK Advani, Chandra Sekhar, Deve Gowda, IK Gujral and others landing at Bhubaneswar airport to pay their last respects to the departed soul. Now it became all the more important to take the body to Puri instead of waiting for the VVIPs, which would mean inviting sure chaos. The family also agreed and by mid-day, the procession was ready to start for Puri.

Before leaving for Puri, necessary arrangements were made for the transport of the VVIPs to Puri which we decided would be in a bus as a carcade would create confusion on the route, adding to the problem of the Puri Police. I rushed to Puri to see the police arrangements. The body arrived as scheduled. The VVIPs also came. Luckily the crowd at Puri was manageable. The funeral pyre was lit at Swargadwar. Next task was to see that the VVIPs who had arrived were emplaned for Delhi. Only after that there was relief. From morning till midnight, running in the scorching sun, with not a crumb to eat, my body had become dehydrated. Next day, I was running temperature and had loose motions and suffered for a week.

Biju had become the symbol of Orissa's pride. Never it was marked more tellingly than when he died. He had all the weaknesses, failings and flaws of an individual. Adventure was in his blood, bravado his forte, but he had a vision for Orissa to make the state rich and prosperous. Politics was the means, but for Biju the politician means became irrelevant, it was end that mattered. He did not bat an eyelid leaving his mentor H K Mahatab; he enjoyed immense patronage of Jawaharlal Nehru, but later left Congress. JB, his arch political rival, gave him the handsomest and most apt tribute. He was "jhadara eagle" — the eagle of the storm.

The end of my police life was drawing near. I was somewhat disturbed by a feeling that the Anjana incident might have ruffled the feelings of JB. But there was no such indication. In me he had found rock-like support.

JB by then had set a record in Orissa politics, becoming Chief Minister for three terms, two successively and the third after a break. He was an astute politician and knew all the tricks of the trade and how to use them against his political opponents. I have served in all the three terms in different capacities and by the time I became IG Crime, my contacts with him grew and became more frequent. When he staged a comeback in 1995, I was DG Vigilance. He chose to retain me as he could trust me and the level of trust and mutual respect grew after I became DGP. He had seen at least four DGs before me. It was said that there was interference in police affairs. During my tenure as DGP I did not come across a single unreasonable request from JB, except of course the Anjana case. He would not interfere in my proposals of posting of IPS officers. Maximum number of requests coming from MLAs, MPs and ministers for posting of subordinate police officers were dealt with by Bipin Mishra, Spl IG (admn).

Apart from being a politician, he is an intellectual of high order with profound knowledge in Sanskrit, History, Art and Culture. He is a writer of eminence, having written and translated some of the finest books. Though not a demagogue, he is a speaker with substance and it is a pleasure listening to his speech which he would invariably finish within the allocated time.

During my tenures as vigilance chief under Biju, then JB, and as police chief under JB, I never felt uncomfortable because my sense of dignity was never affected and I was able to hold my head high.

I superannuated on October 31, 1997 and before that I called on JB. It was morning and he was sitting in his ground floor drawing room with some people. When I entered, he paid me handsome compliments using a cricket term – Orissa Police had a glorious innings under me. Then he called me to the anteroom and told me that he would continue to utilise my services which he would work out after his return from Delhi. BB Panda (1963) was appointed my successor.

I retired at the age of 58 and soon thereafter the retirement age was raised to 60. Some of my colleagues rued the fact that the order came a bit late. For me there was no difference. Had I continued I would have at best continued till the end of 1998. In 1999, when JB was changed, I would have been changed and sent to a side post.

I had prepared myself and advised my family to live like ordinary citizens after retirement. I had seen many AIS officers suffering from retirement blues, finding it difficult to lead a life sans the comforts of bungalows, manpower, cars and other perks. Our transition to `aam admi' life after retirement was not only effortless but also graceful.

A chapter in my life had come to an end.

Part- 7

The Great Human Drama

- 1998-99: Against the Might of the State
- Naveen and I: A Brief Affair
- Foray into Filims
- Ravenshaw University: Despair and Hope
- Human Rights-NHRC: No Ground Connect
- Heritage Preservation—INTACH
- Humiliation in Buddha's Shrine
- Industry, CSR and Human Rights

Chapter-28

1998–99: Against the Might of the State

I call my post-retirement life the great human drama, because I have been a witness to so many facets of human life. My life for more than 35 years in police was in a way an exclusive life where I acted more in consonance with the government apparatus, enjoying all comforts of life. The moment I came out of that cell I landed on a roller-coaster ride for the next two years. I was catapulted to a position of eminence, which some liked and others resented. I became a media hero, darling of the press, adversary of the government, a social outcast. My life was threatened, I was defamed enjoying at the same time the adulation of a large number of people. All this was the fallout of the Anjana–Indrajit case.

The usual speculation about my post-retirement assignment was in the air. Since the post of Chairman, Orissa Public Service Commission was going to fall vacant my name was very much in news. I was sounded to become a member, which I declined. Sensing danger, Fida Rasool IPS (1960), a member, put in a representation with the absurd and ridiculous argument that an officer two years junior to him should not be made Chairman. A group of MLAs met the Chief Minister and made a case for another member for appointment as Chairman. SB Mishra, the Chief Secretary, suggested to me in Delhi to take over as Vice-Chancellor of Sambalpur University. I declined as I was not prepared to remain out of Bhubaneswar where we had settled. Sanjib Hota, who was in the search committee, rang me up to say yes so that my name would be included in the panel. But I declined.

Starting life as a footloose rebel in police, I had finished the last line perhaps as a fairly successful voyager in life. Some of my friends in Delhi advised me to shift to Delhi which was a fertile ground for creative activism. That would have been possible if I had retired in Delhi, now it was not . We planned to shift to our residence in Bhubaneswar which we did in April 1998. My social relationship with Indrajit had continued to remain warm. After my retirement, I found a sudden change, telephone calls were rare and when I rang up I was told that he was busy discussing with the DGP. That was surprising as the Advocate General having frequent discussions with DGP was a rarity. Then I found a certain cooling in the attitude of JB towards me.

When on some matters of public interest I rang up JB he would not receive my call. Then in one or two functions at Cuttack when I met him, he hardly spoke to me. Gone was the warmth that he used to exude only a few days earlier. My apprehension that he was being poisoned against me was becoming true. The reason was one and simple, I did not help Indrajit in warding off the criminal case against him. The investigation into the case by CBI was on. The discovery of the tampered FSL report, a copy of which found its way to a small-time reporter in Cuttack, the source obviously was some FSL employee, had led to filing of a PIL in the High Court with prayers to give directions to CBI to examine all senior officers who were initially in the picture. And strangely, the High Court, instead of passing a simple order to that effect in which case I would have been examined as a witness under section 161 CrPC, gave direction in April 1998 that the DGP should file an affidavit on the case.

The original case took a whole new turn with me in the picture to file an affidavit. This was early 1998 and I was asked to file my affidavit by May. This was big news and the opposition parties, including the dissidents in Congress, wanted to make capital out of it. I was not very happy with this order as I knew it would open a Pandora's Box whereas my statement to CBI under section 161 CrPC would not have become public. Leaders of political parties started fishing in troubled waters. I took further time for filing my affidavit while speculation was running high.

The Biju Janata Dal, which had just been floated with Naveen Patnaik as president, was gaining ground. That was when I came in contact with Naveen after I did not encourage any leader of that party to talk to me. One evening, when sitting in a puja, a telephone call came from Naveen who wanted to see me. I agreed and we met next evening at the residence of his very close friend AU Singhdeo over drinks. A journalist friend was there. The purpose of the meeting was to persuade me to file the affidavit as soon as possible. The future of Orissa politics was writ large on the wall: resignation of JB, a beleaguered Chief Minister, total rout of the Congress in the Assembly elections to be held in 2000 and anointment of Naveen as the Chief Minister. I said I would file it as per my convenience. At that time what intrigued me was the total absence of any effort on the part of JB's supporters in Congress to establish contact with me.

Either they were on the defensive or failed to realize the implication of the High Court order.

To escape limelight I with my wife went to Nahan, a district headquarters town in Himachal Pradesh, where my younger son-in-law Subhasish Panda was undergoing his district training as an IAS probationer. We went to a place called Renukaji and spent more than a week in an IB facing a lake, surrounded by mountains. As I drafted my affidavit, I was torn with anguish with what I was writing as that would put JB on the irreversible path of his exit. We came to Delhi where I gave the final touches, came to Orissa and filed the affidavit in the High Court on September 16, 1998. By evening, there was explosion of news in the press. I went out of my residence and remained incommunicado.

The days that followed were feverish, surcharged with suspense, with allegations and counter allegations from the protagonists and antagonists. The opposition parties, particularly the BJD and BJP, were gloating, so also many Congress politicians headed by Basant Biswal who was effusive in his admiration of so many qualities in me which he had not discovered when I was DGP. JB's supporters cried foul, abused me, condemned me, called me disloyal, ungrateful, ascribed my affidavit to payment of huge sum of money, God only knew by whom.

There were threatening phone calls, which compelled me to go to the Governor and move the High Court for security. The Home department instructed the DGP to provide security and the DGP sent a DIG to me who explained the proposed security arrangements that would make my house a foolproof fortress and me a prisoner. I politely declined and on the DGP's insistence gave in writing that all that I wanted was a home guard round the clock, a personal security officer, and proper lighting arrangements in front of my house.

JB was obviously shocked as he did not have any

inkling of what was coming, total failure of his intelligence machinery. Then began the orchestration of the worst vilification campaign, which was a painful experience for me. I became the devil incarnate, corrupt, disloyal, unprincipled, immoral and what not. The ministers condemned me, politicians denounced me. Retired and senior officers were asked to question my credentials, all in highly intemperate language and tone. One of the first retired IPS officers to file an affidavit to rebut the contents of my affidavit was my classmate and friend Amulya Patnaik, who is no more. He became an object of ridicule for quite some time. The constables and havildars association, which had described me as their saviour, now stated that I was a disgrace to police, so also some junior officers, including the lady Inspector attached to Anjana, under political pressure.

The Chief Secretary and Home Secretary issued press statements rebutting the points made in my affidavit. Frantic efforts were made to find out my weaknesses, the Director Vigilance was asked to find any single loophole, however insignificant, to pin me down. He drew blank. My supposed weaknesses for wine and women were sought to be exposed by putting pressure on Prafulla Mishra and Bata Krishna Tripathy to make statements. They left Bhubaneswar and remained out of reach. Bipin Mishra, who was my Spl IG admn, was asked to question my affidavit. He declined. But the IPS as a whole kept me at arm's length for fear of incurring the wrath of the authorities. Some even thought twice before inviting me to their social functions.

When the Congress politicians supporting JB were showering abuses on me, only one politician, Niranjan Patnaik, a close relative of JB, issued a sensible statement.

I was threatened with criminal and civil defamation which did not worry me much as I had sworn the affidavit on an order passed by the apex court of the state. In the end nothing of that sort happened and the court passed orders, directing the government and CBI to take appropriate action. The CBI started a separate inquiry into the FSL report. The original case registered by Anjana ended in conviction and Indrajit went to the higher court in appeal.

Of the retired IPS officers, PC Ratho was in regular touch with me. So also was SC Mishra. In my time of distress, my IAS friends, mainly PC Hota, RK Bhujabal and Pyari Mohan Mahapatra, remained in touch with me. Two persons who showed immediate concern for my welfare and security were late BR Patel, an IAS officer of 1950 batch who had demitted office as Vice-Chairman CAT, and Professor Bidhu Bhusan Das, my English Professor in Ravenshaw. I was moved by their gestures. While I stood as an outcast, sad and solitary, four persons who dragged me to their occasional drinking sessions were Debendra Mishra, who was State Election Commissioner, Braja Patnaik of IPS, my classmate, Gopal Mishra, a well-known journalist and close aid of JB, and Ananta Mahapatra, who also had an excellent equation with JB.

My affidavit had a cascading effect on Orissa politics. Even in the Congress, demand for Indrajit's resignation became vocal and a time came when he had to resign. Circumstances conspired to make the continuance of JB as CM untenable. A missionary, Father Graham Staines was burnt alive in Keonjhar. There was revulsion throughout the country. It was the last straw. Sonia Gandhi, who I was told had gone through my affidavit, asked JB to step down which he did in February 1999. Giridhari Gamang, a Union minister in Rajiv Gandhi's Cabinet and who had one of the longest tenures as MP, nearly 40 years, became Chief Minister.

My younger daughter Anuradha delivered her first child, our grandson Ankit, in January 1999 bringing joy in an otherwise gloomy atmosphere.

With the impending exit of JB and the denouement

my stock skyrocketed. Political parties wanted me to join their outfits. Some BJP leaders came to my residence with the proposal. Naveen was in regular touch. From being a pariah, I suddenly became most sought after. Basant Biswal and KC Lenka called the shots in the new Congress ministry. Chief Secretary SB Mishra and DG BB Panda were changed. Biswal, who was instrumental in making Panda DG, now ensured his exit. Dilip Mahapatra (1965) took over as DGP. JB was so peeved with me that in a few social occasions when we met he would not look at me. It was only in November 1999 when I had gone to see the super cyclone affected areas with Secretary General NHRC G Gopalswamy and Special Rapporteur Chaman Lal that I came face-to-face with JB at Patkura and wished him to be greeted with a smile and exchange of pleasantries. Thereafter he attended some functions organised by me and invariably enquired about the affairs of Ravenshaw College which was our alma mater.

By mid-1998 I had been sounded by the National Human Rights Commission to join as Special Representative/Special Rapporteur. I was not in a position to say yes as I was in the midst of the affidavit storm which had peaked by the end of 1998 and continued till mid-1999. Apart from pressure from Sankar Sen (1960) and Chaman Lal (MP 1964) to say yes, I received a letter from Secretary General N Gopalswamy to accept the assignment. But by mid-1999 I was struck by a setback in my family.

A malignant lump was discovered in my wife's body. Without any dithering I took her to the Tata Memorial Hospital for treatment. My sister-in-law Shobha Rani Basu of the Income Tax, who was on deputation to the Engineering Projects of India as Chief Vigilance Officer, came, so also my elder son-in-law Vishva Pavan Pati, who was then working in the Central Vigilance Commission. My classmate and friend Bibhudendra Mishra was Chief Commissioner

Income Tax, Mumbai. PC Hota wrote a letter to the Director (admn) whom he knew when he was Secretary Personnel, to help us. With the help of these people, my wife was admitted, successfully operated upon in the third week of July. Then she had to undergo the full regime of treatment till the end of October.

After the treatment we were booked to Bhubaneswar on October 29 by an Air India flight. We went to the airport, checked in, were asked to proceed to the aircraft when suddenly it was announced that the flight was cancelled. We were told that the aircraft would not be able to land at Bhubaneswar airport which along with several other places in Orissa was getting ravaged by the super cyclone.

Given a choice either to go to Kolkata or Chennai, we chose the latter and were stranded in Chennai for the next 4-5 days. Then it was on November 3 or 4 when we could come to Bhubaneswar. On arrival we found a ghost city, roads full of uprooted trees, no electricity, no water, no telephone connection. As we drove home with difficulty, it was apparent that the government machinery had collapsed as even after 5 to 6 days of the cyclone if the state capital was in such a state of paralysis, condition of other places needed no imagination.

As we were settling in our home, which gave a desolate look, the telephone, as if by miracle, came alive and rang and I heard the voice of Justice JS Verma, Chairman NHRC, who said, "Mr Tripathy, we have taken suo motu cognisance of the super cyclone in Orissa. Please visit as many affected places as possible and give us a report in a week after which NHRC team will go to Orissa." That is how my formal assignment in NHRC began.

After filing of the affidavit, Basant Biswal had become a great admirer of mine. Earlier he had threatened to send me to jail. Now with JB, his arch-rival going downhill, he was in great spirits. He told me to give a formal reply to the privilege motion and appear before the committee after which the motion would be dropped. I consulted PC Hota, who had been Secretary Parliamentary Affairs, Narasingh Mishra, the Law Minister in Biju's cabinet and a member of the privilege committee and submitted my reply, which contained my contradictions which luckily I had issued when the news was flashed in the papers. I appeared before the committee and gave my reply which the Chairman and the members heard for the sake of it and the Chairman was pleased to announce that the privilege motion against me stood dropped.

Chapter-29

Naveen and I: A Brief Affair

I have mentioned earlier about my meeting with Naveen at the residence of AU Singhdeo where they motivated me to file the affidavit in the High Court. File I had to as that was the order of the High Court. A rapport of sorts developed between us and our exchanges became more frequent. He was then the Union Minister for Steel and Mines in Atal Bihari Vajpayee's Cabinet. I used to meet him during my visits to Delhi and once accompanied him to the residence of LK Advani with whom he had excellent equations. A coalition with BJP had been formed in Orissa and in the ensuing assembly elections victory of the coalition was a foregone conclusion with Naveen as the leader.

Naveen, younger son of Biju, was a party-hopper in Delhi with no interest in Orissa and people of the state, occasionally dabbling in writing on environment. He was dragged to Orissa politics much against his wish when his elder brother Prem refused to leave his business interests in Delhi. Unlike the ambitious Napoleon who said "I came, I saw and I conquered", a reluctant Naveen came to Orissa, saw and conquered, becoming its undisputed leader for three terms and now a record fourth one.

During my interactions with him he used to enquire about Orissa politicians, more about his party politicians, majority of whom he dismissed with a shrug. He took full advantage of my affidavit and it will be neither an exaggerated statement nor bravado if I say that my affidavit contributed to his victory in no small measure. As we started becoming close, I was apprehensive that in no time the hangers-on would try to poison his mind against me, their weapon was the registration of criminal case against Biju when I was DG Vigilance. This I told him in no uncertain terms. He brushed it aside by saying it was all rubbish.

During my interactions with him I did try to find out his positive qualities. I noticed that there was a certain earnestness in his tone to uplift the lot of the people of the state. Perhaps he thought it was Biju's legacy which he must fulfill. In a series of articles in a prominent Oriya daily on the socio-political conditions of the state, I wrote that he symbolised the hope of people in the murk and filth of Orissa politics. In the aftermath of the super cyclone in 1999, he was closely in touch with me getting all information about the failure of the state government in responding to the warning and chaotic relief operations which became tools to beat the government with.

By the time the assembly elections were held in March 2000, I was a privileged visitor to his house, Naveen Niwas, privileged because while the BJD and BJP politicians would be waiting in the lounge and the verandah to meet him, I would walk straight to his bedroom or the dining room to talk to him. When he was sworn in as Chief Minister, he rang me up every now and then about the portfolios and the likely inductees. Many BJD politicians made a beeline to my residence to request me to put in a word in their favour for a berth in the cabinet.

During those hectic days, Pyari Mohan who was Secretary to Biju, dropped in my place obviously with the purpose of finding out my closeness with Naveen. He knew Naveen who used to visit Orissa once in a while with his friends. But I did not know how close he was. As we were talking, two telephone calls came from Naveen, asking my views on certain aspects of portfolio distribution. Pyari learnt what he wanted to know as he heard my conversation with Naveen and proposed that I look after matters relating to administration while he would take care of politics. I was least interested as I had a premonition that this honeymoon with Naveen would be short-lived and I was not far off the mark. In a few months, the frequency of telephone calls came down, so also the level of interactions. I was not surprised and was happy in a way that it had come early.

Pyari had taken over and ruled Orissa as his alter-ego for the next 11 years only to have a colossal fall from that pedestal in mid-2012. I had no bad feeling for Naveen as I sincerely thought that he, starting with a clean slate, would strive for progress of the people of the state. I have met him on quite a few occasions in connection with work of some organizations with which I am associated like—the Ravenshaw University Development Trust, the INTACH and Western Orissa Forum—and found his response positive.

Chapter-30

Foray into Films

During the Nabakalebara of Lord Jagannath in 1996 we had made a short documentary on the police arrangements, which was aired on Doordarshan. We had also decided to produce a documentary on police-community relations during the Diamond Jubilee celebrations of Orissa Police. But it did not materialise. BK Tripathy, an IPS officer who was the Managing Director of the State Film Development Corporation, was helping us. At that time, I met Soudamini Mishra, a senior actress in Oriya films with BK Tripathy and the idea of producing some documentaries on the socio-economic-cultural life of Oriya people took roots. She knew Gautam Ghosh, a well-known Kolkata-based director, and was ready to rope him in for the venture.

At that time my favourite subject was Kalahandi, one of the most backward districts in Orissa which had brought Indira Gandhi in 1966 following a massive drought, Rajiv Gandhi in the eighties and Narasimha Rao in the nineties. Gautam readily agreed to direct the film.

In mid-1998 he visited Kalahandi with Soudamini who would be the producer and Subrata Joshi, a genial and highly knowledgeable person who had retired as the Deputy Director from the Public Relation department. Being a man from Kalahandi, he would be the nodal point for the shooting team. After their return and discussion and, with my knowledge of the area, I prepared the concept paper and the shooting was scheduled to start after Puja vacation. I also arranged a financier who assured that he would take up the marketing outside India. Then the affidavit mania took over, spilling over to 1999, followed by the illness of my wife, followed by the aftermath of the super cyclone which kept me busy.

Gautam was also not able to spare time. When we were ready to start shooting, the financier understandably backed out. I had to locate another. Shooting was taken up in early 2000. I accompanied the team to Kalahandi and, thanks to Manoj Chhabra, who was SP, all logistic arrangements were made. We stayed in Kalahandi for a week, visited several places and saw the manifestation of poverty and backwardness in a variety of forms. Prime Minister Narasimha Rao had started the KBK Scheme for development of three backward districts—Kalahandi, Bolangir and Koraput. But in 2000, we saw little impact of the development schemes in Kalahandi. The much flaunted scheme of providing drinking water in the villages through borewell was a non-starter as the borewells were dysfunctional.

We saw women in groups digging the dry bed of river to extract some drinking water. We saw people of a whole village with crooked limbs because of high fluoride content in the water without medical attention. We saw hordes of people migrating to Vizag, Raipur, Nagpur and even Mumbai to earn some money after the single crop harvest.

We saw villages only with women, children and the old in the absence of the able-bodied who had migrated; we saw the ground operations of the gem stones merchants from places as far away as Gujarat and Mumbai employing local people to dig earth to pick precious stones and the law enforcing agencies arresting the poor diggers while the rich culprits went scot free; we saw hapless women cutting trees in the forest and proceeding home with the fuel and getting arrested by the forest department for violation of law; we saw schools without teachers, hospitals without doctors and infant mortality rate clocking 115 to 117 per thousand, highest in Asia while the state government figure stood at 80.

We had an animated discussion with PK Deo, former Maharaja of Kalahandi, a long-time MP opposing Congress and famous for a late night brawl with Biju in their hey days over changing loyalty of MLAs, ascribing the misfortunes of Kalahandi to the whims of men and government, not the wrath of nature illustrating how thousands of water bodies had been filled up and the dense forests had been decimated. As he said this, something hit me hard. I remembered the days in 1972–73 when as SP Vigilance, I used to drive from Bhawanipatna to Nuapada, then a sub division, on the roads covered on both sides by teak trees for which Kalahandi was famous. And this time when we drove, the road sides were empty. It had become a big scandal then, but the culprits then enjoyed political patronage and went scot-free.

The film was ready in 2001 and it was sent to the 49th National Film Festival to compete in the non-feature category. It was adjudged the best investigative film and I was nominated for a special jury award. When I received the award from President Abdul Kalam in Februrary 2003, I thought I had legitimate reasons to pat myself for getting a presidential award in my maiden venture. This laurel lasted for some time. I persuaded Bhubaneswar Doordarshan to produce a series of documentary films on human rights. The Director, Baikuntha Panigrahi, readily agreed. I prepared the concept and theme and the serials were directed by well-known theatre and film personality Ananta Mahapatra. I got an invitation to act as a member in the jury for the non-feature films in 53rd National Film Festival in 2006 in New Delhi and acted as Chairman of the State Film Festival in 2007. My journey in filmdom ended.

Chapter-31

Ravenshaw University: Despair and Hope

I have already written about Ravenshaw College. This great institution was virtually crumbling both physically and qualitatively by the eighties due to faulty educational policies of the government. Now there is a lot of debate on the neglect of higher education and fall in standard throughout India. But in spite of this adverse tide, many institutions have been able to retain their pre-eminence or are on the road to recovery.

In case of Ravenshaw, the catastrophic fall was avoidable. It was enjoying a pre-eminent position in the educational hierarchy and no other college grudged it or complained about it. Then came the disastrous concept of declaring some colleges as lead colleges in Orissa and in that list Ravenshaw was placed on par with several other colleges in various parts of the state. The prestige till then enjoyed by the Principal of Ravenshaw nosedived, so also the Director Public Instructions, invariably promoted from the post of Principal Ravenshaw College. The bosses of higher education became subservient to the politicians and mandarins in the secretariat and literally lost their voice.

With Ravenshaw becoming one of the many lead colleges, the staff became transferable and the quality of teaching faculty took an alarming downturn, affecting the excellent standard of teaching that was maintained till the seventies. The other offshoot of this policy was increasing politicking involving transfers and postings. Teachers enjoying the protection of politicians started the business of tuition, which flourished like never before. Many teachers marking their attendance in the college would brazenly advise the students to join coaching classes run by them in two, three or even four shifts, earning huge untaxed money.

Treated as just another college, the politicians played havoc with the institution. Plus II, which is invariably a part of school education, became the starting of college education due to some quixotic decision by the government and the strength of students soared without corresponding provision of classrooms, laboratories, hostel and library.

The infrastructure remained same. In fact, the famous building of Ravenshaw had started crumbling. The roofs were collapsing. The famous college hall which housed the Assembly after the formation of the state in 1936 till the capital was shifted to Bhubaneswar after Independence and the Kanika library were declared unsafe by the PWD. The strength of students stood at nearly 8,000 whereas it was about 2,500 when we were studying in early sixties. Due to the faulty principle of lead colleges, the seniority of senior teachers remained in limbo, as a result government often failed to find a Principal who would last a three-year term. Out of more than 45 posts of professors, about 40 were vacant.

The cumulative effect of all these ill-conceived, ill-considered, opportunistic and populist measures had started showing by the nineties and shockingly there was no sense of urgency or concern shown by the government. At non-official level, Ravenshaw lacked an active and vibrant alumni forum. Then some of us decided that it was high time we came in the picture.

Two articles written by Girija Bhusan Patnaik, who was once the president of the college union and had brought Jawaharlal Nehru to the campus, and one written by me had by then touched the chord of many a Ravenshavian. Girija babu took the lead in organizing a preliminary meeting and I remember ,it was a summer evening in 1994 when we gathered in the botanical garden of the Ravenshaw College to discuss the issue. In the meeting, which was attended by many prominent former Ravenshavians, we decided to first call on Chief Minister Biju Patnaik to ask for funds to take up urgent repairs and constitute a forum to chart out our future course of action. We went in a delegation to Biju, a Ravenshavian himself, who listened to us with great patience. We had taken G C Mitra, then Engineer-in-Chief and Works Secretary, a thorough professional, dedicated to the cause of Ravenshaw, who outlined the urgent repairs that would need more than Rs 1 crore. After taking PWD to task in his usual manner, he readily agreed to provide the funds. He also fully supported our thinking to constitute a forum which we wanted to be recognized by the government. He told us: "Go ahead."

After extensive deliberations, we decided to constitute a Trust that would be the instrument for achievement of our noble objectives and simultaneously launch a membership drive to activate the moribund alumni association. It was yet another historic meeting on July 11, 1994 in the Chemistry lecture theatre. In the presence of a galaxy of former Ravenshavians, bureaucrats, eminent educationists, lawyers, businessmen and social activists, the Ravenshaw

College Development Trust was born in an emotionally surcharged atmosphere.

The founder trustees named an 11-member board of trustees and I was asked to assume the responsibility of Chairman of the Trust. The other members of the Trust were RK Bhujabal, then Additional Chief Secretary, SB Mishra, Chairman IDC, SC Mishra, former DGP then Chairman of the Staff Selection Commission, Sanjiv Hota, Home Secretary, Bijay Mohanty, eminent advocate who later became Advocate General, Samareswar Mohanty, senior advocate who had drafted the Trust deed, Anant Mahapatra, eminent theatre person, Girija Bhusan Patnaik, the inspiration behind and Trilochan Kanungo, Mayor of Cuttack Municipal Corporation who became a member of Lok Sabha and the principal, Ravenshaw College.

It was decided that the principal would act as the secretary of the Trust as that would serve twin purposes of associating the government with the Trust and ensuring better coordination. The deed along with other particulars was sent to the government for approval which readily came. In pursuit of 'excellence in education', while the Trust deed incorporated several noble objectives to restore the lost glory of Ravenshaw, we identified two thrust areas: a) delinking the college from government control; and b) raising a corpus fund to finance some of our activities. While on the first front we were confident of getting government support, in the latter a rosy picture was painted about flow of funds from our non resident Oriyas (NROs) in America and Europe apart from contributions from public and private sector undertakings and countless former Ravenshavians. But that remained a pipe dream.

We started with a bang in our fund collection drive and kept the tempo on for the next 2-3 years, but it proved to be a damp squib. We sent printed appeals to as many NROs as possible in the US and Europe, identified two former

Ravenshavians – Digambar Mishra, a former professor of Political Science in a university in America, and Rajendra Das based in Germany who by dint of his perseverance had gone very high in the ladder of the steel conglomerate Krupps and Dimag, for Europe. Every year when the NROs came to Orissa during their usual sabbatical in December/ January, we invited them and held discussions over lunch or dinner and received promises and assurances which they would forget after reaching their land of adoption. To sum up, the results of our efforts were marginal, there was hardly a generous flow; it was just a trickle and was capped by irony when a cheque of a NRO bounced.

But I must say Digambar in USA and Rajendra in Europe made very sincere efforts in the initial years but gave up. The response at home was also disappointing. It was only the Tatas which gave a generous amount of Rs 10 lakh, thanks to the efforts of Trustee SB Mishra and Nanda Patnaik who was the chief liaison officer of the Tata Group in Bhubaneswar.

In the March 1995 Assembly elections, Biju gave way to J B Patnaik, who also being a Ravenshavian, took keen interest in the affairs of the Trust. We renewed our efforts for a special status for Ravenshaw. By the early nineties, government had conferred autonomous status on some colleges and that included Ravenshaw. But the autonomy was a mockery as other than conducting the examinations, the college had no financial and administrative independence. We were toying with the idea of making Ravenshaw a deemed university and were working in that direction. Principal Prafulla Kumar Mohanty was more than a willing worker and would go out of his way to work with us. He was succeeded by AK Panda, who sent a formal proposal in mid-1995 to UGC for conferring "deemed to be university" status on Ravenshaw.

Around that time I invited CM JB Patnaik to interact with the members of the Trust and some other eminent persons. In the packed meeting held at the Circuit House in Cuttack, JB declared his government's decision to move UGC for making Ravenshaw a deemed university and also announced provision of Rs 50 lakh as corpus as stipulated by the UGC. There was great jubilation over the news. After I became DGP, I remained so busy that it was not possible to keep track of the proposal. At the end of 1997, when I retired, I found that the matter was dragging with correspondence and counter correspondence between the principal and UGC. Three principals had gone. By 1998, there was a need to rethink our strategy.

In January 1999, a UGC team came and discussed the subject with the Trust and college executive committee. The discussion centred particularly on the inadequacies in the college infrastructure, which the UGC had been harping during the previous two or three years, and which the government was not able to make good. In informal discussions, some members thought aloud of a unitary university which the state government was fully competent to start by enacting a law in the Assembly. In January 2000, the UGC expert committee report came, listing various deficiencies which had to be removed after which the college would be given deemed university status. The prospect looked bleak.

Naveen came to power in March 2000 and appointed Prasanta Nanda as the Higher Education Minister. I motivated him to take initiative in the college affairs and he convened a meeting in May to discuss the various issues raised by the UGC and other problems of Ravenshaw. By that time we had inducted Dr PK Mishra, former principal, Ravenshaw College, DK Ray of the Income Tax Service who was then Chairman of the Orissa Electricity Regulatory Commission and Dr S K Sahu, an industry man, to the Trust against three vacancies.

I had been inducted as a member of the college

executive committee, which was headed by LI Parija, former Chief Secretary of Orissa. Parija to say the least complemented our efforts by extending full support. The May meeting was attended by the members of the Trust and executive committee and in the meeting the idea of a unitary university was broached. Now our goal was clear, converting Ravenshaw to a unitary university by enactment of a law in the state legislature.

In September 2000, we met Naveen Patnaik who expressed full support to our proposal. The government requested PK Mishra, Principal Prof. RK Kar and me to draft a project report for a unitary university. We co-opted DK Ray to the group and after examining the structure, constitution and other aspects, prepared a note on the JNU model and submitted it to the government in March 2001.

It was followed up by a draft Act on constitution of Ravenshaw University. By then Prasanta Nanda had been divested of his ministerial responsibility and his successor sat tight over the file. We met Naveen again in 2002 to remind him of his support. Things, however, started moving only in 2004 when Samir Dey, a BJP politician, took over as minister. He being an MLA from Cuttack took keen interest, processed the proposal, and got the bill approved by the state cabinet and the assembly passed it in 2005.

By the time the university became functional it was November 2006. Devdas Chotray, a retired IAS officer from Bihar cadre, was given appointment as the Vice-Chancellor. We all welcomed him, hoping that rooted firmly in Cuttack, Devdas with his administrative background would put the nascent institution on the right track. After the formation of the university, the relevance of the Trust had to be dealt with. All members and the Vice-Chancellor were emphatic that the Trust should continue. The Trust in effect became an effective pressure group on behalf of the Vice-Chancellor. It was also decided to organize an annual lecture highlighting the theme of excellence in various fields.

Started in 2008, the annual lectures have been delivered by Lord Meghnad Desai of the London School of Economics, former Army chief General Shankar Ray Choudhry, telecom wizard Sam Pitroda, former Chief Justice of India Justice M N Venkatachaliah, and former Lok Sabha Speaker Somnath Chatterjee.

I wanted to call it a day in 2007, but that was not to be and I continue to lead the Trust. Devdas, after two years of discretionary appointment by government, continued for another three years duly screened by a search committee. In 2011, the Trust needed an academician, a fact we impressed on the Chancellor and Prof BC Tripathy from JNU was appointed as the Vice-Chancellor.

Now the moot question is whether Ravenshaw will be able to regain her lost splendour. The path ahead has many obstructions, impediments and handicaps. Having been derailed from the path of excellence and fallen from the pedestal of pre-eminence, Ravenshaw is now confronted with many challengers in the form of universities and institutions both in government and private sectors. Coping with that challenge will be tough, but will be possible if the university authorities are given a free hand and full political support, factors that appear to remain elusive.

The Ravenshaw Students' Union was generally a Congress bastion till recently. The ruling BJD now running its fourth term has systematically corroded that base and the internal dissensions in the party, mainly rivalry between two city MLAs, created student unrest on minor issues leaving the Vice-Chancellor helpless. The Chancellor had to take our help to find a solution. Citing the general fall of standard in higher education, there is a tendency on the part of the so-called intellectuals of Orissa to oversimplify the cause of Ravenshaw's downfall. They forget that many general education colleges in other parts of India, which had attained very high standard in teaching, have retained it and some who lost it midway have started regaining it like the Presidency College in Kolkata and Allahabad University. For us Ravenshavians who have an emotional attachment to their alma mater, we wish and pray that Ravenshaw is back on the path of glory.

Chapter-32

Human Rights–NHRC: No Ground Connect

As I have mentioned in the preceding pages, my actual assignment in National Human Rights Commission started in the first week of November 1999 when Justice Verma, Chairman NHRC, rang me and asked me to visit the cyclone-affected areas and I said yes, little realizing the magnitude of devastation the cyclone had wrought in the state. Next day when I made enquiries, I found the Chief Secretary was on leave in the USA, the administration limping without being able to gather momentum to face the huge task ahead.

During this period two other responsibilities kept me engaged. Troubled by the apathy of the State Government towards proper implementation, of various development schemes of Western Orissa of which Kalahandi and Balangir are a part some of us B.R.Patel, Debendra Mishra, Braja Patnaik and me among others sat in a dharna some time in 2002 in front of the Assembly and there emerged the Western Orissa Forum, a pressure group to take up issues with the Government. I functioned as its Convenor in the initial years. In no time we landed into a conflict situation with the Western Orissa Development Council a creature of the Government whose Chairman, a political appointee was spending money like the MP/MLA LAD funds.

In 2005 the Government of India formed a committee under the chairmanship of P.C. Hota former Chairman UPSC to examine various aspects of civil services reforms. I was co-opted as a member and our report containing several recommendations formed the basis of the report of Administrative Reforms Commission headed by Virappa Moily on Civil Service.

Since I had to take the help of the government for my visits, I went to the office of the Relief Commissioner and found him surrounded by print and electronic media. He gave me a simple solution, to make an aerial visit for which he would place a helicopter at my disposal, but that was not on my agenda. I had decided to visit the affected areas by road, whatever insurmountable difficulties lay ahead. From there I went to the room of Revenue Secretary Jugal Mahapatra, a conscientious and committed officer, who later became the state Chief Secretary. I told him that all that I wanted was issue of instructions to Collectors and SPs of the affected districts to extend help to me during my visits. He immediately called his private secretary, dictated a crash wireless message to the concerned Collectors and SPs, gave me a copy. I thanked him, if not for anything, for his promptness.

Next day I started my week-long journey to the affected areas, starting every day early in the morning and returning late in the evening. I first visited the two worst-affected districts, Jagatsinghpur and Kendrapada, where along the coast the high tides in the Bay of Bengal, rising up to 30 feet with a wind velocity of more than 200 km had submerged vast stretches of fertile land, killing thousands of people and animals and destroying houses and crops. Although it was the seventh or eighth day after the cyclone, the state machinery appeared to be in a state of paralysis..

Roads were littered with trees, electric and telephone poles, yet to be cleared. When I reached the Collectorate in Jagatsinghpur, the sight was to say the least surreal. The Collector had not reached the office, gheraoed by victims of the tragedy at his residence. Hundreds of trucks carrying relief materials from all over the country, from several international organisations had jammed traffic, all asking for directions and instructions and finding none were getting restive and agitated. The lone ADM in the office was confused, feeling lost and helpless. A team of doctors from Delhi, many of them Oriyas, thoughtfully chosen by the Delhi administration, were waiting for hours without knowing what to do and where to go. When I was sitting in the Collector's office, a convoy of trucks arrived from Punjab headed by the Health Minister, a lady who sought instructions about the distribution of relief materials which were not forthcoming. Showing her disgust she went to Bhubaneswar and handed over the materials to the Gurudwara for distribution in the affected districts.

In the midst of all this chaos and confusion, the district administration was preparing for the visit of Revenue Minister KC Lenka, the first political executive to visit the cyclone-hit areas after more than a week. I considered it prudent to leave that place and went to the affected areas with the ADM.

The sight on both sides of the ravaged road was heart-wrenching. I saw hapless people taking shelter in high places, polythene which was promised had not reached even after a week, animal carcasses were yet to be cleared, houses razed to the ground. About 8,000 people had died and I learnt that the sweepers employed by the state government refused to clear the bodies. It was in fact the much maligned Anand

Margis who had taken initiative in disposal of the bodies. I went to the port town of Paradip and saw a whole colony of people marooned by the tides sitting under the sun, crying for food and shelter. I visited some places that had not been reached by the district administration and was gheraoed by people. In many places, people wanted to know what the government was doing about their rehabilitation. There was no clear answer to their questions.

When I returned to Bhubaneswar and enquired about the polythene, I was shocked to learn that hundreds of trucks of polythene were lying undistributed as there were allegations of bungling in the purchase. This was a blatant case of trading on human misery. CBI took up investigation into the polythene scandal, nothing came out but people suffered. In Bhubaneswar, I ensured that wide publicity was given to the measures taken by the government to rehabilitate the affected people through print and electronic media. This wisdom dawned on the government after more than a week.

I visited Kendrapara, another very badly affected district, and heard a similar litany of woes from the dazed victims. I visited Jajpur, a district which had remained cut off for a week due to collapse of a bridge, preventing relief distribution. I visited Bhadrak, a town on NH-5, which was flooded due to criminal negligence of the Irrigation staff in the upstream Salandi river barrage. I visited Cuttack where the residents were flooded with the effluents of drains, which was avoidable had the municipal authorities been vigilant. The young Collector was helpless. The fury of the cyclone was such that it had penetrated into the non-coastal districts of Keonjhar and Dhenkanal, which was unusual. Days before the supercyclone, another cyclone had hit the district of Ganjam in the south, causing considerable damage.

Bhubaneswar was the central point of receiving the

relief materials which were pouring in and there was total chaos in coordinating the receipt and dispatch of trucks to different places by the transport staff who were unequal to the task. I advised acting Chief Secretary SM Patnaik to put some police officers in regulating the movements of the trucks, but to no effect. At Patkura in Jagatsinghpur there was another relief camp where I saw the relief materials stacked as high as mini mountains with a directionless staff. The ADM, who was in charge, had reported sick on the day of my visit. Some truck drivers of Andhra Pradesh carrying cooked food materials complained that the packets, two to three days old, had started rotting.

A team from NHRC consisting of Secretary General Gopal Swamy, who later became the Union Home Secretary, and Special Rapporteur Chaman Lal visited Orissa and I accompanied them to some places for the second time on November 17. It was at Patkura that I came across JB Patnaik and his wife Jayanti Patnaik face-to-face after the filing of my affidavit and we exchanged pleasantries.

While visiting the affected places I felt a little uncomfortable that I was not able to participate in the rescue operations which I would have done had I been the police chief. Later, Andhra Pradesh DGP Anjanaya Reddy, who had come to Berhampur with a relief team, told me about the lukewarm response he got from Orissa Police.

A team of Andhra Pradesh electricity staff took lead in restoring electricity in Bhubaneswar and other areas. While they were repairing the line in our area of residence, the state Gridco staff were discouraging them to show any unusual haste. My wife who was standing near the gate heard this from an Assttant Engineer of Andhra Pradesh. Even in crisis, malpractices abound about which I have written earlier, a sense of urgency in service was totally lacking.

Perhaps that is our nature. After all "Lord Jagannath" is there to take care of everything.

My proactive role in the aftermath of the super cyclone had attracted media attention. This coupled with some of my writings in local newspapers had made people aware of the presence of NHRC in Orissa. The State Human Rights Commission was yet to come up. As a result, complaints started pouring in and people came to put forth their grievances. Single-handed it became impossible to manage and a formal arrangement was necessary.

On the request of NHRC, the state government identified the IG/Director of the Human Rights protection cell as the nodal officer and required secretarial assistance was provided to me. NHRC, which was created in 1993, had started with a bang with Justice Ranganath Mishra as its first Chairman. With his good equation with Prime Minister Narasimha Rao, Justice Mishra was able to put NHRC on a solid footing.

In the initial years, the emphasis was more on violation of individual human rights which, when statistically reflected, put police as the worst violator and the easiest target to beat with were the Punjab policemen and officers who had wiped out terrorism in Punjab and ensured the integrity of the country. It is needless to point out that in operations of such massive magnitude and dimension, some innocent people will be victims. The Commission started taking cognizance of the complaints of the relatives of the dead people and put many policemen on the dock by directing institution of criminal cases and putting many behind bars.

In the process, the Commission forgot the plight of the families of the dead policemen. The focus started changing when Justice Venkatachaliah took over as Chairman. The Commission adopted an issue-based approach, which covered not only violation of individual human rights, but their protection in several areas such as health, primary education, poverty alleviation, rights of the differently-abled, conditions in prisons and weaker sections who continue to remain marginalised, neglected, exploited and suppressed.

Justice JS Verma continued with the tempo, suo motu cognizance of the super cyclone in Orissa was a case in point. In a way, the concept of right to food originated in Orissa following complaints of malnutrition deaths in Kalahandi district, which was taken cognizance of by the Commission. A PIL was filed in the Supreme Court, which requested the NHRC to monitor the development programmes in the KBK (Kalahandi, Bolangir and Koraput) districts initiated by Prime Minister Narasimha Rao for a 10-year period (1996–2006). Special Rapporteur Chaman Lal was entrusted with the task.

As many states did not have Human Rights Commissions, the NHRC had a system of having its representatives in some states and, when I joined, the number varied between eight to ten, out of which two were retired IAS officers and rest retired IPS officers, all of the rank of Secretary to Government of India/Chief Secretary and DGP. While the two retired IAS officers, Rao and Medhi, covered Andhra Pradesh and Assam respectively, IPS officers NN Singh (1961), SVM Tripathy (1961), Arun Gurtoo (1962) and Nambudiri (1964) and I looked after Bihar, UP, MP, Gujarat and Orissa I also got the additional charge of Jharkhand, which necessitated my visits to Ranchi and other places from time to time. Sankar Sen (1960) and Chaman Lal (1964) were attached to the head office. It was indeed a compliment to IPS that the Commission, the majority of whose members were from the judiciary chose to select IPS officers who led police forces against whom the Commission received maximum number of complaints.

I not only had a clear perspective of the nature of my responsibility, but also the determination to educate and enlighten the people about their rights and motivate the deprived and oppressed to voice their sufferings. My approach to human rights highlighted their protection in various fields where a man suffers from deprivations and neglect. As a result, complaints came from areas as wide and varied as healthcare, neglect of primary education, malnutrition, poverty alleviation programmes, sufferings of the deprived and marginalized sections of society like women and children, tribal communities, people displaced by big industrial sectors, prison population, witchcraft, infant mortality and many others.

I visited several children's home supported by the Social Welfare Department and was surprised to notice that the total monthly expenditure on a child was less than Rs 250, food, clothing, medicines, books all included, and initiated steps to raise it to Rs 500 and succeeded. I visited some old age homes and tried to redress the grievances of the infirm. I visited as many jails as possible in Orissa and Jharkhand and brought the plight of the inmates to the notice of the government. I visited some of the remotest places in distant Kalahandi, Koraput, Bolangir, Sambalpur, Sundargarh and Phulbani districts and saw the slow pace of development activities, healthcare without doctors, pharmacists and medicines, primary education without teachers and education material, tribal development schemes without staff.

For creating awareness, seminars and conferences were organized either in collaboration with the government or NGOs in places like Bhubaneswar, Cuttack, Balasore, Koraput, Bhawanipatna in Orissa and Ranchi in Jharkhand where the response used to be overwhelming. In all these activities, I had the opportunity of interacting with the NGOs in these states. Many were after money and many came to me to act as their advisor/patron or chairman. Knowing that this would land me in a tricky situation, to the extent of being labelled as partisan, I decided in principle not to lend my name to any NGO and later I found that this stood me in good stead.

I organised a NGO consultation seminar of the eastern states comprising Orissa, Bihar, West Bengal, Jharkhand and Sikkim in Bhubaneswar, which was attended by NHRC Chairman Justice JS Verma. Another similar NGO consultation seminar was organised in Guwahati with the help of Justice Phukan, who was Chief Justice Orissa High Court and then Chairman of Assam's State Human Rights Commission.

Orissa State Human Rights Commission was created in 2002-03 and over a period I found that it lacked the creativity and dynamism of a proactive, responsive and empathetic body. It seems to have started with a predetermined mindset that police is the violator of all human rights and would gleefully dole out statistics to press and in meetings on police brutalities displaying its inability to comprehend the larger perspective on the concept of human rights. This mindset seems to be continuing till today as I find members while talking to media still harping on the same point. No wonder their contribution to promotion of human rights in the state can at best be termed as marginal.

Justice Verma was succeeded by Justice Anand in 2003. The NHRC was involved in several areas of human suffering, like super cyclone in Orissa, the 2002 communal riots in Gujarat, child labour in Andhra Pradesh and Tamil Nadu, displacement of Kashmiri Pandits, conditions in the mental asylums, trial of the under trial prisoners lodged in jails,food security, health care and care of the differently-abled among others.

My term in the NHRC ended at the end of 2006 and, at the end of the day, I felt richer in terms of my experience, understanding of human sufferings and empathy with the poor. While I was in service, I was bound by the shackles of rules and regulations, the years thereafter gave me a deep insight to the real India in her villages. The other day I was reading an article on the hollowness of the Delhi intellectuals -- discussing, deliberating, cogitating and ideating on India in five-star comforts over sumptuous lunches in the day and cocktails at night. I wish the conclaves shifted to remote villages for deliberations under a hot sun in the midst of thatched houses, sitting on a charpoy and eating rice, chapatti and dal.

Chapter-33

Heritage Preservation–INTACH

Currently, I am deeply involved in our heritage preservation through the well-known Indian National Trust for Art and Cultural Heritage of which I am the state convenor. My love for heritage came not by virtue of being a member of INTACH but much earlier during my childhood when I used to be fascinated by the majesty and the grandeur of our monuments, the ancient temples, forts and palaces and the imperial structures.

My visits to the famous temples of Orissa during my school days and the equally famous monuments in North India during an excursion in intermediate college years coupled with reading of ancient history strengthened my interest in our rich heritage. After joining service and acquiring my first new Fiat car I along with my wife embarked upon a road journey to explore the South in 1971. With petrol costing a little over one rupee, the total fuel cost I remember was about 600 rupees. After acquiring my second Fiat car we along with our two daughters covered the North in 1976, beginning from Ranchi on way to Srinagar and then Anant Nag. We were young, carefree and enjoyed every bit of our discovery of the South and North.

When I returned to Orissa in 1983 and saw the pictures of Lord Jagannath being used in a vulgar and obscene manner as the mascot of Orissa Tourism, my sensitivity was deeply hurt which prompted me to write some articles in leading Oriya daily Samaj. In fact, my writing in newspapers on contemporary affairs can be traced to these hurt feelings. The articles that followed were on the old imperial structures of Cuttack, some of which were in a state of utter neglect.

Girija Bhusan Patnaik, a social activist, and Trilochana Kanungo, Mayor of the Cuttack Municipal Corporation, both friends and well-wishers, joined me in successfully persuading the government to conserve three old grand buildings in Cuttack -- the Circuit House, the Kanika Library and the old assembly hall in the premises of Ravenshaw College. I met Nalini Mohanty, the PWD Minister in Biju's Cabinet, who readily acceded to our suggestions.

Girija Babu, who had successfully organised the celebration of 1,000 years of Cuttack, suggested that we take up the restoration of the Barabati Fort. Trilochan readily provided his technical hands and with the help of the PWD we prepared a project report for the restoration of the moat. The State Tourism and Culture Department agreed to participate if we were able to get funds from the central government.

I sent the project report to Srikant Jena, who was the minister in charge in the Union Cabinet. He readily agreed to provide Rs 50 lakh to start the work on the condition that it would be executed by the Cuttack Municipality, reposing total faith in the commitment and integrity of its Mayor, Trilochan. But in the ensuing municipal elections, Trilochan took a beating, and Srikant Jena backed out as he did not have much faith in the newly elected body.

We protested against the government decision to construct a second stadium in the premises of the Barabati Fort. Guru Mohanty, my classmate in Ravenshaw, a well-known PIL activist in the High Court, filed a PIL praying to restrain the government to start work and the government had to rescind its decision.

I had been indulging in acts of heritage activism, often going against the State, while I was holding the sensitive posts of vigilance chief and police chief. To my good luck, neither Biju nor JB viewed this adversely.

INTACH was started in 1984 by Rajiv Gandhi with a corpus fund of rupees five crore given by the Government of India. The signatories to the original INTACH documents were prominent people from Delhi, including Naveen Patnaik. Its Orissa branch was started in the late eighties and Orissa was perhaps the first state where INTACH with collaboration with the state government took up listing and documentation of neglected monuments.The figure stood at around 2,800.

Anant Mahapatra who was one of the original members of the regional chapter formed in Bhubaneswar functioned as the Convenor. Seeing my interest and activities in heritage conservation, he motivated me to start a chapter of INTACH in Cuttack. Girija Patnaik extended all help to me in starting a chapter including the hall of the Universe, his NGO, free of cost. A chapter was started in 1995, with about 35 members, all reputed people in various fields with B K Tripathy, an IPS officer and a culture enthusiast, and Rini Mohanty, a social activist, as the office-bearers.

The chapter remained active by conducting several programmes till I left Cuttack in April 1998 after my retirement. Then it became moribund, which was a bit of a surprise, followed by a lull till it was revived in 2006 by Pradumna Mishra, a former Director of Culture and a dynamic and committed man as its Convenor.

At the national level, vice-chairman S K Mishra, a retired IAS officer of Haryana cadre who was Secretary Tourism in the Centre and was known for his dynamism and resourcefulness, was virtually functioning as chairman as the incumbent chairman, Captain Amarinder Singh, had become the Chief Minister of Punjab. Mishra was subsequently elected as chairman for two terms that ended in 2009. He took the initiative of activating the chapter and sent Lalit Mansingh, former Ambassador to the USA, as convenor of the chapter.

Lalit came to Orissa and started with a bang. A meeting was organised in Hotel Crown in Bhubaneswar which was very largely attended and certainly augured well for INTACH. He involved me and Abasar Beuria, another retired diplomat, to act as co-convenors.

But this experiment did not last long. Lalit was functioning in absentia. Being a resident of Delhi, he came to Bhubaneswar once in a while when some activity was planned. Then the head office for quite some time did not clarify about the identity of the Bhubaneswar chapter and the role of the state convenor. Anant Mahapatra was of the view that the separate identity of Bhubaneswar chapter could not be diluted. However, Lalit continued to function both as state and Bhubaneswar chapter convenor. I extended all my support to Lalit who then developed differences with SK Mishra, who was running INTACH like a patriarch, and submitted his resignation that would land me in a delicate situation.

SK Mishra rang me and requested me to take over as the state convenor, which became a Hobson's choice for me. First I wanted that the confusion about the state chapter and Bhubaneswar needed to be cleared as on no account I wanted to ruffle the feelings of Anant Mahapatra, who was not only senior to me in age but also a very good friend.

SK agreed for a separate convenor for Bhubaneswar

and suggested the name of Abasar Beuria. When I spoke to Abasar, his response was, however guarded. SK sent Major General (retd) LK Gupta, now chairman INTACH, then head of the chapter division, to Bhubaneswar to sort things out. During discussion, I suggested that Anant Mahapatra be appointed as advisor to the state chapter to be followed by the appointment of a panel. Abasar also agreed and accordingly I sent proposals to the head office, which were approved and thus another void was avoided. Subsequently SKB Narayan, a retired Chief Engineer, popularly known as Japani, was appointed as co-convenor of the state chapter.

INTACH has a number of conservation centres located in various parts of the country. The first conservation centre in Eastern India was started in Bhubaneswar with the main objective of conservation and restoration of palm leaves, of which Orissa has a rich storage. Subsequently, the scope of its activities was expanded to cover conservation of documents and painting and execution of conservation projects.

These centres constituted the Indian Council of Conservation Institutes (ICCI) with head office in Lucknow, and were headed by an eminent conservationist, Dr OP Agarwal. Although it was an adjunct to INTACH, it functioned almost independently, resulting in considerable communication gap between the head office and Lucknow. While the conservation centres were managed by salaried employees, INTACH head office and chapters functioned through an elected chairman, a governing body and their nominees as office-bearers of the chapters. For public perception, INTACH meant the chapters in the fields i.e. we the members of the organisation.

By the time I was in position in 2006, INTACH had taken up the execution of two important projects in Orissa – development of Raghunathpur in Puri, famous for Patachitra paintings, as a craft village through the head office, and renovation and conservation of the birthplace of Netaji Subhas Chandra Bose in Cuttack through the ICCI. I found that the state or the Bhubaneswar chapter other than knowing about the projects had no detailed information. This was a situation which I found untenable as I came into to picture only to sort out the administrative and financial problems relating to the projects at the level of the government and had the unpleasant task of answering questions raised by the public. I brought this fact to the notice of SK Mishra and thereafter Dr OP Agarwal, and Arun Gupta, a retired IAS officer of 1966 batch from MP cadre, who was in charge of the Heritage division in the head office, remained in regular touch.

Delay in completion of work at Netaji's birthplace was causing some resentment in Cuttack. Samir Dey, the local BJP MLA who was also Higher Education Minister in which capacity he used to interact with me frequently on Ravenshaw, complained of the delay and brought the same to the notice of Chief Minister who conveyed his displeasure to Dr Agarwal who then became alert and active. For execution of some small items of work, he required my help which I readily extended and got done through the State Police Housing Corporation.

The Raghunathpur project proved to be a big headache due to local rivalry, groupism and intrigues. Arun Gupta and I visited the place several times and tried to constitute a managing committee which would take over the management of the project, but did not meet with much success. Even SK Mishra's visit did not help. Finally, we handed over the project to the Tourism Department.

Mallika Mitra, a lady with remarkable sense of duty, is the Director of the Orissa Conservation Centre through which the projects are executed. She works with quiet efficiency and faces all issues and problems with admirable fortitude. She has displayed her ability in ample measure in the subsequent projects taken up by INTACH, like the State Maritime Museum executed at a cost of Rs 12 crore by renovating the historic Jobra workshop on the banks of the Mahanadi in Cuttack and currently in the restoration and renovation of several monuments out of the 13th Finance Commission grant.

Having worked in the tourism sector, I had a fair idea of the way of working in the Tourism and Culture department, generally without a sense of direction, clarity, definitive policies and going more by acts of adhocism that would flow from the mind of the incumbent Secretary, Minister and Chief Minister. Lalit, having spent his life in the IFS and not knowing the above, got a taste of it when he along with S K Mishra met the Chief Minister and concerned officials. After the meeting, he was not sure what the discussions had achieved. One saving grace in Orissa was that Naveen Patnaik was a signatory to the deed that gave birth to INTACH in 1984 and as such had a soft corner for the organisation.

The Jawaharlal Nehru Urban Renewal Mission started in 2006 had a component of heritage protection. The head office took the initiative of updating the listing of monuments in Bhubaneswar and Puri, which were covered by the scheme. It was done by the Bhubaneswar chapter under the supervision of Abasar by a team led by Sadasib Pradhan, professor of Ancient Indian History in Utkal University. They did excellent work and two very useful documents were produced and presented to Naveen Patnaik.

\We motivated the state government to associate INTACH in planning out the heritage zones and their protection. Initially INTACH was invited to some meetings, which were attended by Anant Mahapatra, Abasar and me. But later we were cut off the loop. When sometime in 2010, in a meeting taken by Debi Mishra, then minister in charge, I pointed this out; he expressed ignorance of JNNURM and asked the Secretary to put up the file.

While Bhubaneswar has visibly benefited from the JNNURM scheme, it just did not take off in Puri because of lack of proper planning, foresight, coordination and awareness at the district and state levels. INTACH's advocacy of city planning has always been embarrassing to the government. During the nineties and later in 2006, the Bhubaneswar chapter had prepared project reports, conducted seminars and brainstorming sessions on the development of this beautiful temple city.

Old Bhubaneswar till the seventies had the potential of being declared a World Heritage site but the builders came and, in the absence of enforceable heritage regulations, raised ugly concrete multi-storied structures, all with the blessings of politicians. In the lanes and by lanes of the old town, the old houses of the local inhabitants gave way to faceless concrete structures, encroaching upon road and government land in many places. The famous Rajarani and Mukteswar temples are today surrounded by tall concrete buildings. The ASI, which protects these monuments, remained silent; perhaps a willing spectator to the rape of the ambience.

In Puri, the situation was worse. There was a mushroom growth of hotels and rest houses along the beach, violating all norms, rules and regulations. They have come up within the Coastal Regulatory Zone and in the absence of proper drainage system, discharge their affluent into the sea which sends it back to the sand mass. The district administration and the Puri Development Authority turn a blind eye to this uglification of the beach, why a blind eye, even collaborate with the violators. The issue went to the High Court, which issued demolition orders which remained unimplemented.

Regardless of all this mayhem, the ministers and mandarins declare from time to time that Puri and Bhubaneswar Old Town area would be declared World Heritage sites. There is no plan, no thought, no research which I discovered in a meeting taken by UNESCO in 2010 on World Heritage sites in Bhubaneswar. The minister and his officials, other than a list, did not have any data, but next day all newspapers told the people of Orissa that so many sites would be declared World Heritage sites.

INTACH has taken some steps to put such populism to rest by organising discussions on this subject in 2013 and it was generally agreed that if properly planned and developed the Buddhist circuit of Ratnagiri, Udaygiri and Lalitgiri can be developed to a World Heritage site. In the past INTACH had prepared extensive documentation on the heritage site of Ekamra Kshetra (old Bhubaneswar).

Around 2006-07, Nilamadhab Mohanty IAS (1962) joined as Member Secretary in INTACH head office and was of great help to us in Orissa. Amongst our various programmes, foremost was the expansion of INTACH to other parts of Orissa and a concerted drive was made in that direction. Cuttack chapter was revived. Our co-convenor Japani took initiave in opening chapters in Mayurbhanj, Balasore and Koraput. DK Mishra, a retired IAS officer and member of the state advisory panel, took the initiative in opening a chapter in Sambalpur.

Presently we have as many as eight chapters of INTACH, spread along the length and breadth of the state, with listing and documentation of neglected monuments as one of their main activities. Japani subsequently took over as convenor of the Bhubaneswar chapter. At the national level, in 2009 Major General LK Gupta was elected as chairman of INTACH for a three-year term, defeating the redoubtable S K Mishra. He was re-elected in 2012.

The Archaeological Survey of India at the national level and the State Archaeology Department at the state level take up conservation of ancient monuments in Orissa, but the number is very small. While the ASI is in charge of 67 monuments, the State Archaeology looks after about 200, leaving a vast number of nearly 3,000 monuments in a state of neglect, at the mercy of greedy builders and unscrupulous encroachers. Moreover, the popular perception of an ancient monument in Orissa, a temple or a place of worship, a math or a fort, does not extend to the numerous palaces. Orissa has more than 50 palaces, and old institutions and buildings, both official and private. I have already mentioned about the absence of a coherent heritage policy in the state

The 10th Finance Commission for the first time gave grant-in-aid for conservation of ancient monuments to the states and Orissa got Rs 10 crore during the period 1995-2000. The 11th and 12th Commissions, gave much larger grants amounting to Rs 40 crore and Rs 50 crore, part of which either remained unspent or spent violating the guidelines of the Commission. New buildings were constructed while old buildings were languishing in neglect.

The 13th Finance Commission gave a grant of Rs 65 crore which we in INTACH decided to take up with the government for its planned and purposeful expenditure. Gen Gupta after being elected as chairman in 2009 came to Orissa and we met Chief Minister Naveen Patnaik, where amongst other subjects, conservation of monuments out of the 13th Finance Commission was discussed and Naveen was receptive to the idea of setting up a committee for selection of monuments and associating INTACH in the exercise.

I had suggested that in order to ensure quality not more than 100 monuments should be selected. Three years into the life of the Commission in 2013, the government offered INTACH about 30 monuments for conservation at an estimated cost of Rs 10 crore. During dialogue, we learnt that the department had identified a huge number of 300 monuments for conservation. This is yet another example of lack of application of mind at the level of the government. We signed MoU in April 2013 and the time schedule is supposed to be March 15 when the 13th Finance Commission expires. What was happening for three years, who will tell?

In 2008, INTACH signed a MoU for starting a maritime museum by renovating the 150-year-old irrigation workshop at Jobra on the banks of the Mahanadi in Cuttack at an estimated cost of Rs 12 crore. This was a pet project of Naveen, who used to visit the place to review the progress of work. Because of his personal interest, the execution progressed smoothly and the museum, now the largest in India, was inaugurated by Naveen on April 1, 2013. The state government has recently entrusted INTACH with the renovation of the building of Janakinath Bose, father of Subhas Bose, in Puri at an estimated cost of rupees four crore.

As part of advocacy, INTACH highlighted the casual approach of the ASI to some famous monuments maintained by it, like the Sisupalgarh, one of the earliest forts in Eastern India built between fourth and second century BC and the Konark Temple, a World Heritage site.

Sisupalgarh, located on the outskirts of Bhubaneswar, said to be the capital of Kharavela, the first recorded king in Orissa history, lay buried and was excavated in 1948 by B Lal, the then Director General of ASI. Dr HK Mahatab, a historian, the then Chief Minister, transferred nearly 600 acres of land to the ASI for excavation, conservation and maintenance. That was in the early 1950s. At the end of the century all that had remained was a little over one acre of land where some pillars, a gate of the fort excavated in 1948 and a portion of the moat remained. The remaining land encroached upon, has hundreds of buildings, all concrete structures below which lies buried the precious heritage of Orissa.

Sisupalgarh is an unparalleled example of negligence by its protector ASI and state government and a heritage being raped and killed and buried by the people of Orissa. I sent a RTI query to the Bhubaneswar Development Authority to find out if the buildings constructed in Sisupalgarh had the approval of the BDA. The answer was in the negative. We filed a PIL in the Orissa High Court to save the area in 2007. Seven years later, it is yet to come up for hearing.

The famous Sun Temple is in an unenviable position of dithering and delay by the ASI and passing on the buck game by the state government. Several committees and expert groups have been constituted by the Government of India after 1950 on the issue of conservation of this temple, but the basic issues are yet to be addressed by the ASI. The exquisitely carved stone sculptures, which are disintegrating, are being replaced by plain stones that will reduce the temple to a stone mass. A variable conservation policy adopted by the ASI, which had allowed carving on marbles in the recently restored Humayun Tomb in Delhi, another World Heritage site, a project executed by the Aga Khan Trust of Culture, baffles the people of Orissa. The ASI is dragging its feet on evacuation of sand from Jagmohan, which was filled up in 1902-04 to guard against collapse to judge the extent of damage. INTACH along with other civil society groups has taken a vocal stand on this issue, which will remain on the top of its agenda.

INTACH's Charter is in tune with my love for heritage, the conservation of which has become my passion not a pastime.

Chapter-34

Humiliation in Buddha's Shrine

One of the organisations with which I was associated was Mahabodhi Society of India, Orissa branch which at the beginning of the century, torn by strife, allegations of malpractices, counter allegations, factions and litigation was in a state of stupor and of which I was pressed and prodded to take over as president in 2004 by two emissaries from Kolkata, its head office They were general secretary Rewatha Thero, a Sri Lankan monk, and vice-president A K Samanta, my batchmate in IPS who has settled in Kolkata. I pulled it from the morass, brought it on a solid footing and I left it in 2008 facing public humiliation.

The Orissa branch of the society standing on a prime land in the heart of Bhubaneswar was the result of united efforts of three ardent lovers of Buddhism, Dr Mayadhar Mansingh, a famous romantic poet of Orissa, Dr Pravat Mukherjee, my teacher in History in Ravenshaw College, and Dr RK Sahu, a devoted Buddhist based in Puri. They had persuaded Dr Harekrishna Mahatab to allot a land for spreading Buddha's message. U Nu, the Burmese Prime Minister, had planted a sapling of a banyan tree brought from Anuradhapur in Sri Lanka.

Later, the Orissa branch became a part of the Mahabodhi Society of India which had been founded in Kolkata by Anagarika Dharmapala, a brilliant young Buddhist monk from Sri Lanka whose erudition used to dazzle people. He along with Swami Vivekananda had participated in the World Religion Congress in Chicago in 1903 and it is said that he was a bigger attraction in the various sessions for his wisdom, exposition, brilliant oratory and open mindedness.

He lived in Kolkata and founded the Mahabodhi Society of India in 1915 to preach Buddha's message. His yet another mission was to free the Buddhist shrines from the clutches of Hindu priests in which effort he received full support from Pandit Jawaharlal Nehru, then a freedom fighter and a lover of Buddha. This holy institution, apart from centres at Bodhgaya, Sarnath and Lumbini, had branches in Orissa, Lucknow, Mumbai and Chennai and had several patrons overseas in the USA, UK, Japan and South-east Asia. The centres had considerable immovable assets.

The broad arrangement as per the society deeds was that while the religious rites of the temples would be under the charge of Sri Lankan monks, the management committee would consist of Indians, Sri Lankans, and nationals of other countries irrespective of religion but believers in the preachings of Buddha. By the end of the century, many monks and members, falling prey to greed and other worldly temptations, had created problems in many centres and Orissa was no exception. One monk had signed a MoU with a private education society for opening a school, which was vehemently opposed by others. A PIL in High Court had brought things to a standstill.

By the time I started in 2004 there was an atmosphere of distrust, hostility, intrigue and mutual recrimination in the organisation. The first task of the managing committee was to settle the PIL to enable the temple activities to run smoothly. In a general body meeting convened to discuss the various issues, I found many members vociferously opposing the idea of the school which was run by SK Mahapatra, nephew of Pyari Mohan Mahapatra, who was the all-powerful prime mover in Orissa politics and administration. Personally, I found the idea of the school not objectionable, so long as the Mahabodhi Society had full control over it. Over the next few months, the PIL was settled, opposition to school overcome and steps taken to start other activities.

The school was formally opened by Chief Minister Naveen Patnaik. The 2550th birth anniversary of Gautam Buddha was celebrated in a befitting manner in 2006 and the branch which had zero balance in its account had more than Rs 1.5 lakh after the celebrations. While SK Mahapatra had won over all his critics who were shouting hoarse against him and had ingratiated himself with Rewatha Thero, the general secretary, he had one person to contend with, one Paresh Naik, who was unauthorisedly occupying a makeshift hall and was Thero's most trusted man in Orissa.

The managing committee had taken note of this illegal occupation and directed him to vacate within a stipulated time, which he delayed flaunting his proximity to the general secretary, which I had to mention in the Governing Council meeting in Kolkata and Thero was asked to keep his hands off.

Now Thero was a wily fox, not believing in leading a spartan life of a Buddhist monk but enjoying the worldly comforts of life and that whetted his desire to acquire absolute power over the affairs of the Mahabodhi Society, which he succeeded in gaining by virtue of his hold over the majority of the people in the society.

In 2003, when he was running his third term, an amendment was introduced in the constitution limiting the term of the general secretary to three terms, which would end in 2004. But he kept this under the carpet and became general secretary for the fourth term in 2004 and fifth term in 2007. With only the printed constitution of 2001 before me, I was blissfully unaware of his illegal continuance. When Dr BK Modi of the Modi group of industries became president in 2006 they had good sailing for some time as Thero was instrumental in getting him elected, but the bonhomie was shortlived.

In a Governing Council meeting held in Bodhgaya in 2008, while discussing various programmes of the society I pointed out certain anomalies in the constitution which Thero was quick to pick up, suggesting constitution of a committee to examine amendments which was readily agreed to and I ipsofacto became a member of the committee. Little did I realise that Thero had a hidden agenda and I was only furthering its realisation without having any idea about it. He took very prompt action in convening the first meeting of the committee in Kolkata which I attended, thinking that the modalities and procedure of the proceedings of the committee would be discussed.

Instead, I found a draft of the proposed amendments along with the printed copy of the amendments of 2003, the most significant suggestion of which was the removal of the restriction clause on the term of the general secretary. I protested, suggesting that we should call for views of members on amendments. The meeting ended in a state of ambivalence, the members not daring to oppose me in the open meeting, not supporting me either.

I sent a strong note of protest to Modi, members of the committee and Thero giving my views. While Modi was in agreement with me he did not like to join issues with Thero.

In the next Governing Council meeting held in August

2008, which was stage managed, Thero wanted to get the amendments passed. Modi remained absent and designated Justice Bhagabati Banerjee, a vice-president to preside over the meeting and sent a letter suggesting that the amendments should not be passed in a hurry and be deferred. Banerjee read out the letter. I was the only person to oppose the farce that was going on. Even Modi's men remained silent. Stage managed as the meeting was, Thero was already circulating a printed paper asking for view, "Do you support the amendments? Yes/ No." It was a big yes. Justice Banerjee fainted and collapsed, I was looking like a fool. Shamed and humiliated, I left the place to join my co brother-in-law A K Basu over drinks. Then I sent my letter of resignation, thus ending my four years of association with the Mahabodhi Society of India.

But nemesis takes over. Thero, while he was the monk in charge of Sarnath before becoming general secretary, was accused of misappropriation of huge amounts of money and the Directorate of Revenue Intelligence, which had taken cognizance as foreign funds were involved, had found him guilty and imposed heavy penalties. A CBI case was also instituted. He was also accused of channelizing foreign contribution in violation of Foreign Contribution Regulation Act. He was evading legal action by manipulating the provisions of law. A non-bailable warrant was issued against him in Varanasi in 2012 which he successfully dodged. These were no secrets and his unpopularity was growing.

The society land at many places was in litigation and the mess had started stinking. Monks started leaving him and staging demonstration against him. In later part of 2013, in a meeting in Bodhgaya, he was seen in a questionable position with a lady. That was the last straw. He was asked to resign.

In January 2014, a general body meeting was called in

Kolkata to ratify his departure and approve the appointment of a new secretary. Several members from Kolkata rang me up, asking me to attend the meeting as I still continue to be a member but I decided to keep out.

Chapter-35

Industry, CSR and Human Rights

My association with Tata Steel started in mid-2008. By then I had developed some familiarity with Kalinga Nagar, the emerging steel complex in Orissa, in my capacity as the NHRC Special Rapporteur.

Conceived in the early nineties, Kalinga Nagar was the baby of Biju Patnaik who was then obsessed with starting a second mega steel plant in Orissa. Biju's dreams of having industries at panchayat level in the sixties, when he first became Chief Minister, failed to take off primarily because of an inexperienced and rule bound government machinery entrusted with the task.

When JB came to power in 1980, he proceeded more methodically by encouraging medium- and small-scale industries and inviting entrepreneurs from private sector. His statement, "A thousand industries in thousand days", with its trappings of populism did show a certain missionary spirit. It was in fact in the eighties that several small industries came up in the fields of electronics, textiles and handloom, leather, information technology and tourism in both private and public sectors. Konark TV became a well-known brand in the country. Factories were set up to produce chips, watches, garments for export and leather products. But JB failed to give importance to the management side and relied heavily on the bureaucrats who managed the industries like any other government department. I underwent this experience while I was MD of Orissa Tourism Development Corporation. By early nineties many industries like Konark TV, Leather Corporation, the textile and garment units, units in electronic sectors had closed due to mismanagement leading to misappropriation and defalcation of funds. As vigilance chief, I saw my staff inquiring into this state of affairs and coming out with scathing reports. Konark TV which became a popular brand in other parts of the country was looted with impunity by the staff led by a politician.

When Biju conceived the idea of a steel complex, the site at Dubri near Jajpur Road Railway Station was appropriately chosen and about 8,000 acres of land was earmarked. The State Infrastructural Development Corporation became the nodal agency for acquisition (a misnomer as most of the area was government land under occupation of tribals) and allotting the land to the intending industries. The tribals, who had to face displacement, were given a meagre per acre compensation of Rs 30,000. Biju invited Swaraj Paul from England who announced to build a mega steel plant at a ceremony conducted with a lot of fanfare. He backed out and Biju's dream died.

When JB came, he increased the per acre compensation to Rs 50,000 and by then two medium size steel plants, the Nilachal Ispat Nigam in state sector, and MESCO in private sector owned by Rita Singh were in the pipeline.

By the beginning of the 21st century, demand for steel in the international market grew and there was a rush of big houses —POSCO, Tatas, Jindal, Bhushan and Mittal—to Orissa. Naveen saw requests pouring in which his father could not have imagined. MoU after MoU was signed and Orissa became one of the top states in attracting investment. It is another matter that many MoUs remained stillborn and some are inching ahead.

In Kalinga Nagar, MoUs were signed for 13 steel plants, biggest being Tata Steel. Government added another 4,000 acres of land and handed over the same to IDCO, which by now was collecting Rs 3.50 lakh per acre from the investors and paying Rs I lakh per acre to the displaced families. The state did not have a rehabilitation policy. The uprooted tribals accustomed to living in their tribal ambience were dispensed with a paltry compensation. The Nilachal Ispat Nigam, which had built a colony for the displaced, was only a cluster of concrete houses, lacking in the basic needs of the tribals, like burial ground, place of community worship—and did not have plantation, which is their lifeline. Discontentment was brewing and the situation was becoming explosive.

In 2004-05, trouble erupted in the land allotted to the Maharashtra Seamless factory and there was a clash between the tribals and police. The ADM and several policemen were injured with similar casualties on the other side.

I went to enquire into the incident on behalf of the NHRC to specifically look into the issues of displacement and rehabilitation and was surprised to note that the state government did not have any concrete scheme or policy. I met Finance Minister Prafulla Ghadei, a powerful politician from the area, and conveyed my impression to him. In my report, I mentioned about the tense atmosphere prevailing in Kalinga Nagar and likely eruption of violence at any time. The state government finally came out with a Relief and Rehabilitation Policy in 2006.

The Tata Steel, which had been allotted 3,200 acre of

land to build a steel plant, was not in a position to start work as the villagers put up stiff resistance. Although the MoU had been signed in 2004 there was no initiative to address the various issues raised by the people. There were occasional skirmishes which the government and Tisco ignored. Prodded by some over enthusiastic top-ranking functionaries in the government, the Tisco authorities decided to have Bhoomi Puja on a day in January 2006. The villagers would not allow it and the government would not advise postponement of the event ensuring violent confrontation with the police. Force was used and 12 tribals were killed in what can be called as one of the worst police-public encounters in Orissa.

As if that was not enough, innocent women were rounded up and put in jail and there were allegations of inhuman conduct at the time of autopsy during which the doctors allegedly cut off the palms of the deceased.

After the ghastly incident, while the work on the site came to a standstill, normal government administration was also paralysed. The villagers blocked the road to Dubri and for more than one year, the blockade continued preventing vehicular movement while the district administration turned its eyes away. In 2008, Samuel Thangaraj, Advisor, Social Development Tata Steel, accompanied by Nandini Sarangi, a social develpoment expert at Kalinga Nagar and wife of Orissa cadre IPS officer Sudhansu Sarangi, who is currently on deputation to ARC, came and met me and explained their scheme to constitute a working group/ committee to monitor the relief and rehabilitation activities at Kalinga Nagar, to listen to the grievances of the displaced persons and take steps for their redressal. They requested me to act as Chairman. I asked them to give me some time while making it clear that the group possibly would not be a creature of Tata Steel and there would be no employer-employee relationship to ensure its independence.

By then the euphoria created by the Naveen Patnaik Government in the early years about industrial investments in Orissa was fading with all major houses facing obstacles and controversies. The Vedanta Alumina group headed by Anil Agarwal, which had its mining plants at Niyamgiri, had inducted me as a member of their advisory group by telling me that they had complied with all the conditionalities laid down by the Supreme Court before mining Niyamgiri.

I visited the sites with some members and was impressed with their rehabilitation measures, but later when I found discrepancies in their compliance on the conditionalities, which had come to the fore, and noticed certain desperation on their part when they requested me to write articles in Oriya newspapers in support of the plant and even brought a draft article requesting me to lend my name, my discomfort grew and I decided to quit.

Work at the POSCO site in Paradip had come to a standstill with the local people putting stiff resistance. I was requested by some people to visit the site and study the situation. While I had an open mind on this issue, I had serious reservations about the provision of swapping iron ores mined in Orissa with the ores from foreign countries on the ground that local iron ores were of inferior quality. Then why did you come? How did you make the state government agree to such an absurd clause? Around that time the CMD of POSCO who had come to Bhubaneswar from South Korea, visited my residence and sought my help and co-operation, I failed to comprehend, how.

As regards Kalinga Nagar, keeping the tragic incident of January 2006 in mind, I decided to accept the responsibility and see if I could do something to sort out the vexatious issues.

Next meeting with Samuel, Nandini and Tata officials was devoted to the modalities and procedure of the group, which was designated as 'Independent Grievance Redressal

Group', with Nandini as our main line of communication with the management. As regards the composition of the Group, they apart from me as chairman had one name in mind. It was Tulsi Munda, a tribal lady, Padmashree awardee and social activist. I was asked to suggest some names. I suggested the name of Dr CR Das, an environmentalist, and advised them to meet Pyari Mohan Mahapatra, apprise him of their scheme and ask his suggestion for any other name. Pyari Mohan suggested the name of AV Swamy, a Gandhian from Kalahandi district, and the list was complete. CR Das left after sometime to accept an assignment in government.

They wanted to discuss the issue of compensation to me which I ruled out and suggested that they should bear my establishment and secretarial expenses only in line of what I was enjoying in NHRC. They readily agreed.

When we met for the first time and discussed the issues, the challenges seemed formidable. About 1,200 families from 12 villages were to be displaced to vacate 3,200 acre of land allotted to Tata Steel. The relief and rehabilitation division of the management was quite active and had succeeded in persuading about 700 families to shift to transit camps. But the hardcore would remain stubborn, refusing to enter into any dialogue.

A Visthapan Virodhi Manch (VVM) had been formed after January 2006 and in the absence of any initiative by the government and emboldened by the success of more than one year of road blockade, the Manch had grown in strength and stature and would refuse to have any dialogue openly.

Apart from the collective functioning of the Group, I found that I had to take initiative at my personal level to start the process of dialogue and create an atmosphere conducive for the management to start work. I wrote appeals to the leaders of the Manch, explaining my role as a protector and guardian of their legitimate rights rather than a functionary of the management. Response was lukewarm, but the ball started rolling. I met the DM and SP separately and found them wary of any negotiation with the leaders.

While the DM explained that any dialogue started by the district administration would appear as taking up the cause of Tata Steel, the SP informed about pendency of more than 60 criminal cases against the leaders. I met Finance Minister Prafulla Ghadei, the local BJD politician, and his rival Sarat Rout of Congress and felt that they would like to fish in troubled waters. I came to the conclusion that the district administration had to show some teeth even if that was not ideal or desirable and wrote to Naveen Patnaik to intervene. I met Pyari Mohan and discussed the issue with him. He seemed to be aware of my letter to Naveen. These steps were showing some results.

- In the meetings we found by 2009 that nearly 800 families had been shifted to transit camps and a contiguous area of more than 2,000 acre of land was available on which work could be started and this was impressed on the management. They, however, were uncertain, saying that bits of construction undertaken during the day would be demolished after sunset. But that risk had to be taken. The evacuated families who now constituted the majority were getting restive and clamouring for work to begin. One village, Chandia, where some of the hardcore leaders lived with nearly 200 families and 1,100 acres of land, was deliberately left out of our outreach programme as we realised that if work started, their opposition would melt in due course.

Luckily, by 2009, Naveen took cognizance of the situation and issued instructions to the district administration to intervene with due diligence to avoid direct confrontation. The SP, who was complaining of inadequate manpower, was given additional force and levelling of land and construction of boundary wall at the plant site began. In the beginning, there were minor incidents, but the opponents had become careful and also the police, not to precipitate a crisis, keeping the tragedy of January 2006 in mind.

By 2010, work in other sectors had started. When I visited the plant site I had a sense of satisfaction that in my individual as well as in collective capacity as chairman of the Group, we had succeded in acting as an effective and successful catalyst in what in the beginning had seemed to be an irreversible imbroglio. In the hectic efforts of the Group, two persons of the management who made signal contribution by extending all help and support were BP Singh, the vice-president of the Orissa project and a gentle soul who was totally committed to start work at the site, and the indomitable Nandini, our lady with the lamp who guided us through the dark mazes of confabulations.

As regards rehabilitation of the displaced persons, the management had taken several measures by supplementing the mandated package laid down in the 2006 policy, keeping the tribal ethos and traditions in view like construction of houses, plantation and capacity building by providing technical, agricultural, vocational and other educational training programmes. By 2012, plant activities were in full swing, belying the forecast of some of my colleagues in 2008 when I took over the responsibility that the project was a non-starter.

At the end of 2012, I decided to call it a day and sent a letter to the management to relieve me with effect from 1.1.2013.

Part-8

Concluding Chapter

➢ I Keep Walking

Chapter-36

I Keep Walking

The previous chapters are a narration of my life. Very consciously I have refrained from discussing any subject like police, policing, governance, security and integrity of the nation, development, corruption, conduct of bureaucracy including IPS as that might have appeared to be sermonizing from a high pedestal. I have lived the issues and leave them to the readers to judge my failures and successes. Having said this and in spite I feel compellingly drawn to some issues on which I will air my views briefly in this concluding chapter.

Having been a policeman for more than three and half decades , I have all along been an enthusiastic advocate of Police reforms. It has been my firm belief that it is the IPS leadership which can bring about substantial reforms in Police. There is a lot of talks on Police reforms and I find IPS leaders find it convenient to pass on the buck to someone else, Executive, Judiciary, Politicians depending on situations and of course dearth of funds . Now allocation of funds is not much of aproblem, what is lacking is the will, a condition that suits the politicians and bureaucracy eminently. The implementation of the Supreme Court judgment in the PIL filed by the indomitable Prakash Singh in which the centre after prolonged procrastination took the stand that the Police being a state subject, the states should formulate their own laws, directing the states to enact laws is only in form and not in spirit leading to the likely consequences of the loss of majesty of the Indian Police. I have been an ardent votary of that unity although there is constitutional impediment in the form of the seventh schedule in which Police is placed in state list.The IPS officers must give serious thought to this.

The NDA government which swept the May elections getting comfortable majority after thirty years made promises in all sectors, but was silent on Police. I wrote a letter to Mr. Rajnath Singh suggesting adoption of a uniform Police act by examining the relevant provisions in the constitution. I received a three line reply indicating that the centre has no role in it.

Then comes the subject of the greatest democracy in the world, i.e., India romanticized as a state of functional chaos. But what is the health of this democracy introduced in a country in a most unique manner through nonviolent struggle? Over time with the erosion of democratic values, principles and traditions the leaders have forgotten that they are to serve the people having been elected by them. They brazenly serve themselves and for that they do not bat an eyelid to indulge in crime, corruption and other nefarious activities. As advisor to the National Election Watch of the Orissa Branch I have come across startling facts which are derailing the smooth march of democracy in India. One of the most disturbing factors is the money spent in election campaign by candidates. The ceiling imposed by the Election Commission has no meaning and relevance. The role of the election observers is marginal. The amount of money spent in 2009 and 2014 elections has baffled me, no wonder several scams have erupted, chit fund, coalgate, mining scam to name a few.

The political parties are required to submit returns to IT department about their income and expenditure. There are 6 national parties, 47 regional parties and about 1600 unregistered parties. With the exception of the national parties and a few regional parties, others don't send their statements to the IT department and the income they show is a fraction of the expenditure incurred by them, all hidden and not shown. In 2014 election the tilt of the corporate houses in favour of BJP was markedly visible. In Orissa BJD which is into its fourth term is one of the worst defaulters in submission of statements. As regards the criminal background of the legislators the less said the better. It remains to be seen if the recent judgment of the Supreme Court will bring about any qualitative improvement. If corruption is to be fought one of the fundamental needs is electoral reform. The Election Commission is doing a commendable job in the conduct of election but in matter of money and muscle power it is a toothless tiger. And mere amendment to the Representation of People Act will not help unless institutional arrangements are built in to rein in money and muscle power.

In the last 3 panchayat raj and urban bodies' election in Orissa I have witnessed the high pitch of electioneering comparable to Assembly elections. Money flows, where from, that defies all explanation and logic. In a convention organized by the ADR and National election watch at Bhubaneswar I was presiding over a session on election to the panchayat bodies. A sarpanch, a semi literate lady spoke with remarkable candor about the funds she spent in the election which had to be made up once she was in office. Whither democracy?

A few words about Bureaucracy. Without going to the theory and the principles of governance, I will cite my experience as a common man with the higher echelons of administration. Senior officers in the All India Services are increasingly becoming inaccessible to people. In this respect the Indian Forest service officers have the unique advantage of minimum exposure to public by virtue of the posts they hold, but that is not the case with the IAS and IPS officers who have to interact with the public on a day to day basis. In my experiences I have noticed that it is impossible to talk to a secretary to the Governmentt, he is busy in a meeting, in a conference or is out somewhere. I have found it easier to talk to the chief secretary but not to his secretaries. In Police what saddened me most is inaccessibility of the district Superintendent of police, if you ring, he is busy in a meeting or is out, and there is no call back. I feel tempted to narrate an experience; I wanted to communicate the grievance of a central government employee about inaction of Police in a complaint of molestation of his girl child studying in class two by an old man to the SP. From morning till afternoon I kept on ringing the SP to the residential and office phones, his mobile, the phone of the Addl SP but nobody would pickup, although they were not out on tour as I learnt from the DIB. Then I sent an e-mail to the SP, but I am yet to get the response.

While I was in the NHRC that was till 2006, I was shocked to see that the CM's grievance redressal cell for which a big building was given was virtually dysfunctional. A public friendly mindset will find it very difficult to reconcile itself to such a state of affairs.

Such ramblings will go on but as far as the out pourings of the country cousin are concerned they have to come to an end with a last thought.

The theme of Raj Kapoor's film "Mera nam Joker" is my all time favourite. Raju, the do-gooder going about his life's journey through sorrow and happiness, agonies and ecstasies, rejection and disappointment singing the soulful song 'jina yahan, marna yahan, iske siwa jana kahan'. The sum of my learning whether from my icon Jawaharlal Nehru drawing inspiration from Robert Frost's poem " I have promises to keep, and miles to go before I sleep" or the quest of Siddhartha the Bramhin for Mokshya which he ultimately found through the medium of a flowing river, or Hemingway's passionate dialogue with self and the big fish he caught in the sea in the face of the defeat staring at him, Lord Krishna's teaching to Arjuna on "karma' or Raju's ability to laugh, then cry and yet march on reveals the inherent dictum "go, march, don't stagnate", 'charaivati' as an ancient sage would invoke in the Upanishad preceded by that self igniting and illuminating verse.

"Charanbai madhu vindati
Charantsvadu mudamburam
Suryasay pasya sreemana
Yo no tandrayate charan"

Index